Offbeat Food

Adventures in an Omnivorous World

Alan Ridenour

SANTA
MONICA
PRESS

SANTA
MONICA
PRESS

Published by:
Santa Monica Press LLC
P.O. Box 1076
Santa Monica, CA 90406-1076
1-800-784-9553
www.santamonicapress.com

Printed in the United States

Santa Monica Press books are available at special
quantity discounts when purchased in bulk by
corporations, organizations, or groups. Please call
our Special Sales department at 1-800-784-9553.

*This book is intended to provide general information.
The publisher, author, distributor, and copyright
owner are not engaged in rendering health, medical, legal, financial, or other professional advice
or services, and are not liable or responsible to
any person or group with respect to any loss, ill-
ness, or injury caused or alleged to be caused by
the information found in this book.*

ISBN 1-891661-09-4

Library of Congress Cataloging-in-Publication Data

Ridenour, Alan, 1961–
Offbeat food: adventures in an omnivorous
world / by Alan Ridenour.

p. cm.

ISBN 1-891661-09-4 (pbk.)
1. Food--Miscellanea.
2. Food--Social aspects.
3. Food habits.
I. Title.
TX355 .R532 2000
641.3--dc21

99-059930

Book and cover design by Ken "Design Boy" Niles
Illustrations by J.T. Steiny

The publisher and author would like to thank Mike
Carrig for his heroic effort in locating and obtaining the majority of the images used in this book.

Table of Contents

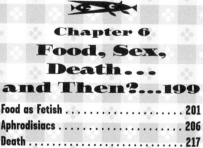

Yes, there are insects in the pages of this book. Discussions of offbeat food invariably seem to wind their way rather quickly toward the topic of bugs and who eats them. But just as insects have become a sort of stock-and-trade shorthand for all that's unusual in the gastronomic universe, they've also begun to lose something of their shock value. The practice of eating insects has slowly infiltrated Western awareness—first as an ethnographic curiosity, later as the novelty in novelty suckers, and later still as an exotic delicacy on the menus of restaurants catering to cosmopolitan tastes. Insects are no longer "inedible" . . . just very, very exotic. And it's not much of a stretch to imagine a day in the not-too-distant future when insects will be a popular snack food—as common, for instance, as potato chips.

Yet if we look back to the 1896 classic, *Anomalies and Curiosities of Medicine,* we find the case of a 6-year-old girl who habitually consumed "slugs, beetles, cockroaches, spiders, and other repulsive insects." At the time, her eating habits were characterized as a "depravity of appetite" and classed alongside clay-eating as symptomatic of mental disturbance. Though, in a sense, this girl could have been considered a culinary pioneer, we also know that many things kids shove in their mouths are undeniably dangerous.

How do children learn what does work and what doesn't work as food? By being told, of course. Language is the handy medium whereby we transmit and store the results of our collective and dangerous experimentation. Language as a distinguishing feature of *homo sapiens* is also one of the reasons our species (unlike others) will eat things that, upon first taste, we instinctually spit out.

You can see this in the individual context, as children are culturally acclimated into an enjoyment of spicy foods, coffee, alcohol, and other initially noxious substances. Despite the protestations of the gag reflex, young initiates are told these foods are "safe" and even good, and the acquiring of "acquired tastes" is an important signifier of membership in adult culture.

On a societal level, it's similar—foods valued as hallmarks of higher civilization are never the simple "natural" foods, but are those involving a strange, sophisticated (and possibly revolting) process of production. Wine and cheese, for instance, produced by fermentation and curdling, are nothing more than the outcome of carefully controlled decay. Hindsight tells us that alcohol turned out to be a clever way to keep beverages free of bacteria, and cheese turned out to be a good way to preserve milk, but it must've been a fool of heroic proportions who first chose to down these rancid provisions.

Foolhardy behavior, accidents, and the acts of the "mentally deranged"—these appear to be the forces behind our evolving definition of "food." It's a bumbling process of mutation and mistake, sometimes dead-ending in hairballs and poison and other times advancing to wine and cheese. Darwin would call it natural selection, and Frank Buckland went ahead and took Darwin's theory to its culinary extreme.

Hold That Tiger!

Frank Buckland was the son of William Buckland–the famously eccentric professor of geology and mineralogy at Oxford in the early to mid-1800s, and generally considered to be the father of modern paleontology. Trained as a surgeon, the younger Buckland, like his father, was a popular scientific author and lecturer. Serious scholars like to remember Frank as a proponent of fisheries, but it was not only fish that Frank's appetites inclined toward. As founder of the "Society for Acclimatization of Animals in the United Kingdom," Frank believed that exotic species should not merely be imported for display in zoos but should be judiciously selected, acclimated, domesticated—and eaten.

On his own estate, Buckland kept an edible menagerie and experimented in his kitchen with a variety of recipes and dishes including kangaroo, buffalo, crocodile, whole roast ostrich, giraffe, porpoise heads, mice on toast, elephant trunk soup, rhinoceros pie, slug soup, and earwigs.

It's even said that upon returning from his travels and learning that the resident leopard at the London Zoo had expired, Buckland rushed to where it had been buried and disinterred the creature in order that he might perform a few culinary experiments with its meat. Of the hundreds of recipes he concocted, only two (stewed mole and bluebottle flies) were deemed inedible by this second-generation eccentric.

In addition to his menagerie, Buckland also kept a collection of relics including a lock of hair from Henry IV and the heel bone of the poet Ben Johnson. The most precious object in Buckland's reliquary, however, was one bequeathed to him by his father, who had purchased it from a certain Lord Harcourt, who in turn had obtained it from Jacobin defilers of the royal tombs at St. Denis in Paris. This jewel in Buckland's collection was the embalmed heart of the Sun King, Louis XIV.

Despite the immeasurable value of this relic, Buckland himself is said to have destroyed this precious object before the eyes of one very alarmed dinner guest, according to an 1886 article in *Popular Science Monthly*. Before disposing of this little bit of history, Buckland is said to have uttered these words, "I have eaten many strange things in my lifetime, but never before have I eaten the heart of a king," and with that, Frank Buckland began eating away at Louis' heart.

Clearly, gustatory pleasure was not the aim in chewing up this leathery bit of mummified meat. So why had Frank suddenly gone cannibal? And why had he chosen to start with this immeasurably valuable and immeasurably unappetizing specimen?

Probably for much the same reasons the cannibals in Papua New Guinea eat the heart of a rival warrior—to acquire the dead man's desirable qualities. Clearly the gesture was symbolic, and clearly Buckland was obsessed with enriching his gastronomic experience. And who in all the world came closer to living out the Epicurean ideal than Louis XIV? This method in Buckland's madness, which might be lost on the typically noncannibalistic reader of *Popular Science Monthly,* would no doubt make perfect sense to the tribal practitioner of ritual cannibalism.

Playing with Our Food

Hopefully, Buckland's spirit can guide you through *Offbeat Food*, reminding you of the essential symbolic potency of food, a power that can spill out over the most unlikely substances, turning the inedible into coveted morsels. Its terrific symbolic force can manifest itself in the desiccated heart of a long-dead monarch, but it can also inhabit a humble loaf of bread or a sculpture made of yak butter.

Is there really any objective definition for food? Can we let the physiologists strong-arm us into the definition of food as "nutritive substances consumed"? How can we let them so glibly exclude foodstuffs (i.e. chewing gum) that are obviously psychological rather than nutritive in function? Even if the physiologist were to back off and decide to offer a more humble definition of food, describing it negatively as "nontoxic substances consumed," we can still raise a fuss, pointing to the vast spectrum of mild to lethal intoxicants enjoyed by various cultures throughout the world.

Throughout the ages and throughout the world, food has been used ritually to bring luck, work magic, bless marriages, bond neighbors, cure and improve the body, placate the dead, and affirm unity with the divine.

With power like that, it's only natural that civilizations should eventually develop an obsession with the form and details of food. It follows that societies would eventually devote intense scientific and artistic energies toward the preparation and presentation of food, and that mankind should eventually fixate on food as a decorative motif and metaphor, eventually anthropomorphizing food, creating animated personas for food, having sex with food, and building homes and driving cars that look like food.

Offbeat Food documents a few of the thousands of ways our species has and continues to play with its food. Smearing it around a plate is only the beginning.

—Alan Ridenour

Divine Eats

Who gets to eat whom? This is one of nature's most convenient ways for establishing hierarchy. Not surprisingly, it's also a favorite model for man's social hierarchies, as well as an inspiration for myths of cosmic order.

Eating a "whom" is generally frowned upon within the human family. It's so basic that the understanding is unspoken, leaving us few mythic stories explaining why men don't (and shouldn't) snack on each other. However, *what* we eat, what we *can't* eat, and why it's so are all hot topics for mythmaking; discussion of these topics forms the backbone of many cultural traditions worldwide.

■ FRUITS & VEGETABLES ■

In the Beginning

Common to Judaic, Christian, and Islamic traditions is the story of Adam, Eve, and the forbidden fruit. Despite their diversity, all intricacies of social hierarchy and law in each of these cultures can be related to this single myth.

And not one of these cultures has a problem with apples.

It's all about the deed. It's not about biting, chewing, or swallowing that fruit; it's about reaching *too high* for it, about snatching at God's own goods. Man's first sin was a big one, namely trying to appropriate divine privileges.

As the snake says to Eve, "For God knows that in the day you eat from [the tree] your eyes will be opened, and you will be like God . . . " What is forbidden in Genesis is actually breaking the "cosmic food chain." Even the literalist, curious as to whether Adam and Eve had navels, knows the fruit is only important as an abstract symbol.

The Forbidden Fig

You don't have to open a Bible to know that the fruit Eve gave Adam was

Adam and Eve prepare to break the cosmic food chain.

> **Y**ou don't have to open a Bible to know that the fruit Eve gave Adam was an apple. In fact, opening the Bible won't help you with this at all, since nowhere in the book of Genesis is this particular fruit mentioned.

an apple. In fact, opening the Bible won't help you with this at all, since nowhere in the book of *Genesis* is this particular fruit mentioned.

Ancient Hebrews wouldn't have known an apple from a hole in the ground. They knew figs, however, and specifically mentioned fig trees growing in Eden, and traditionally leaves from these have been the source of man's first underwear. A few scholars have, therefore, suggested that the fig was the fruit intended. Others have postulated that pears or apricots could've

Many scholars believe that it was the fig, not the apple, that caused the uproar in the Garden of Eden.

been the fruit envisioned. In keeping with the natural and obsessive association of "original sin" with sex, the Koran plants a banana tree in Paradise and implicates this phallic fruit in man's downfall. Stranger still, a representation of the Eden in a thirteenth-century cathedral of Indres, France, depicts the tree in question as bearing an uncanny resemblance to an immense mushroom of a kind known to be hallucinogenic.

The idea that the fruit was an apple comes from medieval Europe, where, in fact, "apple" served as a sort of universal catch-all for any mysterious fruit. Evidence of this is found in the word "pineapple" as well

> **S**tranger still, a representation of the Eden in a thirteenth-century cathedral of Indres, France, depicts the tree in question as bearing an uncanny resemblance to an immense mushroom of a kind known to be hallucinogenic.

as in the archaic "Persian apple" (for lemons) and "apples of Carthage" (for pomegranates). Even in the Middle Ages there must have been controversy, however, as the name "Eden apple" was actually used to refer to the apricot.

In the end, it was probably a translator's pun that pinned it on the apple. We don't know when or where it happened, but it's easy to imagine the wan smile that might've crossed the face of a monk as he notes during his translations that the Latin word *malum* is the correct translation for both "apple" and "sin."

Damned Farmers!

After the fruit was downed, the pleasure garden turns into a farm. Adam is condemned to hard labor. The sentence doled out equates work, suffering, and sustenance: "Cursed be the ground for thy sake; in sorrow shalt thou eat of it all the days of thy life; thorns also and thistles shall it bring forth to thee; and thou shalt eat the herb of the field."

Farming is getting a bad

rep here, and it only gets worse with the story of Cain and Abel in which Yahweh graciously accepts the sacrifice made by Abel (a shepherd) while turning up his nose at the one made by Cain (a farmer). There has been much scholarly

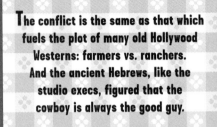

The conflict is the same as that which fuels the plot of many old Hollywood Westerns: farmers vs. ranchers. And the ancient Hebrews, like the studio execs, figured that the cowboy is always the good guy.

spin-doctoring of Yahweh's fussiness here. One of the most provocative theories calls attention to the description of Cain's murder of Abel, and the curious biblical turn of phrase describing the blood shed: "the earth accepts his blood." According to this theory, Cain, as the father of the Canaanites (arch enemies of the Hebrews) is evil from the get-go, and with the murder of his brother, he is watering the fields with the blood needed to insure good harvest. The earth deity *accepts* the murder as a sacrifice. This is correlated with the historical reality of human sacrifices offered by the agriculturist Canaanites.

As a pastoral people, the ancient Hebrews understandably regarded the permissive ways of the shepherd as more "blessed" than the more advanced and "corrupted" life of those who claimed ownership of land and practiced the science of agriculture. The conflict is the same as that which fuels the plot of many old Hollywood Westerns: farmers vs. ranchers. And the ancient Hebrews, like the studio execs, figured that the cowboy is always the good guy.

M E A T

Chickens Are Filthy Too!

Everyone knows the Law of Moses forbids Jews from eating pork. But no one seems to care that the meat of the camel, rock badger, pelicans, swans, and bat is also forbidden. Why has avoidance of pork, above everything else, become a cultural rallying point for Jews from the most orthodox to the more liberal?

What's wrong with pork anyway? Certain schools of academic second-guessing attribute to Moses an anachronistically advanced understanding of trichinosis and public hygiene, but much of this is just pig-headed. Laying an almost paranoid emphasis on the health risks presented by swine, these scholars blithely ignore the chicken's nasty habit of scratching through its own filth, as

The death of Abel.

well as the obvious susceptibility of the Hebrews' sheep to anthrax and burcellosis.

The story behind Hanukkah actually sheds a clearer light on the issue. In 167 B.C.E., after kicking some Egyptian butt, the victorious Greek-Syrian general Antiochus Epiphanes IV returned to his throne in occupied Jerusalem ready to throw his weight around. His tyrannical efforts to homogenize and hellenize his Jewish subjects included installing temple prostitutes and foreign idols in the Temple of Solomon and instituting the sacrifice of swine within the holy site.

It was against this tyrant that the Maccabean revolutionaries fought, eventually liberating the temple again so that it could be purified and rededicated (the event commemorated by Hanukkah). Many historians believe that it was during this period, and in reaction to this insult, that the taboo on pork rose to preeminence over other dietary restrictions.

The Yahweh Diet

The common notion of the "uncleanliness" of pork is related to that of

pigs wallowing in their own filth. But it's a modern mistake to exclusively interpret this word as "dirty." Drop open the book of *Leviticus* anywhere, and right alongside "unclean" you're likely to find the words "without blemish" or "perfect" describing the sorts of materials or animals permissible and impermissible as temple sacrifice.

The ancient Jewish concept of "uncleanliness" has much more to do with a sort of cosmic *fitness* than with soap, Bactine, and Lysol.

The bat. Unclean? A freak of nature? A mouse with wings? You be the judge.

Traits, like limbs, should come in predictable patterns, and the bat, for instance, was unpredictable and, therefore, regarded as unclean, not because of its living habits but because it was a freak of nature. The Hebrews didn't trust it either as a bird lacking feathers or a mouse with wings.

The food fit to enter our bodies, like the food fit to enter the temple as a sacrifice, has to be unblemished and perfect. Offering God an animal without all the appropriate parts or traits would be like offering food that's been nibbled on. A deformed animal missing a limb would be unacceptable just as would an animal

Pig-Out!

Buddha Got Some Bad Pork

For many people, the ubiquitous presence of "Buddha's Delight" as a vegetarian entrée at Chinese restaurants is all that is needed to prove that Buddhism prohibits the eating of meat. Oddly enough, however, there is no recorded instance of the Buddha ever suggesting to his followers that they give up meat. In fact, there is a hotly debated episode in Mahaparinibbana Sutta ("Last Days of the Buddha") in which the aging Buddha is understood to eat meat himself, in this case some "bad pork," which in fact appears to be involved in his death. While this same passage in Chinese translations has the Buddha eating "fungus," the issue remains unsettled and unsettling, particularly in consideration of the teacher's First Precept of nonviolence. Yet in light of his doctrine of the "Middle Path" of moderation, it's entirely possible that the Buddha intended to offer a sort of alternative to the self-righteous and strict vegetarianism practiced by the wealthy Brahmin caste from which he arose. Perhaps the Buddha wants you to order the Kung Pao Chicken every once in awhile.

The founder of Buddhism is on record as forbidding his followers to eat the flesh of humans, elephants, horses, dogs, snakes, lions, tigers, boars, and hyenas. So why didn't he mention chicken, fish, crab, squid, or any of the other creatures that find themselves on Asian menus?

While Zen Buddhists in China remain strict vegetarians, Japanese Buddhists allow themselves meat so long as it does not come from an animal specifically killed for them. In Tibet, their idea of playing it safe means eating any meat they choose, except fish (associated with aggression) and fowl (associated with desire).

> The founder of Buddhism is on record as forbidding his followers to eat the flesh of humans, elephants, horses, dogs, snakes, lions, tigers, boars, and hyenas. So why didn't he mention chicken, fish, crab, squid, or any of the other creatures that find themselves on Asian menus?

with an extra limb or one spotted with irregular pigmentation or stained with filth. None of it sits well with Yahweh.

Traits, like limbs, should come in predictable patterns, and the bat, for instance, was unpredictable and, therefore, regarded as unclean, not because of its living habits but because it was a freak of nature. The Hebrews didn't trust it either as a bird lacking feathers or a mouse with wings. Similarly, shellfish were unclean because they live in water but do not have scales like fish. Like cattle and sheep, the pig had hooves, but it was not a ruminant. Because it "divideth the hoof, yet cheweth not the cud," it was a troublemaker of a cosmic sort, probably somewhat damned, and definitely "unclean."

> The biblical injunction "Thou shalt not seethe a kid in its mother's milk" is the basis for the meat and dairy separation practiced in orthodox households.

How to Kosher

OK. Say you've got an animal obliging enough to both divide its hoof *and* chew its cud. Let's call it a cow. You've taken your cow to a *shochet* specially trained in *Shechitah*, the subset of the *Kashrut* (dietary law) dictating how animals are to be slaughtered. After the throat's slit, and the blood's been properly drained, you're still not ready to make brisket. What if your outwardly holy cow is actually an unclean freak of nature on the inside? Better call the *bodek*!

The *bodek's* job is to inspect all your cow's internal parts for anything unnatural. He'll also want to remove the sciatic nerve from your cow's thigh. In species where this is impractical, the entire rump is discarded. If you ask him why, he'll start telling you the story in Genesis where Jacob wrestles with the Angel of the Lord, who touches the patriarch's hip and thus causes him permanent injury in the area that the ancient Hebrews identified with

the sciatic nerve. Just nod, and say, "I see." You don't really need a sciatic anything anyway.

One more pointer. If your theoretical cow had a kid, and if you happen to have been saving milk from the mama, and if you have a hankering for veal, please, please, don't simmer the poor baby cow in the mama's milk! And to be on the safe side, don't cook *any* meat in milk. In fact, better get two entirely separate sets of kitchenware.

The biblical injunction "Thou shalt not seethe a kid in its mother's milk" is the basis for the meat and dairy separation practiced in orthodox households. While the cruel and unusual notion of

A Schochet *slaughters a lamb in accordance with Jewish dietary law.*

boiling a baby in maternal milk seems like something common compassion would preclude, the way in which it is extended points to something more abstract than mere compassion. In this case that something is the desire to keep *clean* the boundaries between the living and dead, between the giving and taking of life, between nursing and slaughter. Shed blood is an indicator of coming death. Shed milk is an indicator of recent birth. Don't even think of dirtying these two pure and symbolic essences with one another; it'd be akin to witchcraft.

The Hebrew *treifah* (literally "torn") is used to describe a mortally injured animal and has been expanded to describe all food that is not kosher. An animal described as *treifah* is half-dead, and that's one very bad (unclean) state in which to linger. Half-dead is a gray realm for spirits, necromancers, and witches.

This desire for a clear-cut distinction between the living and the dead also explains the body of law dictating the sharpness and efficient use of the slaughtering knife. When God ordains deaths, He wants it good and clean, says Moses. Deaths that God doesn't ordain are murder. Since God alone forges the chain of command, sin is anything that breaks this chain—forbidden fruit or murdered meat. OK?

Now go make your brisket.

> It was only after persistent efforts that Cardinal Joseph Ratzinger made special dispensation for the allergic, allowing devout celiac sufferers to partake in the body of Christ with special, gluten-light (though not gluten-free) bread. Special dispensations, however, would not be made without a note from the doctor.

■ GRAIN & BREAD ■

What's in a Wafer?

Today in Europe, the body of Christ comes with a "must sell by" date stamped on it. In 1998, against complaints by Vatican officials that "Communion wafers represent the body of our Lord; they are not like milk or frozen food," the European Union succeeded in forcing this marketing requirement on Italian nuns cranking out those flavorless little wheat chips Christians pop during Communion.

Around the same time, Catholics suffering from celiac disease (a rare allergic reaction to gluten affecting the digestive system) beset the Vatican with petitions demanding that altar breads made without gluten be accepted as a canonical substitute. Unfortunately, this protein is not only the stuff that makes dough doughy, but it's also essential to making bread breadlike—at least as far as the Roman Catholic Church is concerned. It was only after persistent efforts that Cardinal Joseph Ratzinger made special dispensation for the allergic, allowing devout celiac sufferers to partake in the body of Christ with special, gluten-light (though not gluten-free) bread. Special dispensations, however, would not be made without a note from the doctor.

While quibbling over percentages of various proteins in baked goods may seem a frivolous occupation to some, others see these theological sticklers as heroic guardians against excesses such as those perpetrated during Vatican II liberalization in the 1960s, when chips and coke were sometimes substituted for bread and wine by groovy youth priests trying to get on the same wave-length as groovy parishioners.

These sorts of disputes, however, are nothing new for the Roman Church, which by insisting on unleavened bread has been towing the line against the Protestant and Orthodox churches that defile their sacraments with yeast. Already with-in the first few centuries of its existence, Rome was dealing with Gnostic sects such as the Arto-tyrites, who said the body of Christ was in-carnated in sacramental cheese, and the Barsan-ians, who just took a pinch of raw flour and called that a sacrament.

> **P**riests administering the sacrament are always on the lookout for stray crumbs of the divine flesh that might spring from a sloppy communicant's lips. Centuries of cleaning up messes have taught the clergy to keep the *platen* on a *corporal*, which in this case is a fancy Latin name for a cloth folded envelope-style to catch falling crumbs of Jesus.

Sweet Crumbs of Jesus!

Differentiating itself from those Protestant upstarts led by Martin Luther, the Catholic Church has always empha-sized the "real" (though undetectable) presence of Christ in these holy morsels. Great pains have always been taken to treat these wafers with the respect befitting a member of the Trinity. Because the divine presence does not inhabit the bread until it is consecrated by a priest, the wafers are generally shipped from approved bakeries in humble card-board cartons, but in preparation for

their spiritual upgrade, they are normally stored in a gold or silver *ciborium* and laid out before the Mass upon a *platen*, or plate fashioned of a suitably up-scale metal.

Of course, just because a God is gen-erous enough to sacrifice himself to save your soul, doesn't mean He wants you to be wasteful about it. For this reason, priests administering the sacrament are always on the lookout for stray crumbs of the divine flesh that might spring from a sloppy communicant's lips. Centuries of cleaning up messes have taught the clergy to keep the *platen* on a *corporal*, which in this case is a fancy Latin name for a cloth folded envelope-style to catch falling crumbs of Jesus.

Finally, there must be provisions for those inevitable tidbits that do accumulate in the *corporal,* or crumble down into the bottom of the *ciborium*. You can't very well toss them out the window and have unbaptized birds accept-ing Holy Communion, and God forbid you should throw them down the sink and have them rub elbows with the unthinkable in the city's sewage system.

This is where the *sacrarium* comes in. The *sacrarium* is basically a sacramental sink with Vatican-approved plumbing that leads not to the municipal sanitary system but straight into the hallowed ground beneath the church. It is generally found to the right of the plain old secular sink in the sacristy, the room in which priests don their vestments, prepare the Eucharist, and do all this holy dish washing.

This sink comes into play again in another theologically delicate cleanup problem involving altar bread. Besides its use in the Mass, the Church approves the liturgical use of bread in the ordination of priests, cannonizations, several rites specific to particular localities and saints, and, most curiously, as a means of mopping up Holy Oil.

After anointing candidates for confirmation and ordination, the presiding bishop can't very well just wipe the excess oil from his fingers on a towel that's failed to complete confirmation classes or attend seminary. It's not just barbecue sauce he's having a problem with; it's a Holy essence that will confer blessing upon whatever it touches.

Thankfully, Church rubric eases the greasy bishop from his predicament by having him wipe the excess on bits of consecrated bread—in a sense returning the blessing to its source. The crumbs are then dumped down the *sacrarium* with all accidental blessings averted.

Of course you can't blame Jesus for this. He wouldn't have had any of these awkward situations in mind when He started the whole thing with the bread. Even though He instituted some form of this rite at His Farewell Dinner, telling His disciples to commemorate His sacrifice by breaking bread representing His flesh, He was pretty much saddled with the bread metaphor from day one. In fact, as soon as He was laid in a manger (a place for grain) in Bethlehem (literally translated as "House of Bread"), He was on His way to becoming the "bread of life."

Watch out for those crumbs, Father!

Manna Mania

The actual nature of manna—the miraculous food that fed the Israelites as they wandered in the wilderness—has been the topic of some rather idiosyncratic speculation.

Sketchy biblical descriptions leave plenty of room for extravagant flights of fancy. The book of Exodus only states that the heavens "rained down manna for the people to eat," that it appeared in the morning (Sabbaths excepted) as "thin flakes like frost on the ground," and that the food was collected and made into cakes.

Theories ranged from the rather straightforward, yet somewhat distasteful, attempt to explain the miraculous food-stuff in terms of honeydew (a sweet substance secreted on plants by aphids and scale insects) to the breathlessly off kilter, such as those laid out in The Manna Machine by George Sassoon and Rodney Dale, in which these wilderness rations are produced via top-secret (and possibly extraterrestrial) technology associated with both the Ark of the Covenant and the Holy Grail.

Others equate this heavenly bonanza with the anomalous "Fortean" events discussed by pioneering paranormalist Charles Fort, archiver of countless reports of "falls" of skyborne fish, frogs, or other organic matter for which scientific theory cannot seem to account.

Taking a much different, yet similarly iconoclastic, approach to the topic was Russian linguist and psychoanalyst Immanuel Velikovsky. In his 1950 book World in Collision, the scholar suggests that in 1450 B.C.E. the gaseous planet Jupiter spewed out Venus in the form of a comet, trailed by a tail that provided the fleeing Hebrews of Exodus with a carbohydrate sustenance they knew as manna. Despite the crazed grandeur of his astronomical speculations, Velikovsky piles up an impressive mountain of cross-cultural linguistic evidence

supporting his notions of a manna-like phenomena occurring on a planetary level.

Velikovsky connects the Hebrew association of honey and a heavenly paradise—a land of "milk and honey"—with the Olympian ambrosia, which is also compared by the Greeks with honey, a word that for them designated both honey produced by bees and honeydew produced by aphids. The latter was known to the ancient Persians as "raining honey," implying a celestial origin, and was metaphorically referred to by the Greeks themselves as the "sweat of the stars."

Velikovsky finds the same celestial association is made in the Hindu Vedas, which speak of the source of honey as a "honey lash" (generally equated with lightning, but serving Velikovsky's theory here as a comet's fiery tail). He discusses the common practice of making wine from honey in terms of the Greek's "nectar of the gods," the Hindu's beverage of immortality amrta (from which the word ambrosia is derived), and the mead which the gods of Celtic and Icelandic mythology are said to have bestowed upon man.

The grown-up Jesus explains it this way: "I am the bread of life: he that cometh to me shall never hunger; and he that believeth on me shall never thirst." And, later, the Bible tells us that at His final Passover, "Jesus took bread, and blessed, and brake it, and gave to them, and said, Take, eat: this is my body."

He makes His point with physical symbols in the miracle of the loaves and fishes in which He conjures picnic lunches for more than five thousand (including twelve baskets of leftovers for the apostolic cleanup crew) from five barley loaves and two fishes.

Eternity in a Grain of Wheat

Jesus consciously pulled His bread metaphors from sources that were already ancient, calling Himself the "bread from heaven" and likening this to the manna that fed the wandering Israelites centuries before. He updates it a bit, though, explaining that this new bread, the "bread of life," is not just about daily sustenance but about eternal life.

But has He really said something new here? Or has Jesus just reached deeper into the timeless bread box of metaphor?

Roughly a thousand years before, Egyptians were making weird little dolls consisting of handfuls of Nile mud peppered through with grains of barley nearing germination. Once sprouted, these ancient Chia Pets, or "grain mummies," would be wrapped in linen bandages, placed in miniature sarcophagi, and left in tombs as symbols of the eternal return of life. But the powerful image of apparently lifeless kernels of grain springing back to life when given a proper burial probably began stirring symbolic associations even earlier, with the very dawn of

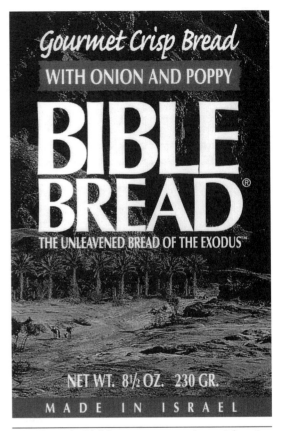

The "bread of life"—gourmet version, with onion and poppy.

> The equation of oven and womb is at least as old as the art of baking itself. Phallic loaves of bread just naturally came out in that shape, and it doesn't take a particularly dirty mind to equate the swelling of bread in the oven to the swelling of its symbolic counterpart on the male.

horticulture in Mesopotamia seven thousand or so years before.

While grain is grain and bread is bread, the Egyptians found the same sort of symbolism in the stuff—whether it was in the field or baked in loaves, as both were used to represent regeneration; bread just made them think more about sex.

The equation of oven and womb is at least as old as the art of baking itself. Phallic loaves of bread just naturally came out in that shape, and it doesn't take a particularly dirty mind to equate the swelling of bread in the oven to the swelling of its symbolic counterpart on the male. Like the Egyptians, the Greeks even made exacting replicas of phalluses out of bread, and they used these creations in rituals of regeneration such as Thesmophoria, a women's harvest celebration dedicated to Demeter.

What Would Jeremiah Say?

But is there any direct connection between ancient Greek fertility rites and those bits of the body of Christ hiding in the *ciborium*? Is it possible that Christians are swallowing a much bigger bite of history than they suppose?

If we back up to a time when the early Christians celebrated eucharistic "love feasts" just down the road from initiation sites of near Eastern mystery religions, we may find some interesting crumbs of evidence. Even when Christianity was merely one of many secretive cults defying the imperial religion of Rome, the form of bread used in communion was already fixed. Paintings in the catacombs depict believers celebrating the rite with *quadra* or small cakes of bread divided on top into *quadrants* by the sign of the cross.

While the Roman Church today derives authority from these ancient roots, those early days were in fact a time of wild and woolly theological eclecticism—a time when the very definition of Christianity was up for grabs. Three centuries or so later, the Church had it all tucked in and nailed down and refused to allow its youth to carouse with Neoplatonists, Zoroastrians, and various Gnostics, but

it seems that these Eucharistic *quadra* were, in fact, a symbol picked up during those early days of more easy going theological exchange.

Cakes representing sacrifice were used throughout the Mediterranean and near East in religious rites. The Greeks made a form of sacrificial cake called *bous* (literally "ox"), so named because its top was marked with a design representing two pairs of horns crossed so as to divide the cake into quadrants. These cakes were used in the worship of Diana, Hecate, and Apollo, and their round shape was intended to suggest the moon, with its four quarters demarcated by the cross of horns.

Throughout Mesopotamia and into the West, the bull and the moon were frequently associated, and the animal's horns were often used symbolically to suggest the moon's crescent. Both were sacred, for instance, to the Canaanite fertility goddess Astarte (the Babylonian Ishtar), also known as the Queen of Heaven and consort of Ba'al, to whom just such cakes were also offered. Old Testament prophet Jeremiah observed these rites firsthand and was none too pleased when the Israelites began picking up idolatrous habits from their Canaanite neighbors, complaining that "the children gather wood, the fathers kindle the fire, and the women kneed their dough, to make cakes to the Queen of Heaven."

While Christians today choose not to associate their holy wafers with moon goddesses, fertility rites, Canaanite temple prostitutes of Astarte, or the babies sacrificed to her hubby, Ba'al, the sacrament's role as a surrogate for a

body sacrificed and mangled on the cross may be gruesome enough for those who do choose to dwell on such things. The association of the Christian sacrament with the Greek *bous* ("ox") also calls to mind the sacrificial bull in whose blood cult followers were "washed" during initiation into some of the mystery cults, including that of the soldier-god Mithras, whose followers are said to have eaten a sacramental bread (a *mizd*, related to the Latin *mass*) marked with the emblem of Mithras' sword (em-ployed to slay a mythic bull).

Whatever exotic heathen flavors of the past these little Christian wafers have absorbed, they remain curiously bland, pointedly flavorless, and inoffensive, perhaps in an effort to lift the mind from the sensual and specific to the spiritual and abstract. After all, a little abstraction is called for when ritual cannibalism is implied, and you've got something mushy in your mouth.

■ **H O L I D A Y   E A T Z** ■

The Cosmic Egg

As many as nine hundred years before the first Easter, the Chinese were decorating eggs for special occasions, covering them with red lacquer to announce the birth of a child. In ancient Greece, Rome, Persia, and Egypt, decorated eggs were also given as gifts. Elaborate beadwork has frequently ornamented eggs in the Middle East and parts of Central Europe,

while in Africa ostrich eggs are often adorned with patterns etched into the shell.

Valued universally for their association with fertility, birth, and the perfection of their form, they are also prized as symbols of cosmic creation. Chinese and related Japanese myths describe the Creation as a primordial egg consisting of a yolk and white, blobs of dark and light, yin and yang, or Earth and heaven. The Greeks, Egyptians, Babylonians, Phoenicians, and the Dogon of Africa all refer to a cosmic egg from which the universe is born.

European alchemists puttered through the Renaissance looking for the "Philosopher's Egg": the matrix from which they would hatch the Philosopher's Stone; the element that would transmute all metals into gold. The egg's four distinct partitions of shell, membrane, white, and yolk clearly suggested (at least to the alchemists) the four primal elements of Earth, air, water, and fire.

Markedly less cosmic, yet much more obvious, is the egg's association with baby-making and all the thrills that this entails. Because of this, it shouldn't surprise us that for centuries the exchange of decorated eggs was more about flirting than faith in any religious creed.

From France eastward into Slavic Europe, young people (almost always female) would pretty up eggs to present to sweethearts like valentines. German suitors were known to scribble sweet nothings on slips of paper and stash these in hollowed and decorated eggs. These blown eggs were sometimes fixed to an Easter tree—a tradition supposedly begun by a love-crazed young man zealously using these trinkets to decorate a tree outside the bedroom window of his sleeping sweetheart.

Alsatian girls took their chances in the dating game by hiding decorated Easter eggs outside their homes and waiting for eligible, and hopefully desirable, young men to come seek them out as a token of their interest.

In Luxembourg, the custom got even more involved. On "Pretzel Sunday," three weeks before Easter, the amorous young

> Another story relates how Mary Magdalen brought a basket of eggs to the Savior's tomb to snack on while preparing the body for burial. Upon her arrival, she uncovered the eggs to find they had been transformed from white to a strange array of brilliant colors.

man presented his lady with an ornately decorated pretzel. To officially accept this advance, the recipient reciprocates with a decorated egg three weeks later.

In associating the custom of decorating eggs with Christ's resurrection, the Church cooked up a number of imaginative rationales. One of the simpler versions simply explains that Catholic nuns in the vicinity of Rome would regularly bring eggs to church as gifts for the needy. Coloring them on Easter Sunday just came to them as a natural way to dress up gifts for the holiday.

In Greece and Germany, eggs dyed red were said to be colored by the blood of Christ. In Poland, they say that while at the scene of her son's crucifixion, Mary begged the centurions to show mercy, offering them eggs as a futile enticement. In falling on the eggs, her tears stained them rainbow hues. Another story relates how Mary Magdalen brought a basket of eggs to the Savior's tomb to snack on while preparing the body for burial. Upon her arrival, she uncovered the eggs to find they had been transformed from white to a strange array of brilliant colors.

Christmas: A Preserving Tradition

While there aren't a lot of Christmas carols about rotting fruit or rancid meat, historical issues with preserving food through the winter have played a tremendous role in determining what European-influenced cultures consider to be the "flavor" of Christmas. In general, the preparation and presentation of most foods associated with the holiday reflect practices that were both fashionable and pragmatic during the Middle Ages.

Because it was generally impossible

The tradition of decorated eggs dates back thousands of years.

The turkey did not replace the Christmas swan on the royal English table until 1851.

for medieval farmers to stockpile enough fodder to keep all their animals well fed throughout the winter—and because there wouldn't be a lot of vegetables popping through the frozen topsoil—the season was generally a good time for meat-eaters and a bad time for livestock.

As the winter reached its most severe around the solstice, a variety of animals would be slaughtered—and this variety is reflected in the diversity of meats found on the table at a traditional Christmas dinner in England. Both fowl and four-legged meats were commonly served, and the ham/turkey schism in America regarding which meat appears on the holiday

table is a domesticated update of the traditional English choice between roasted boar and swan. Imported from America, the turkey did not replace the Christmas swan on the royal English table until 1851.

Because Christmas, like any holiday, is largely a traditionalist affair fixated on perpetuating the past, the presentation of the meat is carefully stylized to evoke atavisitic memories of our glorious hunter-gatherer past.

Even though the Christmas turkey may come from the freezer bin of a thoroughly modern supermarket where we normally purchase conveniently preprocessed cuts shrink-wrapped in single servings, on the holiday table we want to see the entire animal (or close to it) laid out as if freshly bagged by the hunter or slaughtered in our own backyard.

In England, the Christmas swan would be gutted, boned, and then restuffed with its own insides and other ingredients, just as we stuff our American gobblers to retain that all-important shape suggesting an animal just brought back from the hunt.

The same was done for the boar, with special pains taken to retain the head. While the cranium, brains, and bones of the face were removed from beneath the flesh, the boar's jawbone was left in place to maintain some semblance of the original shape. The head cavity was then filled with stuffing consisting of the usual ingredients along with minced tongue. The ears were boiled separately and skewered back to their respective places. With boar rather rarely served in the last several decades, the meat of pigs' heads has sometimes been chopped, boiled, and shaped in a special boar's head mold, sold along with decorative tusks and glass eyes that complete the holiday masquerade.

Sometimes the swan might be stuffed with an entire and slightly smaller goose and a chicken would be crammed inside. This multiplicity

> In England, the Christmas swan would be gutted, boned, and then restuffed with its own insides and other ingredients, just as we stuff our American gobblers to retain that all-important shape suggesting an animal just brought back from the hunt.

of meats, inventively combined or stuffed one into the other, is probably influenced by the combinations found in medieval meat pies. These could contain an entire menagerie of meat: "four geese, three rabbits, four wild ducks, two woodcocks, six snipe, four partridges, two curlews, six pigeons, seven blackbirds," according to one instance reported.

A humbler yet closer relative of such pies would be mincemeat. Originally, mincemeat contained various minced bits of animal along with dried fruits, bread, nuts, and sugar. Though the meat was eventually removed from the pie, it remained in the name. Removing the crust from this pie without meat left a gummy mass of ingredients that through various permutations and cross-breeding with the English Christmas pudding eventually produced the American version of fruitcake.

Yummy! A classic English meat pie (with egg thrown in for good measure).

Perhaps one reason Americans so often loathe this holiday gift item is its relation to the Christmas pudding—a much older dessert that originated in a time of radically different culinary notions.

Also called "plum pudding" because it contained prunes (the only form of plums to be found in mid-winter) along with dried fruits like raisins and citrus peels, the dish might also contain figs, resulting in yet another name: "figgy pudding." And while the word "pudding" may be

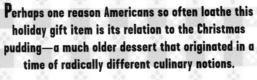

> Perhaps one reason Americans so often loathe this holiday gift item is its relation to the Christmas pudding—a much older dessert that originated in a time of radically different culinary notions.

consistent, it is by no means consistent with the American notion of pudding.

When the English talk about Christmas puddings, it's often with a slight smirk (like the American with his fruitcakes.) Though not quite the joke they once were, these puddings in Tudor and Stuart times were prepared like the notorious haggis or blood "puddings," by boiling the ingredients in the sealed stomach of a pig or other animal. Today, the spongy mixture of flour, sugar, spices,

A typical English Christmas pudding. Note: these are also known to be particularly useful in hand-to-hand combat.

family of baked goods historically prized for their inclusion of ginger, cinnamon, cardamom, nutmeg, and even pepper. Lending these spices additional value at this time of year was their origin in the East—a place loosely associated with stories from the Bible. Their status as a "royal" luxury and their Eastern origin particularly associated them with the gifts brought to the Christ Child by the three oriental magi, or kings.

A primary ingredient of *Lebkuchen* was honey. As a substance that might harden but would never spoil, honey also served as a preservative, and fruits submerged in it for longer shelf life were sometimes removed, exposed to the air, and crystallized into Christmas "sugarplums" or other dainties.

fruits, nuts, and booze is boiled in a cloth bag instead of an animal gut, but traditionalists still insist on beef suet as a primary ingredient, doing little to endear the dish to modern tastes.

Plum puddings are traditionally prepared the first Sunday before Advent (five weeks before Christmas) and are considered inedible until suitably aged. Highly prized puddings as old as five or six years only need to be steamed to prepare them for the holiday table. The use of the animal stomach here for airtight food storage served medieval households in the same way as intestines served them as sausage casing to store ground meat.

> **O**ne further distinguishing feature of the Christmas pudding was alcohol, either ale, wine, brandy, or combinations thereof. This ingredient served not only to heighten the taste but to also preserve the pudding during its prolonged aging process.

The heavy spicing of Christmas puddings and other dishes of the season represents another historic technique for preventing bacteria from partying away on winter rations. The fact that spices were a luxury item imported at great expense from the Middle East also made their use particularly appropriate for festive occasions. Christmas gingerbread, like the German *Lebkuchen* and *Pfeffernüsse* (literally "pepper nuts"), represent a whole

One further distinguishing feature of the Christmas pudding was alcohol, either ale, wine, brandy, or combinations thereof. This ingredient served not only to heighten the taste but to also preserve the pudding during its prolonged aging process. Alcohol, of course, is a time-honored means of not only fighting bacteria but also fighting the gloom of winter, and its warming influence is part of the Christmas traditions of mulled wine, spiked eggnog, and the English wassail bowl offered to chilly carolers.

The technique of preserving fruit in alcohol (as well as the generous sampling of this preservative medium) was probably responsible for the delightfully foolhardy sport of "Snapdragon," an old English Christmas game in which players compete to snatch bits of alchohol-soaked fruit from a bowl of brandy that has been set alight.

Flipping It on Shrove Tuesday

Every year since 1445, the citizens of Olney, England, get a little bit barmy on Shrove Tuesday. While elsewhere the faithful regard Shrove Tuesday as a day to attend a shriving service to get themselves good and shriven, the good people of Olney mark the day by charging wildly through the streets flipping pancakes in their skillets.

Not to be outdone by their fellow pancake racers in Olney, England, these women in Liberal, Kansas have been running the same race since 1950.

In Olney, this day of confession (shriving)—the last before Lent—is the occasion of their world famous Pancake Race. The origin of the race is popularly traced to a particularly thrifty and stubborn medieval housewife hellbent on making good use of her remaining supply of eggs and butter before they were to be thrown out with the beginning of the Lenten fast the following day. Her solution was to make piles of pancakes. However, the task ended up taking longer than she'd supposed, and when she heard the bells calling her to confession, she is said to have grabbed the pan and sprinted to the church, still dressed in her apron and flapping her jacks as she ran. Not to be outdone, her neighbors followed suit, and the one reaching the church first received a kiss from the sexy bell-swingin' sexton.

Today, apron, pan, and kiss are still

> **E**very year since 1445, the citizens of Olney, England, get a little bit barmy on Shrove Tuesday. While elsewhere the faithful regard Shrove Tuesday as a day to attend a shriving service to get themselves good and shriven, the good people of Olney mark the day by charging wildly through the streets flipping pancakes in their skillets.

part of the race, but since 1950 the women of Olney have been joined in the contest by international competitors simultaneously running the same race in Liberal, Kansas. Despite the Brit's five-century headstart, Liberal now stands tied, with American flippers attaining the winning time 25 of the 50 years they've competed.

Massasoit's Guest List

Inclined to see demonic idolatry lurking behind every rock, the pilgrims left the Church of England in a tizzy over corruption they saw manifested in innumerable ways, including the Anglican celebration of Christmas and Easter. The Pilgrims' religion permitted them only three "holy-days," including the weekly Sabbath, and two moveable feasts celebrated as occasion demanded. These were the Day of Humiliation and Fasting, and the Day of Thanksgiving and Praise.

As colonists in the New World, these Puritan Separatists faced problems of a different sort. After losing more than half their number during their first American winter, their prospects looked dicey, and it was only the blessing of a bountiful harvest the following year that pulled them through.

Though their hearts were no doubt filled with thanksgiving that autumn, this was *not* the name they applied to that celebratory feast shared with the Indians in 1621. If anything, they would have casually regarded this celebration as "Ingathering" or "Harvest Home," an old English agricultural festival which, for the Separatists, would have had about as much religious significance as the opening of a farmers' market.

Sadly, the image of feasting Pilgrim and Indian bowed prayerfully together in gratitude for the blessings of an ecumenical God has almost nothing to do with historical Plymouth, and everything to do with wave upon wave of European émigrés arriving on U.S. shores during the early twentieth century. Popularized during those years, when difficulties with immigrant assimilation created a demand for a mythic model of tolerance, this Thanksgiving fable attributes to the colonists a degree

> Originally, only the point man for the Wampanoag, Chief Massasoit, was invited along with his family. But the pilgrims had no conception of the Native American notion of kin. When Massasoit dropped by, he did so with an extended family consisting of 90 or so additional guests.

Chief Massasoit (minus his extended family).

of religious tolerance, which they themselves would have found offensive.

The Puritan Separatist were separatists to the nth degree, having removed themselves from the Puritan movement, which removed itself from the Reformist movement, which removed itself from Anglican Protestantism, which removed itself from the Roman Church. Given this rather poor record in the "getting along well with others" category, how on earth could we believe that the pilgrims would choose to pray side by side with unconverted "savages"? In fact, one of the biggest bones the Separatists had with Anglican doctrine was the decree that made all royal subjects members in the church— a privilege they felt should be reserved for "visible saints" (i.e., those claiming religious experience of saving grace).

Rather than an effort to share their faith or share the wealth of their crops, the invitation of Indians to the feast was above all a political move, an attempt to maneuver the neighboring Wampanoag to deed desirable farmlands to the colonists. From firsthand accounts of those three days spent entertaining the Indians, we know that in addition to some serious power-lunching, the pilgrims

also engaged their guests in competitive sport and sought to impress them with frightful displays of English musketry. The entire affair would've been understood by the Wampanoag in terms of the native American potlatch, an undeniably similar ritual in which neighboring tribes take turns competing not as warriors but as hosts offering food and gifts to visitors in a passive-aggressive spirit of competition—the same sort of spirit of one-upsmanship motivating many a dinner party today.

Even this, however, was more hospitality than the pilgrims initially intended. Originally, only the point man for the Wampanoag, Chief Massasoit, was invited along with his family. But the pilgrims had no conception of the Native American notion of kin. When Massasoit dropped by, he did so with an extended family consisting of 90 or so additional guests.

Noting that Indians now outnumbered the colonists by more than half, Massasoit took charge of the situation by dispatching hunters to the woods to rustle up more food. Returning later with five deer, it was the Wampanoag who provided the bulk of food and guests at the feast. As an affair dominated and catered by Indians then, it may be easier to understand how the first "Thanksgiving" came to resemble a Native American potlatch more than a gathering of pious Calvinists breaking bread.

However, despite the predominance of venison on the menu, traditionalists can rest assured that turkey *was* served by the colonists (along with "waterfowl," cod, bass, and other fish).

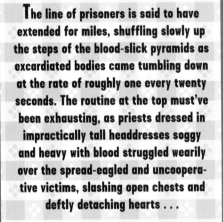

The line of prisoners is said to have extended for miles, shuffling slowly up the steps of the blood-slick pyramids as excardiated bodies came tumbling down at the rate of roughly one every twenty seconds. The routine at the top must've been exhausting, as priests dressed in impractically tall headdresses soggy and heavy with blood struggled wearily over the spread-eagled and uncooperative victims, slashing open chests and deftly detaching hearts . . .

■ THE RELIGIOUS SIDE OF CANNIBALISM ■

New World Man-Eating

The Aztecs knew a thing or two about human sacrifice. The dedication of their Great Temple of Tenochtitlan in 1486, for instance, would've been impressive by any gorehound's standards. During this four-day bloodbath, priests dispatched some twenty thousand victims—a harvest of prisoners taken over several years specifically to meet the needs of these few days. The line of prisoners is said to have extended for miles, shuffling slowly up the steps of the blood-slick pyramids as excardiated bodies came tumbling down at the rate of roughly one every twenty seconds. The routine at the top must've been exhausting, as priests dressed in impractically tall headdresses soggy and heavy with blood struggled wearily over the spread-eagled and uncooperative victims, slashing open chests and deftly detaching hearts, which would then be held aloft to release energy (and spastic gouts of blood) to the Sun, otherwise known as Huitzilopochtli, the war god.

The energy released was called *tonalli*,

Engraving of the Great Temple of Tenochtitlan. Where many a bloody good time was had by all.

derived from *tona*, which means "to make heat or sun," and this is exactly what the priests were doing: making the sun (and the earth below) go on. The heart, the muscle through which the warm blood pumped, was valuable to Huitzilopochtli as the cradle of this energy in man. The rest of the body was just packaging, and after being bounced down those steep stairs, it was skinned and dismembered. Heads were piled as trophies at the pyramid's base, and the limbless trunks were sometimes fed to animals in the imperial menagerie. What became of the legs and arms is, however, the subject of some debate. Most scholars agree that these were eaten. Why and to what extent cannibalism was practiced among the Aztecs remains somewhat controversial.

Though their diet was known to include tropical fruits, vegetables, water fowl, deer, turkeys, dogs, armadillos, gophers, weasels, mice, reptiles, fish, insects, and pond scum (which they made into cakes), anthropologists like Marvin Harris have insisted that Aztec man-eating was the result of limited protein sources. But Harris is pretty much on his own in suggesting that *homo sapiens* were a staple meat, as most evidence suggests that any spare arms and legs cooked up in Tenochtitlan were eaten only by the upper castes, the warriors, and priests.

Noting how, on special occasions, Moctezuma would make a practice of inviting rulers of neighboring peoples to witness sacrifices of prisoners—some of whom came from the regions in question—other scholars have interpreted this cannibalism as a terroristic display of power, an extension of the sacrifice symbolically completing the annihilation of those to be subjugated.

The most convincing theories, however, relate to the idea of strengthening authority within the society rather than outside the state. Cannibalism in this sense is a handy and intimidating means of affirming the godlike position of the upper castes. Costumed as deities for sacrificial rites, their identification with the gods continues as they later share the food (or at least the leftovers) reserved for gods. Above all are the priests and nobility, who during the sacrifice soak up the same blood that feeds Huitzilopochtli. But there is a trickle-down effect, and for the warrior classes, the crumbs of human flesh that fall from the divine table represent the ultimate in class-conscious dining.

Saddled with the outsider legacy of some fabulously biased fifteenth-century European explorers, modern anthropologists tend to be extremely cautious in their discussion of cannibalism among the Aztecs, or other indigenous peoples. Cultural misunderstanding, after all, is inherent in the very word "cannibal," a name that originated with the notorious sailors of the Niña, the Pinta, and the Santa Maria. Believing that the Caribbean natives they chanced upon ate human captives, which may have been true, the crew did a number on the word the natives used to describe themselves, changing *caniba* (literally "strong or brave man") to "cannibal."

Brushes with fearsome man-eating foreigners, a centuries-old feature of any decent traveler's tale, was part of the mythological backdrop against which Columbus and his men recounted their adventures. But the fear of being gnawed upon by unfamiliar races is almost universal and has been reported among African tribes, who have occasionally fled in fear from white men they believed to be on the prowl for human flesh.

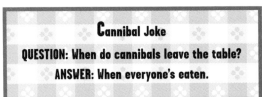

Cannibal Joke

QUESTION: When do cannibals leave the table?

ANSWER: When everyone's eaten.

All the world loves a good cannibal story, particularly one that demonstrates moral inferiority of another group, but the sad truth is that the ubiquitous taboo on human flesh has eliminated the exotic peril of cannibalist cultures from the face of the globe. In the New World, Africa and Polynesia European fortune seekers, followed by missionaries and eventually by colonial rulers, have erased *homo sapiens* from the native diet over the centuries. It's history.

But who made Europeans stop eating each other?

Old World Man-Eating

Beyond the occasional and sinister suggestion of cannibalism that turns up in the study of Western myths and philology, more explicit references can be found in the works of Greek and Roman historians and travelers, who portray human sacrifice and man-eating as a fact of life among the Germanic tribes of Gaul and Scandinavia, the Swedes, the Celts, the Anglo-Saxons, Slavs, and even among their despised neighbors, the Phoenicians and Scythians.

Of course, there's always a possibility of bias and willful misunderstanding in such accounts, as demonstrated by the tendency of the Roman State to literalize the early Christian's "eating" of Christ's flesh, and thereby justify persecution. Once the Christians learned this trick, however, they adapted it slightly for their own use. Recycling the story to smear their Gnostic rivals a few centuries later, St. Augustine, Epiphanius, and other Church fathers accused the heretics of "polluting the sacraments," by kneading the blood of children into dough for altar bread, or grinding up the flesh of fetuses for similar purposes.

While these accusations may have no

Siggy musing on the origins of cannibalism.

laid out in *Totem and Taboo*, the good doctor explains how the "moral impulse" was born amid an ancient tribe of Oedipally motivated male siblings, who rebel against dad, do him in, and then eat the evidence. Chowing down together on the old man's body, they effectively share the guilt that is to become the basis of all future moral dogma and religion. At one point, Sigmund suggests the tribal chief could have been Moses, while at another point he nudges the date back a few millenia, claiming such behavior would be typical of primates in the wild.

Chuckling over Freud's lack of fieldwork, anthropologists of subsequent decades have gone on to create archetypes of their own—typologies such as *endocannibalism* versus *exocannibalism* (distinguishing between human game taken from within or from without the tribe); and *ritual* versus *gastronomic* cannibalism (flesh consumed because of its food value versus flesh consumed to dominate an enemy, acquire his traits, or to create a magical bond, as with tribes that dispose of their dead by reverently eating them).

As swiftly as these models are created, objections are raised. What, for instance, defines "ritual cannibalism"? Some anthropologists dismiss the idea as meaningless. If carving a Thanksgiving butterball or indulging in the ritual of morning coffee can have symbolic weight, isn't it fairly safe to assume that eating the flesh of your neighbor will inevitably have *some* ritualistic import? The controversy over nomenclature now extends to the word "cannibal" itself. Thanks to the cultural misunderstanding that engendered the name, the term has recently fallen out of academic fashion, and polite scholars now demurely refer to cannibals as "anthropophagites." ⬛

more basis than contemporary hysteria regarding a "hidden holocaust" of infant sacrifice at the hands of satanic cults, harder evidence for ancient European cannibalism has been provided during the last several decades by archeologists. From evidence such as the naturally mummified remains of an Iron Age victim sacrificially strangled and dumped in a central European peat bog to clues found at Neanderthal burial sites, where scrape marks on human bones indicate postmortem defleshing, many anthropologists are beginning to take more seriously the accounts of human sacrifice and cannibalism reported by authors of classical antiquity.

Up through the twentieth century, all discussion of cannibalism seems hopelessly entangled in myth and mythologizing. The indelicate Dr. Freud's take on the cannibalistic origins of religion, for example, relies upon a highly speculative bit of anthropology. In the suspiciously Judeo-Christian scenario of primal guilt

> **U**p through the twentieth century, all discussion of cannibalism seems hopelessly entangled in myth and mythologizing. The indelicate Dr. Freud's take on the cannibalistic origins of religion, for example, relies upon a highly speculative bit of anthropology.

Omnivorous Adventures

For some, eating is an adventure. For others, it's an errand. Some go to great pains to acquire interesting food of high quality. They love to eat food, cook food, shop for food, discuss food, and even read entire books about food.

Others just eat so they will have eaten. How does this difference arise?

Children are born into a world that is entirely edible. All they know of it comes through the mouth.

Even before the new-born learns to direct its gaze, it has begun collecting first impressions with its mouth. And once it masters the use of fingers, these are used to seize informative bits of the environment and pass them on to the mouth for further analysis.

But at some point, we start thinking inside our craniums and not our mouths. We no longer need to explore the world by tasting it.

We don't need to put foreign objects in our mouths to understand them. In fact, we've got it all pretty well figured out. After all, we're two years old.

So why do some kids keep putting strange things in their mouths even after they've grown up?

Swiss neuropsychologists may have stumbled upon one part of the puzzle. In May of 1997, the professional journal *Neurology* published a report on the "Gourmand Syndrome," which author Theodor Landis, a neurologist at the University of Geneva, describes as a "rare benign eating disorder strongly linked to damage of the right hemisphere of the brain."

This is not to be confused with bulimia. "Sufferers" of Gourmand Syndrome don't spend their time secretly jamming cheap candy down their gullets or hanging over toilet bowls. Instead, their cerebral trauma results in zero tolerance for mundane fare and an irresistible compulsion to seek out fine foods, exotic tastes, and novel culinary combinations.

Landis' conclusions were drawn after more than 12 years of research conducted with Zurich neuropsychologist Marianne Regard in which they studied 723 brain lesion patients. A significant 36 of the 723 were found to exhibit these traits. Colleagues relate these findings to a general tendency among these patients to express newfound sensual and intuitive tendencies formerly suppressed by the traumatized region of the brain.

But you don't need a hole in your head to become an epicure. For many it's just a continuation of the newborn's ravenous appetite for experience. It's not about filling the gut, but filling the senses. A way to explore the world by tasting it.

And wherever curiosity is key to desire,

> **"Sufferers"** of Gourmand Syndrome don't spend their time secretly jamming cheap candy down their gullets or hanging over toilet bowls. Instead, their cerebral trauma results in zero tolerance for mundane fare and an irresistible compulsion to seek out fine foods, exotic tastes, and novel culinary combinations.

prohibitions only make desire stronger. Those foods our culture locks away under taboos hold a particularly perverse fascination for gourmands driven to leave no food unsampled. This chapter then is a sort of peepshow through the keyhole of that locked pantry door. A chamber of horrors for those who've shaken their oral fixation. An expansive thrill for those stubborn souls who continue to explore.

■ **M E A L   O N   A   L E A S H** ■

Puppies and Protein

In many countries, dogs are allowed on the dining table. These dogs are not spoiled, as Westerners might suspect. They are fresh and nutritious.

In the West, the dog is a sacred cow. In fact, eating dog is practically cannibalistic. Trapping and devouring a stray mutt (much less the family pooch) would be a fairly good way to convert your neighbors into a lynch mob.

We just *don't* eat dogs. But we kill plenty of them. Thirteen million annually. And that's about 120 million pounds of protein rich meat that elsewhere in the world might not go to waste.

It wasn't always like this. Even in the

A Chihuahua dressed in her Sunday finest. The Aztecs gobbled up these puppies at the rate of 400 or so per week.

West, ancient canines didn't always lead the dog's life they do today. Hippocrates— Greek role model to your family doctor— believed that dog was quite good for you and prescribed the meat in cases of waning vitality. Wealthy Romans impressed their guests by serving suckling puppy. The Phoenicians, too, were said to be fond of puppies, particularly roasted ones (of course, they also sacrificed human infants to their gods).

The Chinese also preferred puppies to adults and bred smaller table-sized dogs. This was the Chow (in more ways than one). The Black Tongue Chow was bred specifically for table use. The Chihuahua had a similar culinary heritage. According to early Spanish explorers, roughly four hundred or so of these conveniently "hairless" dogs were sold as meat in Aztec markets every week.

Dog is eaten or has been eaten throughout Southeast Asia and the Pacific Islands, in Korea, and in parts of Africa.

Vietnamese chefs are known for dog chops simmered in white wine, as well as a spicy canine-filled sausage. In Hong Kong, the sale and consumption of dog meat has been officially outlawed but by no means eradicated. Western tourists should be advised that it still shows up frequently on menus. Just ask about the item listed as "fragrant meat."

While Northern Europeans generally do not grow hungry at the sight of a well-muscled dog, it would be wrong to assume that the practice has never existed in these regions. Not only was the canine fox regarded as a delicacy in Russia, but the inhabitants of various Alpine regions at one time would dry and smoke dog meat (*Hundeschinken*) like bacon.

And yes, even residents of one of our fifty states enjoyed the taste of man's best friend at one time (in the years before statehood). In the days before colonial rule, natives of Hawaii, Samoa, Tahiti, and Fiji would regularly roast whole dogs luau-style. Despite their intolerance, Captain Cook's crew did manage to sample the meat before banning it, and the Captain himself recorded a surprisingly favorable response to roast leg of dog, allowing that the meat had a rather tasty resemblance to mutton.

> **H**ippocrates—Greek role model to your family doctor—believed that dog was quite good for you and prescribed the meat in cases of waning vitality.

The Cat in the Bag

No matter how persuasive the purr, cats have not always managed to escape the stew pot. In Spain and elsewhere in Europe, overabundance of strays has frequently resulted in their being employed as a cheap substitute for more upmarket meats. This rural practice of stewing up unwanted felines, however, has more often been regarded as a crime against the taste buds than a crime against God.

The fact that both cats and rabbits are kept as pets, and are said to have a comparable taste, has led to feline being swapped for hare in kitchens where economy is a priority. One result of this is the tradition, still practiced in Old World restaurants, of adorning rabbit dishes with the animal's ears, both as decoration and testimony to the meat's authenticity.

The substitution of cat for suckling pig was a scam widespread enough in seventeenth-century England to have given rise to some common turns of speech. In this case, the ruse involved selling the live animal in a bag (or old English "poke") to an unsuspecting rube. Supposing that he'd purchased an expensive piglet or "pig in a poke," the ruse would succeed as long as no one "let the cat out of the bag."

In China, they pull the old cat switcheroo in *lun fung foo* or "Dragon Phoenix Tiger Soup." While many Chinese will certainly eat tiger if they can get it, this "tiger" is a soup of metaphors, with domestic feline standing in for tiger, chicken for phoenix, and snake for dragon. Cat's eyes sold in Cantonese food markets, however, are the real thing.

Guinea Pigs and Garlic

Who says you can't get pork from a guinea pig? Contributing at least half the protein of the Peruvian diet, they are kept like rabbits in outdoor pens or even in the kitchen where they dispose of food scraps until becoming food themselves. Even in this country, roasted guinea pig with garlic and cumin can be found on the menu in certain restaurants catering to a South American clientele in Queens. The Arawak Indians encountered by

Columbus in the Caribbean also dined on the guinea pig, while North American Indians on the continent hunted its cousins: the groundhog, woodchuck, and prairie dog.

Steak with a Saddle

If American laws were made by sentiment alone, eating dog or cat would get you damned to the very heart of hell, while eating horse would get you a place in hell's suburbs.

Evidence of this passionately protective attitude toward horses can be found in the tone of debate over California's 1998 voters' initiative banning the sale of horse meat in the state, and more so in the success with which this measure was passed.

Maybe this is part of our country's cowboy legacy—a sense of debt to the animal for making possible our westward expansion—but it should be noted that other cultures, equally dependent on the horse, have displayed no such squeamishness about making culinary use of the animal once it lost its giddyap and go.

Slightly leaner, tougher, and sweeter than beef, horse meat was a staple of the South American Gaucho, who happily stewed or made jerky of animals not wearing saddles. A nomadic culture even more reliant upon the horse, the ancient Mongols were not only the first to raise and race horses, but also the first to eat them. Horse was their meat of choice, and in Central Asia it is still valued as a special treat. The modern Yakut in Siberia would not consider celebrating a wedding without

> **T**he substitution of cat for suckling pig was a scam widespread enough in seventeenth-century England to have given rise to some common turns of speech. In this case, the ruse involved selling the live animal in a bag (or old English "poke") to an unsuspecting rube. Supposing that he'd purchased an expensive piglet or "pig in a poke," the ruse would succeed as long as no one "let the cat out of the bag."

Some attribute our aversion to horsemeat to our country's cowboy legacy; others place the blame on Mister Ed.

slaughtering a horse for the marriage feast, employing a boiled head as a centerpiece for the festive spread. Further East, horse was only added to the menu centuries later but is now popular in China and Japan, where it is often prepared as sukiyaki.

The equestrian Germanic tribes of Northern Europe were a bit more ambivalent about the matter, regarding the horse as a tribal totem and consuming its flesh only within the context of ritual feasts. Thanks to these pagan rites, eating horse became the kind of thing that'd put you on a Bishop's blacklist. The Church-enforced taboo became so strong that residents of medieval towns under siege are reported to have devoured rats and the leather of their garments before making a meal of their horses.

Even as settlers were transporting this idea to the New World, Europeans began reconsidering it. First in France and then elsewhere, governments began encouraging the

> The last human morsels we know of were downed around 1950 in the South Pacific, and today it is with a certain wistfulness that ex-cannibals recall their favorite recipes: "beat to death, beat more to tenderize, baste generously with mashed yams, cook on a spit until done."

consumption of horse meat as pragmatic, and chefs made it more fashionable. At this time, horse is sold in butcher shops in France, Belgium, Switzerland, Austria, Spain, Italy, and Sweden, where equestrian meat is particularly popular, exceeding the sales of mutton and lamb combined.

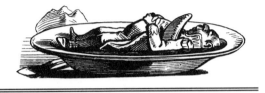

■ "TASTES LIKE CHICKEN" ■

Vanished

Today, all the cannibals have retired. Once common in the Congo basin and other parts of Central Africa, in parts of Sumatra, New Guinea, the Solomon Islands, Java, and among the Maori and Fiji islanders, tribal cannibalism has been wiped out.

The last human morsels we know of were downed around 1950 in the South Pacific, and today it is with a certain wistfulness that ex-cannibals recall their favorite recipes: "beat to death, beat more to tenderize, baste generously with mashed yams, cook on a spit until done" (from an interview conducted by author Michael Krieger). Internal organs and head were discarded. Female breasts and the buttocks (of either gender) were regarded as the most succulent delicacies. And, no, it didn't taste like chicken. They say it was much better.

Necessary Evil

Never in fashion but also never quite out of the question is the consumption

Donner, party of forty eight, er, sorry. Donner, party of forty seven!

ensuing winter, their ranks were depleted by starvation. They took to chewing oxhides, dying, and sizing up the protein potential of the frozen bodies piling up in the snow outside. Forty seven out of eighty nine survived the winter, sustaining themselves on the frozen remains of their fellow travelers.

Similarly stranded amongst snow-covered mountains, the cannibalistic survival technique of a crash-landed Uruguayan soccer team is also familiar to many Americans thanks to the book *Alive*, a best-selling account of this 1972 misfortune in the Andes.

Another widely read book, the Holy Bible, features some fascinating incidents of cannibalism in time of deprivation. Describing the desperation among the Samarians during a siege, the Old Testament reports on one solution: "So we boiled my son, and did eat him: and I said unto her on the next day, Give thy son, that we may eat him; and she hath hid her son" (2 Kings 6:29). Similarly, the Hebrews were cursed with a rather desperate state of affairs caused by a siege in Deuteronomy 28:53: "And thou shalt eat the fruit of thine own body, the flesh of thy sons

Alive is the best-selling account of the Uruguayan soccer team's 1972 cannibalistic nightmare.

and of thy daughters, whom Jehovah thy God hath given thee, in the siege and in the distress wherewith thine enemies shall distress thee."

Such hunger of biblical proportions frequently is the result of wartime

of human flesh in times of extreme need. Accepted as an ugly reality by even the most cautious or politically sensitive anthropologist, "survival cannibalism" may be best known to Americans by the example of those famously famished pioneers in the Donner party, stranded one very scary Halloween in 1846 while attempting to cross California's Sierra Nevada mountains during a snowstorm.

Unable to move throughout the

shortages. This was the case in Leningrad during World War II, as well as during the final days of the ancient Easter Islanders, where cannibalism was so endemic that the most common taunt reportedly was "The flesh of your mother sticks between my teeth." War, famine, and ideological extremism combined in China in the 1950s and 1960s to disastrous ends during the Maoist revolution. In some instances, execution was only the beginning for certain "counter-revolutionaries," whose corpses were said to have been butchered for meat. Less than a century earlier, widespread cannibalism had also been reported in China as the result of a drought-induced famine lasting from 1876 through 1879

Black Market Fetus

More recent accounts of cannibalism in China come from journalists writing for Hong Kong's *The Eastern Express*. In 1995, the newspaper raised a few eyebrows with reports of a black market for aborted fetuses sold as a dietary supplement at a state-run hospital across the border in Shenzhen.

Preferring the delicate meat prepared in a soup flavored with pork and ginger, the doctor responsible for selling the fetuses was said to have admitted to consuming roughly one hundred fetuses himself.

With over 7,000 terminations performed in the hospital annually, the going rate for those not cremated in hospital ovens or devoured by hospital personnel was roughly $1.25 each. The addition of fetus to the diet is believed by some to impart smooth skin, improve immunity, and fight asthma and/or anemia.

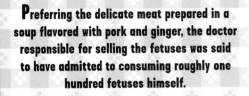

Preferring the delicate meat prepared in a soup flavored with pork and ginger, the doctor responsible for selling the fetuses was said to have admitted to consuming roughly one hundred fetuses himself.

International critics outraged by the story were by no means mollified by comparisons to the use of products derived from embryonic tissue in Western pharmaceuticals, nor by the fact that traditional Chinese medicine encourages mothers who have just given birth to improve the quality of her milk by consuming a soup made with the discarded placenta.

Human flesh is also the key ingredient in an even more archaic Chinese tradition dating from 1100 or 1200 C.E. The self-sacrificial practice of *ko ku* (or *gegu*) involves carving out a chunk of one's own body (thigh, buttocks, or even liver) for use in a restorative soup. This soup was then offered to a dying parent by the carver/carvee, who in this case would be a particularly devoted daughter, daughter-in-law, or possibly son.

The practice was widespread enough that the governments of the Yuan and Ming dynasties issued prohibitions against it. In mythology, *ko ku* is still associated with the Buddhist goddess of compassion, who appears in earthly form as Princess Miao Shan to offer her eyes and hands as ingredients for such a soup.

Rocky Mountain Thigh

The Colorado Cannibal

Sometimes, cannibalism is big business. At least it is in the town of Lake City, Colorado, the approximate location where Alferd Packer murdered five of his companions for food while stranded in a Rocky Mountain snowstorm in 1874.

After being convicted in court for his unsavory deeds, Packer served a brief portion of his term in a territorial prison but was released because of a legal blunder during his trial. The judge, more interested in advancing his political career than the technicalities of the case, is supposed to have sentenced Packer with these legendary words: "There was seven democrats in Hinsdale County, and you've ate five of them, goddamn you!"

After his release, Packer found that his appetite for meat had decreased. He became a vegetarian and pulled a meager income hawking autographed photos of himself—the now-famous "Colorado Cannibal."

Civic boosters picked up on Packer's self-promotion and went to town. They slapped up a plaque at the site of the massacre and rustled up some souvenirs for the Hinsdale County Museum, including shackles from Packer's prison stint, as well as a few buttons and skull fragments from the human leftovers.

But it's local folklore and black humor that really keeps the incident alive. Nearby Boulder University, for instance, boasts an "Alferd Packer Memorial Grill" in the basement of its Memorial Center (complete with marble bust of Packer, unveiled by Colorado Governor Romer). Packer's deed is also commemorated in Boulder's largest burrito, "El Cannibal," in the "Alferd Packer Trail"

Photo of Alferd Packer—the Colorado Cannibal—taken at the time of his 1883 trial.

and "The Alferd Packer Trail Marathon," which attracts dozens of competitors from several states every spring. Most evocative of all is probably the "Alferd Packer Barbecue Cook-off" hosted by the Lake City Chamber of Commerce.

"Alferd," by the way, both is and is not a misspelling. While serving in the military, Packer had his name tattooed on his arm—or at least a version of it. Amused upon seeing the artist's misspelling of "Alfred," the good-natured cannibal eventually adopted it as his moniker.

Celebrity Cannibals

In contemporary Western culture, cannibalism and altruism are infrequently associated.

This is not to say, however, that certain cannibals are without higher motives. Albert Fish, the notorious New York cannibal, might not be known today if it weren't for his charitable intentions.

Fish was convicted of killing and eating 15 children, and it was a letter he sent to the mother of his last meal that resulted in his arrest. In the note, he informed the parent what a delicious repast her child had provided and attempted to comfort the woman by reassuring her that her daughter had died a virgin. Fish's charitable attempts at consolation may have stemmed from the fact that he believed he was Jesus Christ.

Like the first century Messiah, Fish's efforts were rewarded with execution by the state in 1936. After Fish's death, detectives found in the cannibal's apartment a collection of clippings from the 1924 trial of Fritz Haarman, the "Hannover Vampire," who not only drank the blood of the 24 boys he abducted but—like a real life Sweeney Todd—would use their bodies to stock the sausage counter at his Hannover deli.

While Todd, the mythic British bogeyman from the Victorian penny dreadful, *The String of Pearls*, provided inspiration for Christopher Bond's play and Stephen

> **A**lso hailing from the "Cheese State" is Wisconsin native son Jeffrey Dahmer, found guilty of 17 murders in 1992. His confession to cannibalism came after police uncovered a severed head tucked away in his refrigerator, three more stashed in a freezer, a few hands floating in cooking pots, and some skulls hidden in a filing cabinet.

Sondheim's musical *Sweeney Todd: The Demon Barber of Fleet Street* (1979), real life Wisconsin necrophile and cannibal Ed Gein proved to be a meatier subject, inspiring no less than seven motion pictures. *Psycho* (both the Alfred Hitchcock and Gus Van Sant versions), *Texas Chainsaw Massacre I, II,* and *III, Deranged,* and *Three on a Meat Hook* are among the films loosely based on the life of this rural eccentric.

Also hailing from the "Cheese State" is Wisconsin native son Jeffrey Dahmer, found guilty of 17 murders in 1992. His confession to cannibalism came after police uncovered a severed head tucked away in his refrigerator, three more stashed in a freezer, a few hands floating in cooking pots, and some skulls hidden in a filing cabinet. Before Dahmer was killed by a fellow inmate in 1994, he experienced a religious conversion, began a Bible correspondence course, and was eventually baptized by a local

Jeffrey Dahmer's infamous mug shots.

minister in a portable baptistery. Before he received final sentencing, Jeffrey offered these remarks on religion: "In closing, I just want to say that I hope God has forgiven me . . . Here is a trustworthy saying that deserves full acceptance: 'Christ Jesus came into the world to save sinners, of whom I am the worst. But for that very reason, I was shown mercy so that in me, the worst of sinners, Christ Jesus might display his unlimited patience as an example for those who would believe in him and receive eternal life. Now to the King, Immortal, Invisible, the only God, be honor and glory forever and ever.'"

■ E P I C U R E A N   Z O O ■

Beefalo & the Steak from an Egg

Health-conscious Californians are among those at the forefront of a trendy new hunger for exotic game and nontraditional meats. Hunted to near extinction by settlers in the 1800s, buffalo is back on the Western frontier, no longer grilled over a campfire but braised in cabernet and served alongside other dishes typical of Californian cuisine. With 40 percent less fat than chicken,

The Wyoming Buffalo Company offers a wide selection of buffalo (and elk) meats. Hey, check out the buffalo sausage with jalapeno and cheese for something with a little extra bite.

the meat is increasingly popular with health-conscious consumers and venture capitalists like Ted Turner, who is said to own the world's largest herd of 150,000. Sometimes dubbed "beefalo," as a nod to the "cowists," buffalo is still a novelty in many regions.

Ostrich, on the other hand, is today marketed more for its health value than for any exotic appeal it may have possessed a decade ago. Often called the "steak from an egg," ostrich is a red meat, not poultry, yet only has half the fat of beef.

Kangaroo has them both beat. Regarded by the American Heart Association as the red meat with lowest fat per serving, kangaroo is promoted particularly in Australia, where it's consumed now as a matter of national pride. The marsupial has also hopped onto menus in Europe and the United States, where epicures and dieters are beginning to discover its charm.

Perhaps the Serengeti Sampler?

While these meats appeal to health-conscious diners with Earth-friendly agendas, they are also being gobbled up by a curiously different crowd. Tired of decades of carping about calories and guilt trips from Greenpeace, this new generation is rekindling an appreciation for the old: cigars, cocktails, red meat, and wild game. Despite the fact that the ostrich might come from Texas, or the kangaroo grew up on a ranch alongside cattle, the symbolic appeal of these animals as something bagged on the untamed veldt fires an age-old desire for exotic plunder from foreign lands.

Long before the days of white man's safaris into Africa, the upper class in ancient Rome partied competitively, scoring big points for meats that came from far away. The better households served antelope, camel, gazelle, parrots, flamingo, peacock, and other expensive

PANÂCHE
• CHEF OWNED CASUAL ELEGANCE •
802•422•8622

Appetizers

Tempura Crisped California Nori Roll (vegetarian) with Sweet Kumquat Sauce and Crisped Asian Cabbage 9.

Spicy Camel Enchiladas with Corn and Cactus Pico di Gallo 12.

½ Order of 16-Hour Barbequed Wilderbeast Ribs (no, doesn't taste like chicken) 10.

Very, Very Spicy (and expensive) Wok-Crisped Indochinese Style Scorpion Bowl (with real scorpions!!) with Chilled Cucumber Yogurt Dip. Now THIS tastes like chicken!! (Not for the faint-of-heart, and yes, we removed the stingers!!) (Just think "soft-shell crabs") Served Family Style $85 per guest

Scooby Snax: Skewer of Today's Wild Game: Vermont Elk & Apricot Sausage, American Bison and African Waterbuffalo 22.

Add African Lion, American Cougar or African Giraffe for 12. ea

Entrees

The Most Amazing Barbecued Ribs You'll Ever (and they're African Wilderbeast!!) 33.

Pan Seared Five-Spiced Skate Wing, with Crisped Napa Cabbage, Tamari and Hot Hot Tropical Peppers in dark Rum and Coconut 24.

Tender Cubes of African Giraffe with Cool Stuff 38.

Hippo Pot Pie (that's right kiddies . . . have fun!!) 42.

Terryakki Yak, Don't Talk Back with Green Onion Taters 33.

Filet Mignon of African Zebra with Skewered Flaming Pineapple Nuggets 60.

Pan Roasted Loin Chop of African Lion 41.

Serengetti Sampler for Two: American Bison, Vermont Elk Sausage, African Waterbuffalo and African Giraffe 99.

Add Egyptian Cobra on-the-bone, Yak Camel, African Lion or American Cougar for 20.

Add Scorpions for 45.

Please note that all wild game, both domestic & imported, is farm-raised and approved by the USDA/FDA. It is also substantially low in fat & cholesterol.

Panache restaurant in Killington, Vermont attracts urban gastronomes from New York and Boston with edible menageries like the "Serengeti Sampler."

imports. Historically the torchbearers of this epicurean tradition, the French, in classic

volumes on cookery like the *Larousse Gastronomique,* dutifully include recipes for items such as camel's feet and camel's hump.

Today, American restaurants like Panache in Killington, Vermont, attract urban gastronomes from New York and Boston with edible menageries like the "Serengeti sampler," while more adventuresome gourmands indulge themselves at the source with preplanned safari vacations in East Africa.

There, in the dining rooms of urban tourist hotels, at oppulent hunting lodges, and wherever bush camps may be struck, chefs stand ready with supplies of frozen warthog, springbok, impala, zebra, elephant, and lion. Despite the fact that there's not much "African" about these dishes since totemic animal worship (*mutopo*) forbids most locals from touching any

of these meats, and despite the fact that this game is not bagged during hair-raising hunts but is instead weaned and slaughtered on farms, these "safari menus" are big business in the African tourist industry.

Particularly popular are the relatively inexpensive hippo burgers or zebra steaks, but few tourists on these package outings return home without sampling some more elaborate fare such as roast warthog with mint sauce, marinated antelope braised in marsala, or grilled crocodile steaks with cornmeal fritters. Boiled elephant trunk, however, is off the menu. Though you can't beat it for the novelty, this cut of pachyderm was a total washout when some hotels added it to their safari menus in the mid-'90s. One deterrent was the six-hour boiling time required to suitably soften this less-than-tasty morsel, while the other was the difficulty most diners felt in carving away at the trunk while peering up Dumbo's nostrils.

> **P**articularly popular are the relatively inexpensive hippo burgers or zebra steaks, but few tourists on these package outings return home without sampling some more elaborate fare such as roast warthog with mint sauce, marinated antelope braised in marsala, or grilled crocodile steaks with cornmeal fritters.

The Pit of Vegan Hell and the Peak of High Adventure

Notorious even among restaurants specializing in such things is Carnivore, a themed "dining experience" originating in Nairobi, Kenya, and now boasting franchises in Johannesburg, South Africa, and Frankfurt, Germany. In what appears to have been conceived expressly as a vegetarian's vision of hell, tourists at this airport-adjacent eatery are seated outside around a flaming barbecue pit and offered an all-you-can-eat succession of meats "from antelope to zebra." Retrieving skewers from the flames, waiters circulate about, prying huge chunks of flesh off these swords and onto guests' iron plates

Something's Rotten in Denmark

Old Fish, New Fish

For some reason or other, different cultures seem to have disturbingly different ideas as to how long one should wait between catching and consuming fish. In Iceland, they enjoy hakarl, (the flesh of the Greenland shark) only after it's been dead and buried for at least three months. While traditionalists still insist on stuffing the shark in a barrel and planting it under the earth, some Icelanders have updated likewise buried underground by the Innuit, but in this case the actual bodies of the fish are discarded and only the decomposing heads are buried and later eaten.

In the Far East, there is a tendency toward eating fish that are as fresh as possible. This all-important pursuit of freshness in sushi and sashimi can trivialize the distinction between raw and living, and fish are commonly not only filleted while still

A variety of sushi and sashimi. Have you ever experienced the thrill of a piece of extremely fresh fish wriggling its way down your throat?

the tradition by merely isolating the deceased fish for several months in an airtight bag. In either case the stench is the stuff memories are made of, and the ammonia-rich remains strike a familiar note with any visitor to a public restroom in need of a good cleaning.

Extraordinary as this preparation of hakarl may sound, it's not that uncommon. The Norweigian gravlax, or "buried" lox, and the Danish rasatefisk are both "go the way of all flesh" before going into the mouth. In Alaska, "stinkhead" are salmon alive, but also swallowed in that state. It's not at all unheard of for diners to experience a bit of convulsive wriggling as they down their food. As sashimi, squid is occasionally swallowed with suction cups still functioning. But this mollusk is also used to make shiokara, one of Asia's many fermented seafood dishes. This notorious Japanese speciality is made of spoiled squid parts (including guts) that are salted and pickled. Its unearthly purple color, smell, viscosity—not to mention taste—repulse many Japanese. Westerners are not expected to touch it.

Screw Vegetarians

Let's Eat Meat!

where they are torn to bite-sized chunks and consumed without benefit of silverware. Starting off with less exotic fare like goat, patrons build to a carnivorous frenzy, consuming rarer and rarer species like lion, cheetah, and giraffe as they go.

All of this may be good fun for the meat-eater on vacation but would be unlikely to impress members of the Explorers Club, a legendary society of elite adventurers whose members have walked the surface of the moon (Buzz Aldrin, Jr.) and plumbed the depths of the sea (Robert Ballard, discoverer of the Titanic).

The menu of their annual banquet, traditionally held at the Waldorf Astoria, is as daring as members' exploits. Planning begins as much as six months in advance with a letter written to wildlife services of dozens of countries, inquiring not only about export and conservation law but also as to availability of species in question,

since many cannot be hunted and can only be ordered from zoos, where they may be stashed in freezers after expiring naturally. Recent dinners have included ostrich egg canapés, candied boar skin, paillard of penguin, and curried Tibetan ram.

■ CRAWLY THINGS ■

All the World Loves a Snail

Though its meat can be obtained in many backyards, and there's certainly no sport in catching it, the snail is widely regarded as an icon of epicurean adventure.

S—Car—Go

Pack the Car! We're Going to the Snail Farm!

Recently, French entrepreneurs have recognized the attraction a snail farm might have on money-spending tourists. One such farm open for visits in Montlouis, France, offers multilinqual tours along with screenings of a 10-minute documentary that finally lays to rest all your burning questions about Heliciculture (snail farming). Also included in the package is a visit to the rearing enclosures and kitchens, a steamy peek into the "reproduction rooms," and a chance to scarf a few of those little animals you've gotten to know so well.

Marinated, simmered in wine, and served in its shell with garlic butter and herbs, the species *Helix Pomatia*, sometimes called the *gros blanc*, is that most commonly used in Burgundy style escargot. It's not alone; there are over one hundred varieties worldwide, which are stewed, smoked, creamed, baked in pastry envelopes, prepared with anchovies ("Roman style"), or otherwise turned into comestibles.

Europeans have been eating and otherwise putting these slimy things to work for around twenty thousand years. The Greeks ate them, and the Romans used mashed snails in salves and as a nutritional supplement during pregnancy. During the Middle Ages, snails were raised by nuns as an alternative to meats banned during Lent. The Chinese serve them roasted in a dish with shark fin and sandpiper eggs. In Africa, there are several giant species (some as long as one foot), and the Ashanti of West Africa eat these meaty specimens, preferring them to chicken, pork, or fish.

These African giants are occasionally minced in Indonesian or Taiwanese factories and sold as escargot, but French connoisseurs regard these disdainfully as snails fit only for Americans. In the U.S., a few large-scale snail "ranches" raise native species for domestic consumption, but France remains our biggest supplier, exporting roughly $300 million in snails annually, while still managing to hang on to some 35,000 tons of the better bred gastropods for themselves. The French are most fond of homegrown snails from Burgundy and the Alps regions, but will also accept snails from northern Italy, Eastern Europe, and Turkey. Snails gathered from the wild are generally preferred to those raised on farms, where the uniform diet is said to render the taste inferior. Other critical factors in preparation include the removal of the liver, which in some species can be bitter, and the evacuation of the digestive system accomplished by isolating the animal from food for the last three weeks of its life (e.g., starving it).

R.V. "Dick" Johnson of Frescargot Farms demonstrates the finer points of snail farming.

Webbed Toes and Drumsticks

Frog is another dish often regarded as peculiar to the French. The English (regarding the French as themselves peculiar), believe this dish makes an ideal symbol for their neighbors. They, therefore, use the slang "frogs" to denote their neighbors across the channel.

The only part of a frog worth bothering with is the legs, and the French are by no means the only ones to do so. Throughout the Mediterranean, they are sautéed, stewed, grilled, folded in omelets, and set in aspic. In southeast Asia, they're likely to be curried or served in a sweet and sour sauce. In China, there is disagreement on the topic of frog similar to that on either side of the English Channel; in the South they are a great delicacy, in the North an abomination.

In Korea, they eat American frogs, or at least since 1997 they've been trying to. Thanks to overbreeding by a species imported from the U.S., the government's been pushing frog dishes as a way for the country to eat its way out of an ecological bind. Conversely, in this country, ecological challenges have created shortages, and the Cajun frog legs tourists visit Louisiana to sample are now often imported from Japan.

Norman Padgett of Frog Legs Unlimited (West Palm Beach, FL) packages frogs he caught the previous evening.

Reptilian Smorgasbord

In addition to frog, the reptile-heavy diet of Cajun Louisiana includes alligator and turtle. Though gator's not so commonly eaten elsewhere (outside of Rhodesia and a few other African regions), turtles are eaten most everywhere they wash ashore, especially in Mexico, China, Fiji, and Malta.

Grilled or in soup, turtles were at one time so popular in Europe and the U.S. that many species came close to extinction in the nineteenth century and were saved only by their aristocratic price. Where a taste for turtle appeared without the funds to support it, mock turtle soup was concocted, substituting a broth made by boiling a calf's head or ears and often adding calf brains and wine to complete the ruse.

A more abundant cold-blooded critter that's often eaten is the iguana. Tasting something like fish, the pygmy iguana is a popular item showing up in markets and roadside stalls in Mexico, Central America, and the West Indies.

> A more abundant cold-blooded critter that's often eaten is the iguana. Tasting something like fish, the pygmy iguana is a popular item showing up in markets and roadside stalls in Mexico, Central America, and the West Indies.

In the American Southwest, particularly Texas, rattlesnake is sometimes served, though mainly as a novelty for tourists eager to ingest a bit of Old West machismo. Marinated snake is a more traditional item in Asian cuisines, frequently showing up in soups. Asian diners can insure freshness by purchasing live animals from special markets offering everything from the tiny garden variety to immense king cobras. At the customer's request, these are killed, zipped out of their skin, filleted, and grilled on site. The snake's gallbladder is particularly prized for its medicinal power.

■ TASTY RODENTS ■

Better Looking than Sea Slugs

The advertisements called it "super deer." And it looked rather upscale as depicted in the slick little brochure—an artfully arranged kebab photographed next to a costly bottle of Napoleon X.O. brandy. This was the "Super Deer Kebab" offered by the "Superior to Deer Restaurant" opened in Guangzhou, China. Unfortunately for the unprepared Western diner, the animal "superior" to deer in this case was rat.

When the restaurant opened in 1991, it made international headlines in *The Wall Street Journal*—not for criminal fraudulence in advertising but as the only restaurant in the world exclusively dedicated to serving rat.

LL STREE

91 Dow Jones & Company, Inc. All Rights Rese

TUESDAY, MAY 31, 1991

Waiter, There's A Rat in My Soup, And It's Delicious!

* * *

A Restaurant in China Serves Rat 30 Different Ways; We Suggest the Kabobs

By JAMES McGREGOR

Staff Reporter of THE WALL STREET JOURNAL

GUANGZHOU, China—The Cantonese people of south China are legendary for eating anything that moves—and some things that are still moving. The food market here features cats, raccoons, o...

This 1991 article in The Wall Street Journal *detailed the eating of rats in China.*

What was most novel about the venture was not the fact that rats were showing up on plates—rat meat has often been eaten in the form of jerky in China's rural regions. What was unusual here was the way in which the meat was pitched to more urbane tastes. Satayed Rat Slices with Vermicelli, Rat with Chestnut and Duck, and Liquored Rat Flambé were some of the rodent-oriented dishes offered.

Confronted periodically by massive plagues of rats, the Chinese government has for many years actively promoted rat-eating as one solution to the problem. State endorsements such as, "Rats are better looking than sea slugs and cleaner than chickens and pigs" have proven effective in boosting rodent popularity ratings. Today, Chinese restaurateurs interested in obtaining these clean, handsome animals for table use may travel to the famous Guangdong Province mouse market to barter with farmers bringing the rodents in from the fields. There, approximately two thousand animals are sold each week.

We Give Them Cheese, They Give Us Meat

Though stigmatized as disease carriers after Europe's bout with the Black Death, rats and their mousy cousins have nonetheless been eaten by Westerners in the past. The Romans ate dormice, a species not quite mouse, not quite squirrel. They kept these animals in outdoor pens or clay pots in their kitchens, feeding them on nuts until such time as they were called upon to return the favor. Baked into a pie, dormice were regarded as highly efficacious against colds. In ancient Greece, mice were sometimes eaten by priests of Apollo, to whom the animal was sacred.

During the deprivations of the Franco-Prussian war, Parisians made no secret of resorting to rat meat. At the time, it was regarded as a decent substitute for partridge or pork. After the war, certain varieties were still considered quite palatable as evidenced by a recipe for grilled rat *à la bordelaise* found in the venerable *Larousse Gastronomique.* In this case, the rats called for are those indigenous to the wine cellars of the region. Premarinated by osmosis, these rats are simply basted with olive oil and crushed shallots while roasting over a wine-scented fire of broken casks.

In West Africa, rat is also a significant source of protein. In Ghana, a particularly large species, the cane rat, is the featured attraction in spicy stews. Mice, the rat's scaled-down cousin, are eaten by the scaled-down pygmies of Central Africa as well as in the Pathum Thani province of Thailand and some rural regions of Mexico.

Take Away the "Musk" and What've You Got?

Even in North America, where there is serious stigma attached to even having rats in one's home, much on one's table, a number of rat-like animals are eaten.

In Louisiana's Cajun country, in French areas of Canada, and along the east side of Maryland's Chesapeake Bay, the muskrat is not only hunted for its fur but also its meat. As an entrée, there are only two problems with this animal: one is the "rat" in its name and the other is the word "musk." The latter is easily enough removed by extracting the glands at the rear of its leg before cooking, and the former is eliminated by referring to the animal euphemistically as "marsh rabbit." In Louisiana, another cousin of the rat is also on

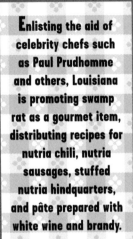

Enlisting the aid of celebrity chefs such as Paul Prudhomme and others, Louisiana is promoting swamp rat as a gourmet item, distributing recipes for nutria chili, nutria sausages, stuffed nutria hindquarters, and pâté prepared with white wine and brandy.

Your basic, run-of-the-mill nutria.

the menu—the swamp-dwelling nutria imported from Argentina in the late 1930s by the Tabasco moguls of the McIlhenny family.

A beautifully arranged serving of Nutria Fettuccini, from the kitchen of chef Philippe Parola of the Cordon Bleu de France.

Originally confined to Avery Island, the creatures broke loose during a hurricane and proceeded to wreck havoc in the bayou ecosystem. The serious danger this presents to local sugar cane crops has prompted the state to form a special task force devoted to seeing nutria hunted down and eaten. Enlisting the aid of celebrity chefs such as Paul Prudhomme and others, the state is promoting swamp rat as a gourmet item, distributing recipes for nutria chili, nutria sausages, stuffed nutria hindquarters, and pâté prepared with white wine and brandy.

In the American Southwest, armadillos pose a similar threat to property by burrowing under homes and gardens. Attempts to control the population have not relied so much on hunting them for meat, but in Texas particularly, the animal is occasionally eaten as "possum-on-the-half-shell." This light, tasty, and tender meat also shows up on tables from Mexico to South America.

Delicious Right Down to the Fur

It might come as a surprise that a good number of U.S. citizens celebrate weddings and other special occasions by feasting on boiled fruit bats. Not in the 50 states, mind you, but in the territory of Guam, where the animal is regarded as something of a cultural icon. The native species, the Mariana fruit bat, is pretty hefty (some with wingspans over three feet), and the larger specimens are highly coveted, fetching up to $50 at roadside stalls or markets. As a sort of holiday treat, these delicacies are frequently mailed to homesick relatives who have emigrated to non-bat-eating regions. Once boiled, the animal is served whole, and eaten thus—meat, wing membrane,

and all. Even the fur is consumed with great relish. Demand for these creatures has been so high as to endanger the native species, and the island now imports twenty thousand bats yearly from other western Pacific countries to satisfy its appetite for flying mammals. According to Bat Conservation International, unregulated hunting has already caused the extinction of some species, and continues to threaten the environmental health of these areas. Bats are also eaten throughout the Pacific Islands, up into Southeast Asia, and even in parts of Africa. In Samoa, they are typically cooked in luau pits or over heated rocks.

> **O**nce boiled, bats are served whole, and eaten thus—meat, wing membrane, and all. Even the fur is consumed with great relish.

■ SNACKS ON SIX LEGS ■

Swarming with Protein

We Americans don't eat bugs. We have no qualms about consuming buttered toast spread with the sticky vomit of the *Apis mellifera* or munching our way around the exoskeleton of a *Penaeus duorarum* drenched in cocktail sauce. But that's ok. Honeybee vomit is not quite honeybee, and shrimp may be close cousins, but insects they are not. A quick check with the gag reflex tells us this is so.

OK. Maybe your neighbor will claim he's slurped down the worm in the last shot of tequila, or perhaps a kid with an adequately receptive audience will crunch down on worm embedded in a novelty sucker. But we're just not on the insect-eating bandwagon with the rest of the world. In Asia, Africa, Australia, South and Central America, roughly fifteen hundred species of insect provide substantial protein in many diets. A 100 gram serving of crickets, for instance, gives you 121 calories, 12.9 grams of protein, 5.5 g. of fat, 5.1 g. of carbohydrates, 75.8 mg. calcium, 185.3 mg. of phosphorous, 9.5 mg. of iron, 0.36 mg. of thiamin, 1.09 mg. of riboflavin, and 3.10 mg. of niacin.

As long as you have the sense to pick off the spiny bits, and fry them a bit before eating, insects generally have a pleasant enough taste. Many are described as "nutty" or "smoky," while others may taste like shrimp. The FDA, in fact, expects

cuisine of both North and South China where fried water beetle and dragonfly larvae are both munched like a cocktail shrimp. Maggots are regarded as particularly nourishing in times of sickness. A rich broth of earthworms helps with fevers. In China, Vietnam, and Korea, silk worm pupa not only provide silk but are eaten after the substance is extracted. These useful by-products of the silk industry are often steamed and served on their own as a street food or occasionally as an ingredient in omelets and soups. The pungent aroma of a big mess of silkworm grubs (larvae) boiling away in their inky juices is sometimes said to be surprisingly pleasant to Westerners (though others compare the smell to burnt hair).

Americans to eat a certain allowance of insects, though "accidental" ingestion is the focus here. Up to 60 mites, thrips, or aphids, for instance, are permitted to stray into a package of frozen broc-

> **E**xtensive use is made of insects in the cuisine of both North and South China where fried water beetle and dragonfly larvae are both munched like a cocktail shrimp. Maggots are regarded as particularly nourishing in times of sickness. A rich broth of earthworms helps with fevers.

coli, and up to 10 fly eggs are tolerated in every 100 grams of tomato juice.

And it's not just the FDA; even *God* says it's OK! According to Leviticus 11:22, any kind of locust, katydid, cricket, or grasshopper are kosher as far as the Lord is concerned. Insect eating was very common in the ancient Middle East and Mediterranean. John the Baptist, the prophet and herald of Jesus' birth, not only knew a messiah when he saw one, but he also recognized insects as good eating and is said to have lived exclusively on locusts and wild honey.

Wok Full of Wasps: Asian Insect Snacks

Extensive use is made of insects in the

In Hong Kong, diners enjoy their scorpions drowned in wine, then deep-fried, and those suffering from headache and "wind-damp conditions" will try to alleviate their ailments by crunching

Cooking up a batch of delicious stir-fried giant silkworms.

Zachary Huang of the Michigan State University Department of Entomology samples a serving of giant silkworms.

even flood their fields just to drive the insects out for capture. Ants are less common in Asian food, but in India you might be able to locate a chutney containing red ants and chili. And the Balinese have many fine recipes for dragonfly.

Grubs and Between Meal Bugs: Africa & Oceana

Throughout North Africa and the Middle East you can get your locusts dried and salted, boiled with couscous, ground and kneaded into dumplings, or mixed with milk into a sort of locust shake.

Further south in Central and Southern Africa, termites are the favorite entomological snack—one often stockpiled for the rainy season. These "white ants" are eaten dried in Swaziland and Rhodesia and occasionally pulverized and used in a nougat filling for pies made with banana flour. Termites are generally caught overnight by placing a bowl of water near a light source and waiting for the insects to be drawn in and drowned.

away at a plateful of these crispy beasts. In China, these creatures are sometimes eaten while still alive, but first swished about in alcohol till the insect's too sloshed to sting. In Japan, cicadas, wasps,

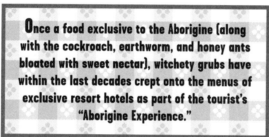

Once a food exclusive to the Aborigine (along with the cockroach, earthworm, and honey ants bloated with sweet nectar), witchety grubs have within the last decades crept onto the menus of exclusive resort hotels as part of the tourist's "Aborigine Experience."

grasshoppers, and the grub of longhorn beetles are boiled and fried. Canned wasp larvae are also sold as ready-to-eat hors d'oeuvres or between-meal snacks.

In Thailand, you can sample roasted tarantulas and bee grubs in a coconut cream with lime leaves. But the insect you're most likely to encounter there is the giant water bug—an insect resembling a particularly large and well-armored beetle. Prized for their aroma, these monsters pack a lot of meat even after their inedible legs, head, and wings are plucked off and discarded. If you can't make it to Thailand, you can also find these eaten in other parts of Southeast Asia and even India. If it's crickets you're after, you'll find them all over this region. In the Philippines, farmers will sometimes

The witchety grub—an Australian favorite—is the larva of an immense moth. Once a food exclusive to the Aborigine (along with the cockroach, earthworm, and honey ants bloated with sweet nectar), witchety grubs have within the last decades crept onto the menus of exclusive resort hotels as part of the tourist's "Aborigine Experience." In Papua-New

Guinea and Borneo, sago "worms" (larva) hanging out in the rotting wood of sago palms are skewered and roasted until golden brown. The nearby Samoans have an interesting trick to preparing grubs: They'll feed the larva on coconut shavings for several weeks to fill them with "coconutty" goodness before roasting them in envelopes of folded palm leaves.

> **In Columbia, paper cones full of toasted and salted ants are sometimes sold like popcorn in movie theaters.**

Entomological Eats in the New World

Most North American Indians ate grubs. Hungry settlers put aside their prejudice

How many licks does it take to get to the center of a tequila pop?

and followed their example, sustaining themselves on larva either fried or simmered in soups. Some tribes also used honey ants to make a sort of mead-like beverage, and this sweet dessert insect is also a traditional wedding food in some rural regions of Mexico.

This brings up the legendary "tequila worm" (actually yet another grub or larva) native to the maguey "cactus" (actually not a cactus but a relative of the lily). Actually it's not even tequila. The grubs are sold in bottles of mezcal, a more generic category of drink of which tequila belongs as a superior example. There are two types of these grubs: the red (*gusano rojo*) and the yellow (*gusano de oro*). These two live in very distinct neighborhoods on the maguey, with the red residing in the heart and roots and the yellow only on the leaves. The red lives in the more upscale property and, thus, swims in more expensive bottles of mezcal. Both grubs have long been consumed as a regular part of the diet of the Zapotec Indians of Mexico.

A variety of grubs are eaten by Indians further south in Central and South America, as are ants. The Jivaro of Peru and Ecuador eat ants when they aren't hunting heads, and in Columbia, paper cones full of toasted and salted ants are sometimes sold like popcorn in movie theaters.

While all this may seem rather remote to the average American, he is still likely to have consumed at least one bug also used by Peruvian Indians. Dried and pulverized, the shells of the cochineal insect (a parasite on certain types of cactus) are used as a dye by these people. It's also imported to the U.S. in great quantities for FDA-approved applications as the primary coloring agent in many red cosmetics, foods, and drinks, such as lovely crimson lipsticks and colinea-licious Hawaiian Punch.

A Little Chocolate with Your Insects?

It takes some serious sweet talk to convince most Americans to eat a bug. That or the bravado-inducing influence of hard liquor. Mindful of these realities, yet also sensing a perverse urge among consumers to break the insect-eating taboo, entrepreneur Larry Peterman whipped up a confection in 1991 that met the demands: a sweet, tequila-flavored sucker with a beetle larva embedded in the center.

It all began innocently enough with clear suckers encasing red candy hearts. This was a special Valentine's item Peterman created at the S.S. Lollipop candy store in Pismo Beach California. But as the season passed, his experiments became increasingly bizarre and he began to incorporate banana chips, trail mix, and eventually bugs into his suckers.

Yet these efforts were not without precedent or success, and his confectionery take on the Mexican custom of plunking a worm-like larva into bottles of mescal eventually became a hot-selling novelty item. The Hotlix line of insectoid candies has since exploded into a booming mail-order business offering crickets implanted in mint, cinnamon, and grape lollies ("Cricket Lick-its"), as well as snack packs of crispy-fried "Larvets"—beetle larvae seasoned with chili, cheddar cheese or barbecue flavoring. A toffee-flavored "amber" candy hearkens back to the Cambrian,

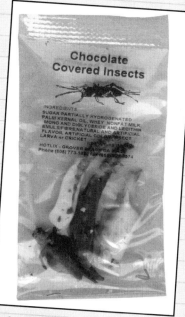

offering a variety of insects embedded in a sugary simulation of fossilized tree sap ("InsectNsides"). Most recently, it's chocolate-covered crickets chirping on Peterman's horizon. Call the Hotlix hotline to find out when they're available: 1-800-EAT-WORMS.

As the business continues to grow, Peterman, like the Colonel, has become a bit protective about the worm frying technique used for the now-classic tequila pops. The secret method evolved out of innumerable less successful experiments with freeze-drying, sautéing, and microwaving (especially messy). "Some of the initial worms were pretty earthy tasting, and some were a little moist in the middle," Peterman confesses.

Exactly which bug you encounter as you lick closer to your destiny was also a major question in the beginning. "We called entomologists and tried regular meal-worms, but some of them squished up too much, and some of them turned black." The urgings of an enthusiastic maggot rancher in Oregon went unheeded. "He said there was more protein in them," Peterman remembers. Eventually, the company settled on the larval offspring of a particular beetle farmed in Los Angeles, and these creatures—shipped weekly by the squirming bagful—have become the centerpiece of Hotlix's entrepreneurial empire.

■ Right Animal, Wrong Part ■

Visceral Aversions

Americans are notoriously squeamish about eating certain organs or parts of slaughtered livestock. Aside from the occasional liver, Americans will not delve very deeply into the animal, regarding most of the viscera as unfit. In fact, lungs were legally declared unfit for human consumption by the 1971 U.S. Wholesale Meat Act, and variety meats such as heart are usually only purchased as pet food. But in Peru, chunks of lamb and beef heart (*anticuchos*) are marinated, grilled, skewered, and served as a national favorite. The English also have a higher tolerance for such things; in the past, beef heart would even show up as the centerpiece of a Christmas feast with poorer families who found this easily stuffed organ to be a good stand-in for the more expensive goose.

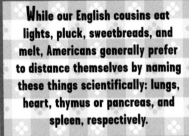

While our English cousins eat lights, pluck, sweetbreads, and melt, Americans generally prefer to distance themselves by naming these things scientifically: lungs, heart, thymus or pancreas, and spleen, respectively.

Our fear of the unknown is intensified by contradictory terminologies used by anatomists and chefs. While our English cousins eat lights, pluck, sweetbreads, and melt, Americans generally prefer to distance themselves by naming these things scientifically: lungs, heart, thymus or pancreas, and spleen, respectively. Collectively, the Brits call these "offal," while we tend to lean toward Webster's secondary meaning of word: "that which is thrown away as worthless or unfit for use; refuse; rubbish." Etymologically, offal does indeed originate from what "off falls" when a butcher opens an animal.

Interestingly, our expression "eating humble pie" also comes from the less glamorous status assigned these meats, specifically from medieval England when variety meats were called "umbles" and guests served umble pie were obviously not being shown the royal treatment.

The Noble Haggis

Served in Scotland and in Nova Scotia on both New Year's and the Robert Burns Night (the January 25 birthday of the bard), the "Noble Haggis" is an uncompromisingly Scottish dish. It is consumed on these holidays as testimony of mortal allegiance to all things Scottish, and though some Scotsmen blithely claim to enjoy the taste, others view the whole ritual as a sort of gastronomic trial by fire.

A sheep being converted to haggis will have its heart chopped, liver grated, and lungs minced. It will also have its stomach yanked out, emptied, and used as a pouch

The noble haggis in all its glory.

to hold all of the above. These ingredients are then gummed up inside the displaced tummy with a spiced mixture of oatmeal and fat. The whole is then trussed up and boiled for several hours.

Though haggis has its fanatical supporters—some even lauding the dish as an aphrodisiac—it is clearly not for everyone. In 1992, U.S. Customs officials banned a shipment of the stuff from entering the country on the grounds that it was "unfit for human consumption."

But what the dish may lack in popular appeal is made up for in presentation. The true Scotsman traditionally ushers his haggis to the table with a fanfare on bagpipes and a parade of accompanying dishes: "neeps, tatties, and nips" (mashed turnips, mashed potatoes, nips of whiskey—the latter in quantities copious enough to turn even the most distant foreigner into a haggis-friendly Scotsman).

From One Stomach to Another

Though they're more discrete about it, the Germans also cook seasoned head, jowels, and other variety meats inside spare animal stomachs. Pigs are usually the organ donors here, and the end result is usually cured as a sausage such as *Preßwurst* or *Schwartenmagen*. Cajuns whip up a similar treat called *paunce bourre*, or stuffed pork stomach.

Even when not used as a boiling bag, cow, pig, or sheep stomachs may be hacked up and served as tripe. Appearing in many dishes throughout Europe, one of its most popular starring roles is in Mexican Menudo, a soup with variable contents but always including tripe and hominy (and perhaps a cow foot tossed in for flavor).

While these dishes are enjoyed by many, a much larger segment of the world's population makes use of a lower segment of the digestive tract: the intestines. Showing up as casing for thousands of varieties of sausage worldwide, the entire length from stomach on down is used in one sausage or another. Even the rectum of the pig is occasionally used for sausage, and should you wish to ask for this segment by name, the proper slaughterhouse term is "bung." In the American South, they don't even bother stuffing the gut with sausage-makings. They just cut it out of the pig, slice it up a bit, boil it with onions, pepper, and vinegar, and call it chitlins.

> **E**ven the rectum of the pig is occasionally used for sausage, and should you wish to ask for this segment by name, the proper slaughterhouse term is "bung."

Like it or not, even cheese has a gastrointestinal origin, at least indirectly. Rennet, the coagulant that turns milk to cheese, is extracted from calf and lamb stomachs. In fact, the first cheese is said to have been created by an Arab wishing to transport milk on a long journey. Inexplicably, it's said that the most suitable vessel he could find for his milk was a lamb's stomach in which rennet was still present. The rest is cheese history.

Clotted, Stewed, or Fresh from the Vein

Blutwurst, boudin noir, morcilla, black pudding. Though the concept really doesn't translate well into American, these are the German, French, Spanish, and British equivalents of blood sausage, a mixture of congealed blood, fat, onions, and perhaps some meal stuffed into an intestinal casing.

Blood is also traditionally used as a thickener in *civets*, French stews containing game. In the Philippines, there's a stew called *diniguan*, made with pork variety, head meats, and blood. The dark color imparted by the blood has suggested the euphemistic name "Chocolate Pork," as one preferred in Americanized contexts. Chinese chefs serve a slick black concoction of jellied duck or pig blood.

In some cultures, the whole rigmarole in the kitchen is bypassed, and blood is sucked straight from domestic animals, as with the horses kept by the medieval Mongols of Central Asia and the cattle kept by the contemporary Masai of Tanzania. In these cases, only a small amount will be sipped, so that the beast is not tapped out and weakened.

Down to the Bone and Beyond

While we normally think of bones as being something even a carnivorous animal leaves untouched, this is not the case with *homo sapiens*. Marrowbones (beef) or ham hock (with a bit of pork adhering) are not just used to flavor soups; the pulp within is used by the French in canapés. Those in search of a traditional English treat should borrow a shinbone from a cow, plug the ends with dough, bake it, then scoop out the inner meat with a special marrow spoon. Marrow of the calf flavors *osso buco*, a traditional Milanese dish of veal in white wine with vegetables. The marrow of the sturgeon is used in the Russian *coulibiac*, a layered pie of salmon, rice, eggs, and mushrooms. The Tibetans prepare a type of dumpling, *momo*, that derives its distinctive flavor from marrow, while the Germans use another part of the skeleton—thin-sliced cartilage from the jaw of a cow—in the German *Ochsenmaul* salad.

> **P**igs feet ("trotters") are one of the cheapest parts of our farmyard friend; they're also relatively healthy, with less fat and 20 percent more protein than ham.

Everything but the Squeal

Pigs feet ("trotters") are one of the cheapest parts of our farmyard friend; they're also relatively healthy, with less fat and 20 percent more protein than ham. They're found in American soul food along with turnip greens, as well as throughout Europe and China, where they may be pickled, jellied, roasted, or stewed. Poached and stuffed, they are *zampone*, a specialty of the town of Modena in northern Italy, and in Brazil they are stewed along with black beans, snout, ears, and sausages.

If you want to make your own pigs feet, don't forget to remove the toenails and soles (once the feet are removed from the pig). And while you're at it, check out those other spare parts: ears and tails, for instance. The ears were once used in England to impersonate turtle in mock turtle soup and in Germany as a garnish for pea soup. Pickled tails are sometimes stewed in France, but beef is usually preferred in the oxtail soup of France, Austria, Hungary, and Italy.

Pork rind sales skyrocketed in the late 1990s thanks to the high protein/low carb diet craze.

While most Americans would probably rather see pigskins kicked than eaten, the deep-fried covering of a pig is regarded as quite a treat in some parts of the country. Whether sold as a member of the potato chip family (pork rinds) or retrieved directly from pork prepared in the kitchen (American: cracklings; British: scratchings), the enjoyment of this treat is rather tightly restricted to regions in the South or Midwest of this country. But in Latin America, pork rinds (*chicharron*) are more widely beloved, showing up in salads, stuffings, snacks, and even ice cream.

Americans who disdain this stuff as a greasy cousin to Styrofoam, may indeed be surprised to learn that in the sophisticated kitchens of France, these crispy tidbits, called *grattons,* are used to flavor a number of dishes. On this side of the Atlantic, French settlers of Quebec took to drowning fried pork rinds in maple syrup and calling them "ears of Christ" (*oreilles de christ*). This treat is an essential element of the uniquely Quebecoise "sugar shack" (*cabane à sucre*)—a traditional gathering place for cholesterol kamikazes, in which foods drenched in sugary maple syrup are the featured item.

I Only Have Eyes for Christmas

Many people would rather not dwell upon the fact that the meat they eat could once look them in the eye and moo, bleat, or otherwise attempt to ingratiate itself. The desire to avoid face-to-face confrontation with our food is one reason that most animals are decapitated before being served. However, this aversion is far from universal. Lamb or sheep heads are boiled or roasted in their entirety and served, soulful eyes intact, in North Africa, Turkey, Norway, and Scotland. The sheep-headed *smalahove* is a West Norwegian dish served alongside *lutefisk* on Christmas Eve. In Scotland, a whole boiled sheep's head shows up in a broth called *powsowdie*, a dish said to have been popular with Mary Queen of Scots.

Sometimes the eyeballs in *smalahove* and these other dishes will be plucked and eaten along with the other meat. Arabs consider sheep's eyes a delicacy unto themselves, and the French have a

Please Sir, May I Have Some More?

Primer on British Cuisine

The cuisine of the British Isles is legendary—much to the misfortune of all involved. To the novice familiar only with staples such as vegetables cooked into a state of despair, some of these terms may prove enlightening.

AMERICAN DINNER
A potluck dinner. Not surprisingly a rather foreign notion in the UK. Would you invite an Englishman to bring food to your house?

BLACK PUDDING
Sausages stuffed with congealed blood.

BLANCMANGE
Powder plus milk equals dessert. A pudding, in the American sense.

BLOATER
As healthy as it sounds, this is fat and salted herring. Bloater paste is sometimes eaten on crackers.

BREAD SAUCE
Very, very white sauce of milk, bread crumbs, and onions served with meat.

BUBBLE AND SQUEAK
Fried leftovers. Usually mashed potatoes and cabbage. Other ingredients as available.

CANDY FLOSS
From carnivals, not the dentist's office. Spun sugar or cotton candy for maintaining those pearly English smiles.

CHIP BUTTIES
Two pieces of bread with French fries mashed between. A sandwich native to Liverpool.

COCKNEY STINKING
A pie baked full of eels.

CRISPS
Potato chips. Many times in very un-American flavors such as shrimp, catsup, roast beef, turkey and stuffing, lamb with mint, and even haggis (in Scotland).

DEVIZES PIE
Specialty of Wiltshire. Pie filled with meat from boiled beef heads.

FAGGOTS
Just as rude as it sounds. A Welsh treat consisting of fried pork liver balls made with suet.

FLUMMERY
Not as frilly as the name. Fruit pudding.

HAGGIS
What you'd get if a sheep could swallow its own organs (Scottish).

HOT POT
Beef stew with vegetables. Not complete without tripe.

JUGGED HARE
It starts well with hare marinated in red wine and juniper berry. But then it's browned, and cream, strained liver pulp, and blood is added.

LAMB'S TAIL PIE
Exactly that. With a few parsnips, turnips, chopped eggs, and barley thrown in (Wales).

LAVER BREAD
Seaweed used as a breakfast dish, or in salad or hors d'oeuvres (Wales).

MARMITE
A brown paste made of yeast extract intended as a spread for toast. Tastes salty and smells like something manufactured for health, not pleasure. Similar to Australian Vegemite.

PIG'S FACE AND CABBAGE
Just that. The skin off a pig's head, baked, and flattened on your plate amidst boiled cabbage (Irish).

PORK FRY
A meat grab bag. Pork, but also lamb. Heart, liver, eyes, etc. Lots of etc.

SPOTTED DICK
Steamed suet pudding with currants for the "spots." English schoolboys call it "dead fly pie," but American adults will probably find the actual name sufficiently offensive.

TIDDY OGGIES
Another nasty-sounding dish. This one turns out to be sausage rolled in pastry.

TOAD IN THE HOLE
An even nastier name for a similar dish consisting of bits of sausage or meat baked in batter.

dish called *des yeux de veau farcis* in which calves' eyes are stuffed with truffles and mushrooms and deep fried in a rich batter. Eye-gobblers the world over, however, share a distaste for the cornea, which is usually spit out or discarded as it remains tough regardless of long hours of boiling.

From Headcheese to Jell-O

Despite the fact that nature packages the meat in a pretty tough shell, cooks all over the world have found it worthwhile to crack open the skulls of cows, pigs, and other animals and scoop out the brains. Austrian chefs scramble their brains with eggs, while the French fritter theirs, and at Mexican taquerias you'll find the grey matter minced and stuffed into tacos.

Getting at the brains usually is made somewhat easier by boiling the head of the animal (usually a calf or pig) to soften the muscle around the skull. Because gelatin is created as a by-product of boiling bones, cartilage, and muscle tendons, this process quite naturally gave birth to a substance little loved in this country, but popular for centuries elsewhere: headcheese.

This heady stuff's also called "brawn" in the UK, *fromage de tête* in France, *sylte* in Norway, or "souse" in rural America.

> **D**espite the fact that nature packages the meat in a pretty tough shell, cooks all over the world have found it worthwhile to crack open the skulls of cows, pigs, and other animals and scoop out the brains.

Not at all a cheese, but in fact akin to sausage, a headcheese is made by removing the bits and pieces of head, tongue, and jowl meat boiled loose, and layering these with gelatin in a mold or cloth bag (the brain is not used in headcheese). The mixture is then congealed into a softish cheese-like consistency and eaten in slices, cold or warmed by those so inclined.

When the animal in question is the more regal boar, artistic attempts are sometimes made to use the outer hide of the head in place of the cloth bag or mold. The intent is to create a more festive presentation by retaining a semblance to the beast's actual head. The inedible bones are removed, and the somewhat more edible "cheese" takes its place.

These deboned examples of edible taxidermy are related to a class of dishes the French call *galantine*. Served cold because they rely on gelatin, which easily melts, *galantine* preparations may consist of boned meat or fish, filled with meat stuffing and covered with aspic. The name *galantine* is related via the Latin *gelatus* (congealed, frozen) to our word gelatin, and thereby distantly related to "America's favorite dessert," Jell-O.

LIVERS & HEADCHEESES

SALCESON BIAŁY   PASZTETOWA WEDZONA   PASZTETOWA

SALCESON PIKATNY   SALCESON OZORKOWY   SAL. WIEJSKI GŁOWIZNA

PASZTET PIECZONY   SALCESON BIAŁY - MACIEK   KISZKA

COUNTRY STYLE PATE   ...ZEWIK HEADCHEESE   L   CHUNKY LIVER SAUS.

PASZTET WIEJSKI   SALCESON — BOLSZEWIK   PASZ. WĄTROBIANA

LIVER SAUSAGE

COUNTRY HEADCHEESE

BARLEY SAUSAGE

Sausage Company
Chicago, IL 60632
Your ⌣ to Quality

Bobak's Sausage Company offers a wide variety of meats. How about some Hot Headcheese to go along with your Chunky Liver Sausage?

Americana

Wonders of science, wartime rations, jet-puffed dainties of the most undernourishing kind. This is American food at its most American. Don't blame us. We didn't think it up. Most of the foods discussed here are actually European. Or they were a century ago. But we've taken that food and run with it—straight to hell as far as most Europeans (and some Americans) are concerned.

WARNING!

The following pages contain Sugar, Pork, Salt, Sodium Nitrite, Chicken Fat, Monocalcium Phosphate, Sorbic Acid, Glucose-Fructose and/or Liquid Sugar, Hydrolyzed Plant Protein, Sugar, Partially Hydrogenated Soybean Oil, Sodium Aluminum Silicate, Potassium Sorbate, Xanthan Gum, Sugar, Sodium Benzoate, Sugar, Dextrose, Polysorbate 60, Artificial Colors and Flavorings.

But at least we ran *fast*.

Most of this food is fast, stuff to eat on the go. It's pulled out of boxes and dumped out of bags—right there on the front seat, and knives and forks weren't along for the ride. This stuff's got color and crunch and sizzle and fizz, and a

- *new color* next month! And taste?
- Well, it's got more humor than
- taste. But if you're in on the joke,
- you'll find it all delicious.

HOT 5¢ COFFEE

BEST YOU EVER ATE

CHILI

A mouth-watering array of the all-American food affectionately known as everything from "Red Hots" to "Death Tubes."

■ DOGS 'N BURGERS ■

Baseball, Apple Pie, and Animal Parts

Hot dogs are often part of the "American as . . . " formulation. Right there in the same ballpark with baseball. In fact, Americans do cram a disproportionate number of these things down their gullets. About 65 per year on average. Collectively, we Americans require about 450 of them every second. And within the last few years, our national hankering has spread overseas to some pretty unlikely quarters.

Since 1991, the leading international customer for domestic hot dog producers has been the Russian Federation. *Sosiska*, a rather garlicky interpretation of the American treat, has become a popular Russian street food and does double duty as a breakfast sausage—fried in butter and eaten with cheese and smoked fish.

The Chinese also have been downing dogs in great quantity, albeit in slightly different form. Their version, the *rouchang*, is served as a warm snack impaled on a stick like a cornless corndog or sold cold and precooked, zipped up in a red form-fitting plastic skin. The plastic sheathed *rouchang* is often tossed into lunch boxes, briefcases, and backpacks to be carried throughout the day until hunger dictates that it be peeled and eaten banana-style.

The hot dog's cultural ascendancy would've no doubt pleased Franklin D. Roosevelt, who was known to serve the all-American sausage to visiting heads of state. Oddly enough it was another Roosevelt—Teddy— who helped raise awareness of the reckless disregard for hygiene exhibited by meat packers, sausage makers, and others in the business of converting flesh to food. Roosevelt's Federal Meat Inspection Act of

Upton Sinclair's The Jungle. *A classic work of journalistic muckraking.*

1906 was the result of outrage shared by the president and other readers of Upton Sinclair's *The Jungle.* In this classic work of journalistic muckraking, Sinclair attacked the Chicago meat-packing industry in particular, detailing quite a number of gruesome meat extenders used in sausages, including recycled rancid meat, sawdust, and rat droppings.

Indeed, from the very beginning, Americans have exhibited a sort of loving distrust of their "favorite" sausage product. In fact, the name "hot dog" was never intended as a compliment.

Called by a variety of names, hand-held sausages had already worked their

> **S**ince 1991, the leading international customer for domestic hot dog producers has been the Russian Federation.

way into ballparks by the turn of the century. By 1893, Chris von de Ahe, owner of the St. Louis Browns, began including frankfurters along with the other menu items (ice cream, fountain drinks, and boiled eggs) sold by the ballpark concession stand he operated.

By the early 1900s, Harry Stevens, concessions director of New York's Polo Grounds, had introduced wheeled hot water tanks that allowed vendors to circulate freely through the ballpark hawking "red hots."

A hot dog vendor does brisk business outside the ballpark in the early part of the 20th century.

The warm frankfurters, sold as "dachshund sausages" thanks to their stubby dimensions, far outsold cold refreshments on chilly days. On a particularly cold April afternoon in 1906, popular sports cartoonist Tad Dorgan is said to have overheard the vendor's cries from his press box seat and absentmindedly sketched a caricature of a steaming hot dachshund lounging on a bun.

A good cartoonist, but a lousy speller, Dorgan made no attempt at the word "dachshund" and simply scribbled in "hot dog" as a caption instead. When the cartoon came out, people seized on the name, taking ghoulish delight in the implication that dog meat might indeed be one of the ingredients of these inexpensive treats. Sinclair's *The Jungle* had just appeared in print that year and mystery meat horror stories were all the rage.

In fact, by 1913, a Chamber of Commerce ban restricted the words "hot dog" from appearing on any signage on Coney Island for this very reason. "Frankfurters," "Red Hots," and "Coney Islands" were all accepted as alternatives, yet the phrase "hot dog" proved too popular to shake.

White Gloves and the Definitive Buns

But exactly who do we have to thank or blame for the hot dog? The name probably does originate with Dorgan, yet there are many names Americans use to designate this meaty treat. Are they frankfurters originating in Frankfurt or are they wieners originating in Vienna (German: *Wien*)? And are these the same thing? Was it the same sausage people were scarfing at turn-of-the-century ballparks in St. Louis and New York and Tyrolean beer gardens by the sea? How can we say for sure, given the notorious mystery and variability of sausage ingredients?

In 1916, Coney Island hot dog vendor Nathan Handwerker took a creative approach to the wiener's image problem by offering free hot dogs to all doctors. The only catch: The medics needed to arrive in their white coats and gobble their dogs out front so that the passing crowd would be assured of the wholesome and healthful nature of Nathan's franks. Today, Nathan's is one of New York's most famous landmarks and, for

Nathan Handwerker (left-center) holds his son and future Nathan's president Murray Handwerker behind the original Nathan's hot dog stand in Coney Island.

many, has become synonymous with both Coney Island and hot dogs. Successfully franchised nationwide, the original location has sold over one million frankfurters.

Yet Nathan's was not the first. Handwerker had been hired in 1913 by Charles Feltman, Jr. whose father had actually founded the Coney Island hot dog empire from a simple pushcart operation in 1871. The Feltman enterprise grew into an immense Tyrolean beer garden with adjacent carousel and three thousand person ballroom. Feltman's white-coated waiters catered to an upper-class clientele dropping by after a day at the races, and by 1916, Feltman's 5-cent franks had become 10-cent franks. Old

> According to legend, Nathan's move to open his own stand, offering good old nickel dogs was instigated by fanatical frankfurter devotees Eddie Condon and then unknown actor Jimmie Durante.

timers were unhappy with the changes. Revolution was in the air, and Feltman's employee, Handwerker, was enlisted to lead it. According to legend, Nathan's move to open his own stand, offering good old nickel dogs was instigated by fanatical frankfurter devotees Eddie Condon and then unknown actor Jimmie Durante.

Before the beer garden, the carousel, and the white-coated waiters, Feltman was just a pushcart vendor selling sausages and rolls like countless other German immigrants in New York and St. Louis in the mid-1800s. Every town in Germany has many local varieties of sausage, and each of these were produced with slight variations as the decades passed. German Americans created rough translations of these in their adopted homeland, and these recipes were altered further under the influence of Polish, Hungarian, and Italian immigrants.

Oddly enough, it seems that the hot dog is better defined by its bun.

So who came up with this notion? Feltman's pushcart operation offered rolls and sauerkraut along with sausages. But a roll, eaten as a side or even pinched around a sausage, is not a hot dog bun. The quintessential hot dog comes in a custom-made bun, one baked specifically to serve as a sleeve for this meaty object of mystery. Years later, Feltman was serving these, but do we know when and where this idea arose? How about 1904, at the St. Louis World's Fair. That's the story anyway.

Two years before Dorgan sketched a dachshund reclining on a bun, it was developed at the suggestion of Bavarian-

> **W**hereas only St. Louis and New York purport to be the birthplace of the hot dog, no less than four cities earnestly claim to be the site of the hamburger's nativity.

American concessionaire Anton Feuchtwanger. In keeping with the grandeur of a World's Fair, Feuchtwanger is said to have tossed the idea of serving his sausages wrapped in the usual greasy paper and instead attempted to dress things up a bit by lending customers white cotton gloves with which to pick up the hot links. Charming as the idea might have seemed on paper, it proved disastrously impractical, and after seeing hundreds of pairs of gloves walk off down the midway, Feuchtwanger, still unwilling to go back to the traditional paper, enlisted the aid of his brother-in-law, a baker, to create a bun custom-made for the job. Americans from all over the country left the fair with a newfound desire to slip their wieners into these form-fitting buns.

Danish Sideways Burgers

A World's Fair makes for an ideal coming-out party for culinary debutantes. All the better if they are jockeying for American icon status. Not surprisingly, then, it's also claimed that the hot dog's arch rival, the hamburger, debuted at this 1904 shindig. But the hamburger's true place of birth is even more embattled than the hot dog's. Whereas only St. Louis and New York purport to be the birthplace of the hot dog, no less than four cities earnestly claim to be the site of the hamburger's nativity.

Ultimately, this probably reflects the hamburger's preferential status in the American diet. Though we may pay patriotic homage to the hot dog, nostalgically respectful of its association with baseball, and Fourth of July barbecue parties, the truth is the average U.S. citizen puts away 156 burgers yearly as opposed to the scant 65 dogs he swallows. And, mind you, that's not counting hamburger showing up as meatloaf, chili, Salisbury steak, and so forth. We're just talking basic hamburger here—a burger, a bun. But in Connecticut they want to talk about toast.

There's a Burger Born Every Minute

Fast & Faster

What really makes the hamburger a hamburger has less to do with the bread or buns or grills or gravy and more to do with the system that pushes this hamburger as an edible widget. Burgers as business epitomizes those all-American values of economy, quantity, and speed. What could be more patriotic than fast food?

Founders E.W. "Billy" Ingram and Walt Anderson strike a pose outside one of their original White Castle restaurants.

Hamburgers as a cultural phenomenon are really the brainchild of fry cook E.W. "Billy" Ingram and real estate agent Walt Anderson, founders of the White Castle hamburger chain. Back in 1921, they raised the first gleaming white steel facade in Wichita, Kansas, with others soon to follow.

The ideal of military conformity suggested by the uniformity of these franchised "fortresses" was further enhanced as White Castle pioneered the use of standardized uniforms and military-style paper hats originally developed by the employees from playfully folded napkins. By 1949, efficiency was pushed further as Castle cooks discovered that poking holes in the already small steam-grilled burgers caused them to cook even faster. Squeezing eighteen one-ounce perforated hamburgers from a meager pound of beef, the Castle advanced the cause of quantity over quality with their influential slogan "Buy 'Em by the Sack." By 1987, White Castle was bucking the trend toward more sophisticated and healthful tastes by marketing precooked hamburgers, complete with bun, in supermarket frozen food bins. As a further affront to effete gourmets, these bags of microwavable sandwiches featured recipes like broccoli "Castlerole" made with chopped burgers, frozen broccoli, Ritz crackers, and Velveeta.

While White Castle, as the nation's first fast-food chain, remains eccentrically committed to more or less unfashionable ideals, McDonald's long ago overtook the competition by adapting both to changing domestic climates as well as international markets. With twenty three thousand restaurants in over one hundred countries, McDonald's adapt-and-conquer strategy for world domination is preposterously successful—as evidenced by the opening in 1994 of the first McDonald's restaurant in Kuwait, where some fifteen thousand eager customers crowded under the arches, and traffic at the drive-thru backed up seven miles. First played by TV weatherman Willard Scott in 1963, the grease-painted corporate shill, Ronald McDonald, is now believed to beat out everyone but old St. Nick himself in terms of worldwide recognizability.

World conquest was probably not on the agenda when Dick and Mac McDonald opened their San Bernadino, California, takeout. Serving hot dogs and fresh orange juice seemed like enough at the time. In fact, they were doing a pretty brisk turnover—a point that was not lost on Ray Kroc when he met the brothers in 1954. But Kroc was not as excited about the orange juice. Kroc's vision of the future included milkshakes.

Lots of milkshakes. And in obedience to this vision, Kroc had mortgaged his home and thrown his entire life savings into distribution rights for a souped-up, five-spindled variety of shake-maker called the Multimixer. Kroc estimated the brothers would need approximately eight; a sale was completed, and business boomed. But Kroc was already 52 at the time and understandably restless to get on with things. He liked the efficiency of the McDonald brothers' "speedy system" and liked the idea of selling more Multimixers. With a little coaxing, the brothers entered into an agreement to franchise the operation.

McDonald's unbounded growth over the years has generated plenty of opposition from various activists. Among the general population it has generated a great body of paranoid rumors, some of which (like the myth that earthworms were being used as a beef extender) have actually cost the company some serious expenditures on public relations.

The worm rumor, believed to have begun circulating sometime in the mid-1970s, spread frantically until 1982, when the corporation was compelled to hold a press conference to rebut the claim. The U.S. Secretary of Agriculture was even called in to provide a letter verifying that the burgers were pure beef, unadulterated by earthworms or other annelids.

However, it was Ray Kroc, as quoted in Time magazine, who provided the bottom line: "We couldn't afford to grind worms into our meat; hamburger costs a dollar and a half a pound, and night crawlers six dollars."

The toast issue revolves around Louis Lassen—a man whom local historians in New Haven, Connecticut, like to credit with the hamburger's invention. Arriving in this country from Denmark in the 1880s, Lassen quickly made a name for himself thanks to the fine slices of steak piled high on the sandwiches he sold from the back of a rented lunch wagon. However, Lassen fed his family on scraps and leftovers rejected as unfit for his paying customers. But this wasn't a bad thing, as Lassen had developed a technique of grinding the meat and broiling it in the form of patties that yielded very satisfactory results.

At some point, these patties found their way onto toasted bread (not a bun, mind you) and, from there, onto Lassen's lunch cart menu. The growing popularity of the burgers paid for a small brick diner, where the Lassen family, to this day, continues to broil burgers sandwiched vertically in peculiar antique gas grills. Another eccentricity of the diner is a fanatical prohibition against condiments. Insisting that the beef be enjoyed in its virginal purity, Lassen's descendants maintain a century-long vigil against sullying the beef with ketchup or mustard. While New Haven's claims are well-authenticated, can we really accept this freakish, sideways-grilled, bunless, ketchupless sandwich as ancestor to our beloved American icon?

We do, after all, have plenty of other choices.

Got the Name, Making the Claim

In Hamburg, New York, they'll tell you that the sandwich originated at the Hamburg (or Erie County) Fair of 1885.

Residents of Stark County, Ohio, have mixed feelings about this claim, as the actual invention made near Hamburg was the work of two brothers from Ohio.

Natives of the Buckeye state, Charles

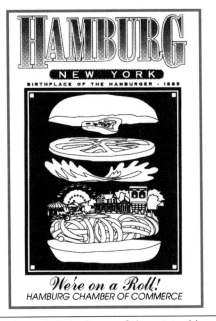

Is Hamburg, NY, the home of the original burger?

and Frank Menches spent the 1880s hauling a tremendous gas stove around the country, frying up pork sausage, eggs, liverwurst, cornmeal mush, and split-pea fritters at fairs, picnics, revivals, races, and wherever people were likely to pay for such food. While setting up for the Hamburg fair, the brothers realized they were short on the pork they needed for their best-seller: sausage sandwiches. Thanks to a miserable heat wave, no slaughterhouse was interested in filling the brothers' small order, which promised little money and lots of perishable leftovers and flies. Instead, the butcher is supposed to have ground up some beef already on hand. Grilled patties, toasted bread, success, and a namesake for the town of Hamburg all followed.

Or so they say. Despite decades of popularity, no one in Hamburg, New York, ever got around to mentioning this story until 1985, conveniently in time for the one hundred-year anniversary of the invention and a commemorative festival organized by Hamburg civic boosters.

Why Wisconsin Needs a Walk-Thru Burger

More dubious, still, is the claim made by the town of Seymour, Wisconsin, where they tell a tale of one 15-year-old entrepreneur, Charles Nagreen, who in 1885 decided to improve his meatball-vending operation at the annual fair by squashing the balls and serving them between slices of bread. Fair after fair, the boy's success as a squashed-meatball salesman increased, eventually earning Nagreen the appellation "Hamburger Charlie" and igniting in Seymour, Wisconsin, a vision of a "Hamburger Hall of Fame" to one day be housed in a four-story, $15-million bit of burger-shaped architecture—though for now the Hall of Fame is accommodated in more modest quarters in downtown Seymour.

Curiously, however, the first mention of Nagreen's claim did not appear in print until 1947, and no contemporary accounts of the 1885 Seymour Fair make mention

Home Of The Hamburger

Celebration

Seymour, Wisconsin

August 5, 1989

Charles 'Hamburger Charlie' Nagreen

The one and only Hamburger Charlie.

Seymour, Wisconsin
"The Home of the Hamburger"

Seasoning the world's largest hamburger. Finally, something to go with that order of super-size fries and soft drink.

of meatballs squashed or otherwise. Nonetheless, Hamburger Charlie's spirit of self-promotion was rekindled in Seymour's 1989 "Home of the Hamburger Celebration" marked by hamburger relays, a ketchup slide, and the creation of the world's largest 5,520 pound hamburger (scaled down to a mere 1,000 pounds in subsequent years once the feat went unchallenged).

Yes, Yes. But Check Out Those Blackeyed Peas!

While Seymour, Wisconsin's municipal fantasy runs toward four-story burgers, Athens, Texas, is more lackadaisical about its claim to be the birthplace of America's beloved staple. Texans say it was Athenian, Fletcher Davis, a.k.a. Uncle Dave, a.k.a. "Old Dave," who started grilling hamburgers in their home state, and eventually went on to flip burgers at the 1904 World's Fair. Though the innovation is noted every October in the Uncle Fletch Davis Hamburger Festival, this celebration tends to take a backseat to Athen's title as the "Blackeyed Pea Capital of the World."

Besides the relative lack of interest and financial motive, Athen's claim is authenticated by a contemporary account from the *New York Tribune*, in which a reporter at the fair mentions a new sandwich called the "hamburger" as "the innovation of a food vendor on the pike." The account is cited by hamburger historians from McDonald's called upon to provide the final word in hamburger history.

And there's a final touch of grim realism that lends the Athens story a ring of truth. Upon returning home from his victorious stint at the World's Fair, "Uncle Fletch" discovered that in his absence, several other cafes had begun selling the local favorite. Lacking the energy or inclination to compete, the

A 1904 portrait of Fletcher Davis, the Lone Star state's heir to burgerdom.

former potter gave up the grill and went back to fiddling with clay.

Raw Beef, Beets, and Eels

The only unexplained aspect of the Athenian creation myth is the name itself. Why "hamburger"?

All accounts (outside that offered in Hamburg, New York) inevitably associate the sandwich somehow with the Northern German port city of Hamburg. Athens' supporters maintain that the sandwich arrived nameless at the St. Louis Fair and received its nickname thanks to the large number of German-Americans living in that city at the time. These immigrants, coming mainly from Southern Germany, were supposedly amused to encounter these ground beef patties, which remind-ed them of the ground meat dishes served by their ancestral enemies in Northern Germany. Somewhat derisively they labeled Davis' creation the "Hamburger sandwich."

That's one version anyway.

Plausible or not, many hamburger historians note that shredded lean beef used in America as hamburgers is simi-lar to beef tartare—a dish introduced to Germany by the Russian Tartars in the fourteenth century. Served cold and uncooked, this delicate blend of high-quality ground beef, chopped onions, parsley, and capers could be related to another cold (though not raw) beef dish, "Hamburg Steak," mentioned in the *Boston Journal* in 1884.

By 1889, the "Hamburg steak" was served warm and was now fairly synony-mous with "Salisbury steak," a dish named after the New York food reformist and crank, Dr. James H. Salisbury. Already in the 1870s, Dr. Salisbury was advocating a bizarre diet of beef (lean and shredded to ease digestion) washed down with copious quantities of warm water as a sort of systemic cleansing to be under-

taken three times daily. Salisbury claimed that he had subsisted on this diet for decades. Though Salisbury didn't dare serve his curative "steaks" on a bun, he was serving up beef patties before any of the other hamburger "inventors."

■ FLAKES FOR SCIENCE ■

Dr. Graham: Wheat and Bran, Joined by God

Cold cereal for breakfast is a distinctly American thing, created in an optimistic country in an industrialist age with "sci-entific progress" written all over it. It was mass-produced, boxed and uniform for efficient stacking, and could be stored for long periods. And, best of all, the factories that churned it out were not just filling boxes with food; they were, in a sense, filling prescriptions. Breakfast cereal was the first food created by doc-tors and engineers.

The story begins with a cracker. One so suspiciously bland it seems to conceal something—and indeed it does. Perennial favorite in nursery schools and nursing homes, the Graham Cracker was named after the nineteenth-century Presbyterian minister Sylvester Graham. It's likely the clergyman would be pleased that his crackers have found a home with the prepubescent and the postmenopausal since he'd particularly prized the snacks as a buffer against troubling sexual desires. But later developments—Cinnamon Grahams, for instance—would have the poor man rolling over in his grave. Rev.

Graham abhorred cinnamon and indeed all spices as "highly exciting and exhausting."

The thing was, Graham didn't really distinguish between "stimulation" and "overstimulation." Health, for him, was the reward for a lifestyle of moderation and simplicity. Right living would put doctors out of business, and Graham wouldn't have minded that a bit. "All medicine, as such, is itself an evil," he wrote in one of his many tirades. Doctors, he believed, were much less likely to understand man's ills than those who followed simple God-given laws of clean living.

> **"All medicine, as such, is itself an evil,"** Rev. Graham wrote in one of his many tirades. Doctors, he believed, were much less likely to understand man's ills than those who followed simple God-given laws of clean living.

Graham also worried a great deal about how we milled flour and insisted

that separating wheat and bran was a violation of "what God joined together." Deep-seated concerns over this were the origin of his own whole-wheat "Graham Flour." Though the meal was later used to make the crackers that bear his name, that wasn't what Graham had in mind when he came up with it.

First he baked it into small rugged loaves. Finding these by no means fit to eat, he crumbled them up and threw them back in the ovens, thereby producing something that he at least considered somewhat palatable. He called the twice-baked grains "granula," and still determined to see the stuff eaten by others, he tried soaking the flinty clumps overnight in milk to soften them. The year was 1863, and this was the rocky start of the breakfast cereal industry.

The fact that chewing a single mouthful of his product presented such a challenging workout to the jaw in no way hindered Graham's sense of success, since more attentive mastication and rigorous exercise were two more essentials to Graham's idea of "right living."

Adventist Crackers and Animal Propensities

Though Graham was certainly in favor of a manly program of exercise, there was one manly part of the body he was all too happy to see exempted. Sexual stimulation for the good Reverend was

The clean-living Presbyterian minister Sylvester Graham.

even more dangerous than cinnamon, coffee, tea, and meat put together. While grudgingly allowing the act some place in Creation, he suggested that married couples confine their coupling to no more than once a month. It was for young unmarried men and their idle hands that Graham reserved the most vitriolic threats of all.

Despite all this seething, Graham remained quite a popular guy up through the early 1840s. Around that time, one of Graham's disciples, Dr. James Caleb Jackson—a Yankee abolitionist and firm believer in the oldworldly science of hydropathy—had opened a health resort in Danville, New York, where Graham's

> **S**exual stimulation for the good Reverend was even more dangerous than cinnamon, coffee, tea, and meat put together. While grudgingly allowing the act some place in Creation, he suggested that married couples confine their coupling to no more than once a month. It was for young unmarried men and their idle hands that Graham reserved the most vitriolic threats of all.

granula was always on the menu. The "Grahamite" movement was in full swing.

Things were looking good, except for one thing: The world was supposed to end—on October 22, 1843, to be exact. Thousands of followers of Rev. William Miller waited for Christ's Second Advent on that day. Unfortunately, the Big Guy failed to show. "The Great Disappointment," as it came to be known, was followed by a few others, until one day some of the "Adventists" came under the influence of Sister Ellen White. (White is generally credited with founding the Seventh Day Adventists, a group that splintered into a number of other apocalyptically minded

The Battle Creek Sanitarium (1911).

sects, including the Branch Davidians of Waco, Texas.) Along with White's visionary tendencies came periodic paralysis, and other psychomotor abnormalities. This is where Dr. Jackson and the Grahamite influence comes in.

After experiencing encouraging results in treatments with Jackson in New York, White returned home to Battle Creek, Michigan, and (with the encouragement of a visiting angel and backers within the church) set up a Grahamite facility of her own: The Battle Creek Health Institute. This high-profile sanitarium did more than anything to popularize the obscure Granula and demonize booze, coffee, tobacco, and meat as the source of "animal propensities."

Harvey Kellogg: Nuts May Save the Race

Now, what Sister White really needed to fight those unsavory "propensities" was a director who was not only serious about Graham's principles, but also those of the Seventh Day Adventist variety. She found this in the surgeon, mechanic, and inventor Dr. John Harvey Kellogg. Borrowing rather directly from Jackson's regimen, Kellogg began immediately manufacturing and

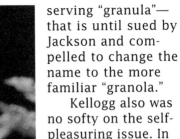

John Harvey Kellogg (1942).

"A remedy which is almost always successful in small boys is circumcision," Kellogg wrote. "The operation should be performed by a surgeon without administering an anesthetic, as the brief pain attending the operation will have a salutary effect upon the mind ... In females, the author has found the application of pure carbolic acid to the clitoris an excellent means of allaying the abnormal excitement."

serving "granula"— that is until sued by Jackson and compelled to change the name to the more familiar "granola."

Kellogg also was no softy on the self-pleasuring issue. In fact, his approach to the topic left Graham looking rather lax. "A remedy which is almost always successful in small boys is circumcision," he wrote. "The operation should be performed by a surgeon without administering an anesthetic, as the brief pain attending the operation will have a salutary effect upon the mind . . . In females, the author has found the application of pure carbolic acid to the clitoris an excellent means of allaying the abnormal excitement. "

Though married, Kellogg's union was supposedly never tainted by sex, and he is said to have spent his wedding night penning the fear-mongering abstinence tract *Plain Facts for Old and Young*. Some biographers suggest a possible sexual dysfunction caused by mumps, while others speculate that Kellogg's obsessive insistence upon a daily enema administered by hospital orderlies may have indicated a preference for other forms of sexual gratification. (Kellogg

The ancestor of one of the world's most popular breakfast staples.

also imposed his preoccupation on all residents of the Sanitarium, subjecting them daily to copious enemas of water and yogurt.)

Personal eccentricities aside, Kellogg managed to crank out quite a number of dietary innovations to accompany his granola. One was a coffee substitute made of toasted and caramelized cereal; the other was "granose," a shredded wheat substance served not only as a breakfast food but also formed into little nests into which sanitarium cooks dumped cheese, mushrooms, bananas, and creamed peas. A pasty imitation of meat called "protose" or "nuttose" also came out of Kellogg's kitchens. (Some historians even credit Kellogg rather than George Washington Carver with the invention of peanut butter thanks to this formula.) Appropriately enough, Kellogg loved nuts, and at one point Battle Creek's medical messiah even composed an essay evocatively entitled "Nuts May Save the Race"!

C.W. Post: The Road to Wellville

Graham, Jackson, and Kellogg—a good assortment of mixed nuts but not quite complete without C.W. Post. Perhaps a trifle less nutty but no less important to the mix, Post gravitated not so much toward medicine as marketing. It was

Post's mystical bamboozling that eventually gave birth to the corporate behemoth General Foods.

A dyspeptic entrepreneur with business interests ranging from ploughshares to suspenders, Post came to the Battle Creek Sanitarium from Springfield, Illinois, for a nine-month stay. Not only did the cure at the "San" resolve his gastric problems,

C.W. Post (1904).

but it sent him off filled with prophetic zeal. His inspiration derived in part from millenialist and spiritualist undercurrents at the spa, and in part from the divine marketability he found in San's products.

Post's religious positivism expressed itself in a miracle of self-healing and a pamphlet called *The Road to Wellville*, after which the T.C. Boyle novel and the Anthony Hopkins/Matthew Broderick film were named. Practicing what he called "mental therapeutics," he suggested to Kellogg that he might help out at the San by praying over patients for $50 a week. When Kellogg rebuffed this proposal, along with Post's suggestion they

Have a Look!

Through a magnifying glass, at

Grape-Nuts

The glass brings out sharply an interesting sight. Upon every golden granule will be seen small, shining crystals of Grape-Sugar.

This isn't "put there."

In the process of making Grape-Nuts the starch of wheat and barley is changed into this sugar and the result is probably the most perfect and beneficial food known for providing the elements Nature uses for rebuilding the brain and nerve centres.

Trial proves.

"There's a Reason"

Postum Cereal Company, Ltd., Battle Creek, Michigan, U. S. A.

Turn-of-the-century advertisement for Grape Nuts.

form a partnership to market a version of the San's ersatz coffee, C.W. took off in a huff and opened a rival institute across town.

This facility, La Vita Inn, was pitched as a sort of halfway house for "graduates" of the San. Its monastic ambiance inspired Post to nickname his cereal beverage "Monk's brew." Even better, his alternative to granula was trumped up as "Elijah's Manna," and the cereal box portrayed the bearded patriarch receiving the divine flake from a heaven-sent bird. This turned out to be a bit much both for indignant Bible-belters and British custom officials, who had laws against products exploiting biblical names. Elijah's Manna consequently was demoted to "Post Toasties," and "Monk's Brew" became "Postum."

> **O**bserving the success of these strategies, Post brought out another product, "Grape Nuts," which contained no nuts and bore only the most tenuous connection to grapes, thanks to a small presence of "grape sugar" (dextrose), a byproduct of the baking process. Further muddling the public, Post advertised the "nuts" with the cryptic slogan "There's a reason."

For Sale: Predigested Food, Some Chewing Required

When religiosity failed, Post turned to science, or a convenient facsimile thereof. Appealing to the hypochondriac in everyone, he claimed that drinking Postum saved one from "coffee heart" and "coffee neuralgia," caffeine-induced accidents on the road and at work, financial ruin, and broken homes.

Observing the success of these strategies, Post brought out another product, "Grape Nuts," which contained no nuts and bore only the most tenuous connection to grapes, thanks to a small presence of "grape sugar" (dextrose), a byproduct of the baking process. Further muddling the public, Post advertised the "nuts" with the cryptic slogan "There's a reason."

Post was the first to mass market his foods as medicines, claiming that because the ingredients were "concentrated," they would enhance the brain's functioning. Gums and teeth were strengthened by the laborious chewing required to reduce the cereal to something that could actually pass through the esophagus. Despite all the hard work required of your teeth—and despite the rather nauseating images evoked—Post advertised the cereal as "predigested" and, therefore, good for modern man's overtaxed stomach.

All of this marketing was ridiculously successful, making Post a billionaire, and forcing Kellogg to compete on Post's terms. The struggle brought John Kellogg's younger brother, William, to the frontlines. Much less worried about masturbation than money, the wily William Keith (W.K.) Kellogg countered Post's scientific pretensions by advertising the Kellogg's products as more "genuine" and urging consumers to accept no imitations. It was at this time that the "W.K. Kellogg" autograph first appeared on cornflake boxes, signifying "authenticity," as well as the older brother's backseat role.

Increasingly cantankerous, old John Kellogg had broken with supporters in the Seventh Day Adventist Church, and his financially mismanaged health resort had become significantly less healthy. While John was away in Europe, William bought up enough shares in the Kellogg Company to give him legal control. Thanks to their wholesome diets and regimens, the two brothers were able to continue their struggles far into their golden years, each dying at the age of 91.

■ MILITARY INDUSTRIAL GOURMET ■

Frozen Dinner Theater

The year was 1954, and Lassie was bounding across American television screens for the first time. The adventures of this fine Scottish lass were sponsored naturally enough by a family with a conspicuously Scottish name, Campbell, and the Campbell clan owned a Soup Company. Coincidence? No more so than the fact that Campbell Soup also happened to produce the perfect product to enhance your viewing pleasure while watching this dinnertime entertainment: TV dinners! That very year, when the famous collie began endorsing TV dinners, Campbell's had acquired the small Omaha-based business C.A. Swanson & Sons, who'd been

test marketing the product between Chicago and Omaha for several years prior.

Gerry Thomas, the inventor of TV dinners, claims that he got the idea while on a flight to Pittsburgh, during which he noted single-serving metal dinner trays being tested by the airline. "It was a case of necessity being the mother of invention," he said.

Though there may have been something inevitable in Thomas' application of aluminum, the association with TV was not as obvious to the inventor, who at the time did not even own a television. "We couldn't afford it," he recalls.

W. Charles and Gilbert C. Swanson, the "sons" in C.A. Swanson & Sons, wanted to premier the product with a traditionalist menu intended to counter any objections from culinary reactionaries, and so they went with the surefire familiarity of the all-American Thanksgiving dinner: roast turkey, gravy, cornbread dressing, peas, and whipped sweet potatoes.

The recipes were said to have been tested on focus groups consisting of a number of prominent hotel chefs and

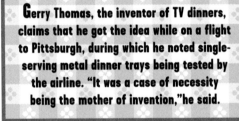

> **G**erry Thomas, the inventor of TV dinners, claims that he got the idea while on a flight to Pittsburgh, during which he noted single-serving metal dinner trays being tested by the airline. "It was a case of necessity being the mother of invention,"he said.

The original TV Dinner (note the absence of the beloved dessert compartment).

The 45th anniversary edition of the TV Dinner (with brownie).

Gerry Thomas, father of the TV dinner, immortalizes the famous tray in cement in the forecourt of Mann's Chinese Theater.

twelve hundred housewives. A survey of children's preferences highlighted their dislike of foods running together, and nasty runaway juices were therefore confined by little metal damns installed between the individual portions. (Perhaps this emphasis on child psychology accounts in part for the TV dinner's continuing role as a "comfort food.") Conveniently enough, the tripartite division of the tray, which also added structural strength to the stamped aluminum, looked a damn sight more "futuristic" than a bunch of old-fashioned quadrangles to boot.

Finally, the packaging was designed to capitalize on America's newfound love for broadcast entertainment, and the box layout depicted the food within a television console complete with knobs.

It didn't hurt that the homemaker's household allowance was set back only 98 cents per meal, and that popping the item into an oven for 25 minutes was even within the repertoire of culinary skills possessed by the typical male of the 1950s.

Roast beef with mashed potatoes and corn was soon to follow, and in the 1960s a fourth compartment for apple or cherry cobbler was introduced, forever endearing the product to kids of all ages. Now, rather than waiting for dessert to be brought to the table at the end of the meal, the sweet was already sitting there, ready to be gobbled as soon as the cover was peeled back.

Public furor over the brownie being dropped from the menu in 1986 attests to the public's sweet spot for that dessert compartment. Today, the brownie's back, but as of 1987, the trays are now micro-wavable plastic. The cultural significance of the original trays being fabricated of "space age" aluminum has been acknowledged by the Smithsonian, which now exhibits one of these American icons among its collections.

While some may blame the introduction of the TV dinner for the breakdown of the family, Americans continue to down roughly 3 million of Swanson's frozen meals weekly, and the company's introduction of a new boneless chicken entree was supported in 1998, ironically enough, by a "Make New Memories with Swanson" campaign designed to recast the product as a nostalgic centerpiece of family interaction.

In April 1999—the 45th anniversary of the product—inventor Gerry Thomas was honored with a ceremony in the forecourt of Mann's Chinese Theater, during which an imprint of the famous TV dinner tray was pressed into wet cement. The slab, however, is destined for display in Swanson corporate headquarters.

Home on the Radar Range

How Percy Spencer Blew Up an Egg and Other Grisly Tales of the Microwave

How did the microwave oven arrive in our kitchens? Largely thanks to Hitler sending his Luftwaffe to bomb the hell out of London, an act that prompted British scientists working with microwave radar to turn to U.S. engineers for assistance in radar production. It was the American-engineered magnetron tube that saved the day, and its creator was Percy Spencer, a self-taught inventor lacking even a high school education.

Spencer worked for Raytheon, a Cambridge-based company that had made its name engineering radio components, and it was while working with the magnetron tube in Raytheon labs in 1946 that he noticed a strange phenomenon that would lead to the invention of the microwave oven.

The chocolate bar he carried in his pocket had melted.

It had not just gone soft from his body temperature but actually liquefied. Suspecting this curious effect might be due to emissions from the tube, he brought in a bag of popcorn, placed it near the tube, and, as expected, ended up with a floor full of popped kernels. By the next morning, he was already cooking eggs, though the process was not yet fully understood—either by Spencer or his curious colleagues—one of whom was said to have been close enough to one egg to have it unexpectedly blow up in his face.

Near the end of that same year Spencer had created a behemoth of an oven as tall as a man and weighing in at around 750 pounds. Pretty soon, these giants were finding their way into factories for industrial applications like roasting potato chips and drying nuts, coffee beans, wet leather, dyed textiles, cork, and books. They were even used to shuck oysters.

It was not until 1952, however, that the Tappan Stove Company, in partnership with Raytheon, introduced the first home model, which with its $1,295 price tag was a bit steep for the average homemaker. By 1967, the militaristically named Amana Radarange debuted, with a lower price and wider market appeal, and by 1975 microwaves were outselling gas stoves in the U.S.

Besides price and size, suspicion about the unfamiliar technology played a large role in deterring sales and manifested itself in a diverse collection of urban legends detailing the grisly ends of babies, cats, and dogs nuked in these ovens. (Though mostly spurious, there was one case of a Baltimore lawyer convicted of microwaving a kitten in 1992.)

Today, though the technology behind the convenience is probably no better understood, an attitude of trust is more common with most parents feeling safer about kids preparing food in a microwave rather than burning down the house or gassing themselves with a conventional oven.

Great War, Bad Cheese

The horrors of war come in many forms, and some of them are edible, as was the case during the height of World War I, when cheese wholesaler James L. Kraft unleashed a substance unlike man had ever seen. It was derived from milk solids, cheese-like, yet not like the Old World cheeses of the past. He applied for a patent and dubbed this wartime wonder "American cheese."

In naming it this, perhaps Kraft had been swept along on the wave of patriotism that had already seen sauerkraut rechristened as "liberty cabbage," or perhaps Kraft just hoped a good nationalist name would boost sales to the military. The cheese was promising little success on the civilian market, but it did at least store and travel well, and Kraft managed to convince the U.S. Army to requisition 6 million pounds of the stuff. Amidst the depravations of war, overseas troops somehow managed to develop a high degree of tolerance—if not a taste—for the substance, and when they returned home civilian sales picked up.

If war was good for American cheese, economic depression was even better. The hard times of the 1930s saw a widespread acceptance of many synthetic substitutes for traditional foods, including Miracle Whip, Parkay margarine, and Velveeta. Though much maligned today, the mellifluously named Velveeta introduced in 1928 at least served to replace the even nastier canned cheeses that once lurked on grocers' shelves.

Real cheese is milk. It's simple. Milk thickened to curds and whey, then drained and pressed into a form. It's cured, it ripens, and then it tastes good. Velveeta begins with real cheese, with a mix of Colby and cheddar leftover from processing, but soon it's on its way to something else. Kraft grinds up the cheese scrap;

Velveeta was originally introduced in 1928.

combines it with milk, emulsifiers, dyes, and flavors; melts it down at 150 degrees; and then pours the glop into brick-shaped boxes lined with foil. This is "processed" or "process" cheese. A step down from this on the "Great Chain of Cheese" would be "Cheese food." Cheese food undergoes the same processing, except the substance produced can start with less than the 50 percent natural cheese required for the coveted "processed cheese" title.

Cheese Man Was Not Meant to Know

Kraft's cheesy machinations, however, did not end there. During the Great War, the military had not only looked kindly upon Kraft's relatively imperishable "American cheese," but had also encouraged the consumption of lightweight dehydrated and reconstituted rations, boosting sales of items like "instant potatoes" in the postwar market. Maddened with a sort of Frankenstinian desire to create artificial cheese, Kraft began experimenting with ways to reduce his American cheese down to its very essence.

The "powdered cheese" Kraft unleashed upon an unsuspecting public, however, was generally regarded as a crime against nature and went virtually unsold.

One day in 1937, a St. Louis salesman changed all that. A devilish whispering in his ear suggested he take a bit of string and bundle the lurid powder up with boxes of macaroni. This was the world's first prepackaged dinner, simple enough for a chimpanzee to make and cheap enough for depression-era households. And it was "instant" too, allowing consumers to "make a meal for four in nine minutes." The Kraft Dinner, or "Blue Box," was also an instant success. When the next war rolled around, households were armed for "Meatless Tuesdays" with this all-American comfort food.

A final milestone in the de-evolution of cheese came in 1952, when Kraft laboratories produced a pasteurized, shelf-stable process cheese spread. First sold in jars, the substance would later be copied and sold in squeeze bottles, and finally, once all inhibitions had been broken down, it would appear in aerosol cans that could spray cheese on crackers or directly into the mouth.

The name chosen for the substance in 1952 was "Cheez Whiz." In the rapture of the postwar economic boom, the word "whiz" would naturally suggest the triumphant sound of jets racing into the future (rather than the jets of urine that might be called to mind today). As if the name weren't bad enough already, the word cheese itself was eventually poisoned by associations with these experiments.

The famous "Blue Box" changed the way Americans prepared and ate dinner.

> **A final milestone in the de-evolution of cheese came in 1952, when Kraft laboratories produced a pasteurized, shelf-stable process cheese spread. First sold in jars, the substance would later be copied and sold in squeeze bottles, and finally, once all inhibitions had been broken down, it would appear in aerosol cans that could spray cheese on crackers or directly into the mouth. The name chosen for the substance in 1952 was "Cheez Whiz."**

Sometime during the '80s, "cheese" began to take on unpleasant associations. In particular, the word "cheesy," which had been used by advertisers to designate products that were cheese-like (without containing genuine cheese), began to be used like the word "corny" (corn being another cheap food filler) had been used in prior decades. "Cheesy" described all that was inauthentic or lacking in quality or substance. Even the "corn" in the word "cornball" was in some places substituted with cheese, and "cheeseball" might be used to describe a particularly smarmy artistic endeavor.

"Velveeta" today is also sometimes used to describe Internet messages (usually advertisements) cross-posted to many unrelated newsgroups. Junk mail of this sort certainly could conjure associations with the undesirable "filler" content of process cheese, but this bit of cyberslang clearly derives more directly from the term for unsolicited personal e-mails, namely "Spam."

SPAM

"Specially Packed Assorted Meats?"

"Super Processed Artificial Meat?"

"Scientifically Produced Animal Matter?"

"Some Parts Are Meat?"

All these possible derivations of the name are part of the mystique and folklore of everyone's favorite mystery meat Spam. The truth behind the name, however, is not nearly so sinister, though it is just as silly. It was during a 1936 "meat naming contest" sponsored by the Minnesota-based Hormel Foods company that the word was coined, and the winning entry was cooked up by Kenneth Daigneau, an actor and brother of a Hormel executive. Whether Daigneau had ever seen, much less tasted, the product is unclear, as the name he came up with was intended as a contraction of the words "Spiced Ham." Not quite the savory Black Forest ham that might be conjured by the name,

> **N**ot quite the savory Black Forest ham that might be conjured by the name, Spam actually consists of ham adulterated with pork shoulder and (less than 10 percent tendons!) "spiced" with salt and sodium nitrate — the substance responsible for its perpetual and preternatural rosiness.

Spam actually consists of ham adulterated with pork shoulder and (less than 10 percent tendons!) "spiced" with salt and sodium nitrate—the substance responsible for its perpetual and preternatural rosiness. In all fairness, it should be noted that Daigneau won his $100 prize at a New Year's party, presumably after an adequate amount of champagne had been uncorked.

Much like its cheesy cousin, Velveeta, Spam consists of the real thing ground up and suspended in an emulsion. In the case of Spam, this means coarser chunks of meat suspended in a slurry of more finely ground meat and water. This goop is then poured in the same metal can in which it's precooked. Cooking in the can sterilizes the product and creates the vacuum seal responsible for the distinctive and welcoming "Spam shlurp" heard upon opening.

Slammin' Spammy & Friends

The durable space-efficient container, the unrefrigerated shelf stability, and ready-to-eat portability were a heaven-made match for the logistic needs of the field kitchens of World War II. Promoted at the time by "Slammin' Spammy," a bomb-chucking cartoon swine, Spam went to war, providing the troops

1940's-era SPAM ad featuring Burns & Allen.

with many meals and many memories, neither of which were necessarily good.

Regardless of its inherent quality, Spam was an integral part of a heroic time in many young men's lives. It was a subject for cathartic humor, a mutual enemy, and sometimes—given the hardship of war—even a welcome meal. Ike may not have liked Spam, but General Eisenhower himself, in a letter to Hormel, expressed grudging recognition of this role, writing, "I ate my share of Spam along with millions of other soldiers. I will even confess to a few unkind words about it—uttered during the strain of battle, you understand. But as former commander-in-chief, I believe I can still officially forgive you for your only sin: sending us so much of it."

Had it only been properly fostered, perhaps this grudging respect for Spam could have prevented the Cold War. Recalling this common bond, Nikita Krushchev, in his autobiography, *Khrushchev Remembers*, writes, "There were many jokes going around in the army . . .

about American Spam; it tasted good, nonetheless. We had lost our most fertile, food-bearing lands—the Ukraine and the North Caucasians (during World War II). Without Spam, we wouldn't have been able to feed our army."

Spam Torta Rustica

Through subsequent decades, Spam continued to fill its role as the meat the world loves to hate, and Hormel does brisk business with its meaty pariah, unloading 140 million cans annually on a public claiming to despise it. Americans chew through 228 cans of the stuff with every passing minute. Alaska, Arkansas, Texas, and Alabama all rate high as Spam gobblers, but Hawaiians, in particular, exhibit an eerie affinity for the stuff, making it the centerpiece of a number of exotic island specialties including Spam Musubi, a kind of sushi featuring thick slabs of the meat product.

Located in Austin, Minnesota (SpamTown, USA), Hormel's Spam museum entices more than sixty thousand visitors annually through the giant replica Spam that serves as an entrance to the collections. Exhibits feature archival materials like back issues of *Squeal*, Hormel's employee newsletter, as well as curiosities like "Wimpy's Hamburgers in

> Through subsequent decades, Spam continued to fill its role as the meat the world loves to hate, and Hormel does brisk business with its meaty pariah, unloading 140 million cans annually on a public claiming to despise it. Americans chew through 228 cans of the stuff with every passing minute.

George Bush hands Boris Yeltsin the secret to the Allied victory in World War II.

a Can" and "Hormel Dog Dessert" in a tube. A nearby gift store opened recently by popular demand features clothing, watches, jewelry, golf balls, and even basketball backboards adorned with the beloved Spam logo. Hormel also hosts the annual "SpamJam," complete with recipe contests and cook-offs. (The 1997 winner was Spam *Torta Rustica,* calling for pink stuff, frozen spinach, and sliced Swiss cheese.) But Spam is celebrated far beyond the borders of its hometown, with Spam-carving competitions rapidly becoming entrenched nationwide as features of state fairs and festivals, such as Seattle's annual Fat Tuesday celebration.

Appearing in groceries in roughly 50 countries abroad, Spam's international following is particularly strong in the UK and South Korea, where as an American import it's regarded as a prestigious gift item. Sold in handsome nine-can presentation boxes, it's a popular gift for weddings and other festive events. There is even a Korean black market for Spam, and hordes of stolen spiced ham traceable to the larders of U.S. Army bases in that country are sometimes recovered by police. Those without suitable means or access to black-market booty will sometimes resort to cheaper domestic imitations of the real McCoy. Korean

Can you say, "licensing revenue"?

knockoffs include Lo-Spam, Dak, Plumrose, and Tulip.

Virtual Ham and Pork Shoulder

Spam also has a significant international presence on the worldwide web—albeit one originating largely with American college students. A classic among the more than two hundred pages of farcically cultic devotion is Bob Gorman's *Page O' Spam*, offering a collection of Spam trivia, a "Find-the-Spam" game, links to pages offering Spam knickknacks, audio clips from Monty Python's Spam song, and an original musical tribute to the miracle meat.

Probably the only thing more frightening than fresh Spam would be Spam that's not so fresh. A grisly concern with the demise of a loaf of Spam exposed to the elements served as the motivation for a two-year online research project focused on a single question: "How does

Museum-quality SPAM.

> **P**robably the only thing more frightening than fresh Spam would be Spam that's not so fresh. A grisly concern with the demise of a loaf of Spam exposed to the elements served as the motivation for a two-year online research project focused on a single question: "How does Spam decompose compared to other organic materials?"

Spam decompose compared to other organic materials?" One of several web projects set up by On and Off Productions, the "Spam Cam" site became notorious around 1998 for its Internet broadcast of time-lapse images from a camera trained on rotting Spam and control subjects that include assorted fruits, cookies, Jell-O, and a Twinkie. On and Off Production researchers describe their experimental method in the following manner:

"Every four days (or so) in the afternoon we photograph the research subjects. After careful analysis, we then upload the photo to the Spam Cam home page. The subjects are never moved from their location (the bedroom), although they remain covered unless photos are being taken. (The cover is a stopgap measure to prevent cats from eating the Spam, particularly as it begins to reek.)"

■ F L U F F & W O B B L E ■

Project Twinkies

Niacin, Ferrous Sulfate, Thiamine Mono-nitrate, Riboflavin, Dextrose, Modified food starch, Sodium acid pyrophospahte, Monocalcium phosphate, Mono and di-glycerides, Lecithin, Polysorbate 60, Dextrin, Calcium caseinate, Sodium stearoyl lactylate, Cellulose gum, Wheat gluten, Sorbic acid.

It may sound like a science project, and it can be. At least it was for researchers on Project T.W.I.N.K.I.E.S. (Tests With Inorganic Noxious Kakes In Extreme Situations) at Rice University at Houston. The findings, published on a web page created by sophomore Todd Stadler, were presented as a malicious send up of stodgy scientific writing documented by amusing images of Twinkie snack cakes in various states of abuse.

Stadler's "Rapid Oxidation Test" consisted of torching a Twinkie with a lighter. Testing of "Gravitational Response" was an excuse to hurl the snack item from a ninth-story window. Practical applications or experiments were also provided. After determining through "Maximum Density Testing" that the cakes were 68 percent air and 32 percent solid, researchers suggested formulas for efficient packing (i.e., squashing) of Twinkies to be transported.

The page was the most frequently accessed student homepage at the university, accounting for more than 10 percent of the traffic on the school's computer system. Unfortunately, it was removed when university officials were spooked by a threatening phone call regarding trademark infringement.

But the call didn't originate with Interstate Brands of Kansas City, Missouri—the maker of Twinkies; it instead came from an anonymous prankster. Interstate Brands had been aware for some time of the web page, and the company was not about to take issue with it. Reaction to the web site at the Kansas City company in fact ranged from neutrality to support.

"I got a chuckle out of the web site myself," Mark Dirkes, senior vice president of marketing remarked some time after the web site's demise.

It's hard to imagine an angry, litigious Twinkie. It's such a friendly, fluffy name.

Not Being Shoes, They're Filled with Whipped Cream

When a product's mainly air, you need a good name to give it a little substance. James Dewar was aware of this back in 1931, wracking his brain, juggling syllables, hoping to string together the perfect name that would sell this new product of his. As the Chicago head of Continental Bakeries, he'd just come up with a new sponge cake item to make use of all the custom pans that only got used once a year during strawberry shortcake season. Even in the midst of the Depression, he figured sponge cakes would sell if you pumped them full of some sweet fluff and packaged them as a two-for-one nickel bargain. Dewar had been thinking of them as "Little Short Cake Fingers" but knew he'd need a zippier name.

It was while he was on a business trip with a friend that they passed a shoe factory bearing the sign that gave them the idea. Thankfully, it was the manufacturer of Twinkle Toe Shoes rather than Dr. Scholls, and thankfully Dewar had the good sense to reject his friend's slightly naughty sounding suggestion of "Twinkle Finger," shortening it instead to "Twinkies."

Death, Eternity, and Twinkies

Much reviled by the health conscious, the snack cake's leading ingredient is, and has always been, sugar. While, for most, the snack cake provides a sweet and slightly guilty pleasure, others find concealed in its fluffy core a seductive invitation to murder. The cake's darkest hour came with the notorious "Twinkie Defense" offered during the 1979 murder trial of Dan White, a one-time star athlete who'd confessed to the murder of San Francisco Mayor George Moscone and

supervisor Harvey Milk. In an attempt to reduce charges from murder to manslaughter, White's attorney, Douglas Schmidt, implicated the snack, citing the consumption of "Twinkies, cupcakes, chocolate bars, and Cokes" by his formerly health-conscious client as evidence for extreme mental distress. Psychiatrist Martin Blinder piped in with testimony to the effect that high sugar levels in the snack had brought about White's state of "diminished mental capacity." After convening

James Dewar, inventor of Twinkies, with some of his offspring.

"RACCOON" :30 TV

(MUSIC: SWEET TUNE, RACCOON STROLLS THROUGH MEADOW)

(RACCOON LOOKS UP)

(RACCOON SEES OBJECT)

(RACCOON IS INTRIGUED)

(RACCOON THINKS OBJECT IS A TWINKIE)

(RACCOON SMILES AND PREPARES TO CATCH OBJECT)

(OBJECT IS FALLING FAST)

(RACCOON'S EXPRESSION CHANGES TO ALARM)

(THE OBJECT IS A SNOWBOARD)

(SNOWBOARD LANDS, MUSIC CHANGES TO ROCK)

(SNOWBOARDER ZIPS OFF)

(RACCOON POPS UP)

RACCOON: Hey! Where's the cream filling?

RACCOON (VO): Now that's the stuff...

Hostess!

Even raccoons love Twinkies!

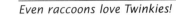

for six days, a jury of health-conscious San Franciscans agreed that the murder charges should be reduced to manslaughter.

True to its impervious nature, the Twinkie, however, withstood this assault on its character. Its folkloric ability to remain eternally fresh was put to the test in 1998 by scientists at the Massachusetts Institute of Technology, when a pair of the preservative-drenched sponge cakes accompanied contemporary newspapers, Nobel Prize-winning papers, and other archival materials into a time capsule slated to be opened in the year 2020.

The Twinkie's powerful appeal to academics is apparently shared by other products in the Hostess family of snack cakes. Art historian Jack Sheffler at the University of Pittsburgh-Bradford offered monumental testimony to this effect with his 1997 10-foot-high, 113-square-foot pyramid constructed entirely of Hostess Sno Balls and cupcakes. Erected in the university's Hanley Library Gallery from three tons of products donated by Hostess, the pyramid suggested intriguing parallels between the ancient Egyptians' yearning for eternity and the enduring nature of the preservative-laden snack items.

As highly disposable products endowed with an epic life span, the cakes are a natural for the mock heroic treatment of pop art. Working in Andy Warhol's hometown, Sheffler acknowledges this, remarking that Hostess products "are ideal for pop-related sculpture because they are an American icon."

Marshmallow

Let's be frank. The marshmallow's not what it used to be.

> **T**he Twinkie's folkloric ability to remain eternally fresh was put to the test in 1998 by scientists at the Massachusetts Institute of Technology, when a pair of the preservative-drenched sponge cakes accompanied contemporary newspapers, Nobel Prize-winning papers, and other archival materials into a time capsule slated to be opened in the year 2020.

Shamefully demoted from their full size, marshmallows have generally been reduced to the more common "miniatures" that now tend to fill grocery shelves and placate our needs to melt things in cocoa and mire things in Jell-O.

If anyone still buys the adult-size marshmallows, it's probably only to melt them into some sort of adhesive for Rice Krispies or impale them on sticks and torture them with fire. The very word itself has come to be more or less synonymous with "pushover."

But it wasn't always like this.

Back in ancient Egypt, a form of marshmallow was the food of the gods, the Pharaoh, and his court. This divine sweet was made from an essence of the marsh mallow (*Athaea officinalis*), a plant native to the marshy banks of the Nile. Sweetened with honey, the substance extracted came from the root of the mallow plant and was believed by many ancient peoples to have medicinal if not magical powers.

The Roman sage Pliny wrote, "Whosoever shall take a spoonful of the Mallows shall that day be free from all diseases that may come

Marshmallow Fluff: The Pharaoh would've dug it.

to him." The Greek father of medicine, Hippocrates, used it as a salve for wounds. During the Renaissance, it was considered effective against sore throats, stomach ailments, urinary problems, gonorrhea, and many other conditions. Herbalists today continue to prescribe *Athaea officinalis* for dozens of complaints.

So why don't you see bags of mini-marshmallows next to the ginseng and ginko bilboa?

Sometime in the mid-nineteenth century, marshmallow the medicine and marshmallow the confection parted ways.

> Taking their cue perhaps from the online endurance tests to which Spam and Twinkies have been subjected, hundreds of Peeps are tortured and destroyed each year, and the results are publicized on Internet "snuff sites." Though the sites come and go, and many colorful and vicious methods are discussed (including fire, boiling, and some exotic tricks with lasers and liquid nitrogen), the classic method of Peep disposal is the microwave.

French confectioners less concerned with effect than taste realized that the mallow's gummy substance, which was used more for body than flavor, could be easily replaced by cheaper whipped gelatin. (Their technique of casting gelatin in molds is still used to make a variety of gummy, chewy sweets.) So they tossed the mallow and kept the name, and by the mid-twentieth century, marshmallows were no more than corn syrup, corn starch, sugar, and gelatin. This sweet goo was no longer molded but was now spit from pipes and cut to length before drying and dusting with starch.

Americans eat, dissolve, and burn around 95 million pounds of these synthetic treats annually—quite a mountain of these little puffballs given the air-solid ratio. Most marshmallows come from factories in Henderson, Nevada, and Kendallville, Indiana. The Nevada factory, Kidd International, just outside of Las Vegas, offers tours where visitors can witness the birth of Smurfmallows, Martian-mallows, and the rare and exotic Penn State Nittany Lion Marshmallow.

Easter, a Time of Sacrifice

Taking their name from their motto, "A great candy isn't made . . . it's Just Born!," the Just Born company in Bethlehem, Pennsylvania, produces around 600 million marshmallow replicas of newborn chicks annually. They're called "Peeps," and they won't hit the shelves until a few weeks before Easter. The first "born" in 1953 was the classic Day-Glo yellow Peep, though fluorescent pink Peeps are not uncommon in the species. Purple Peeps were first sighted in 1995, blue arrived in 1998, and there are rumors of a race of albino Peeps. Marshmallow bunnies are also manufactured by Just Born, but they are not considered true Peeps, even less so are the Halloween pumpkins and Christmas Trees.

> **I**f offered the choice between a bowl of Jell-O or an experimental laxative concocted by a male carpenter named Pearl, chances are most people would go with the Jell-O. Yet a little over a hundred years ago there would be no choice in the matter, as the former and the latter were one in the same.

The world into which Just Born brings its marsh-mallow offspring is a cruel one, populated by individuals with twisted imaginations, web sites, and too much time on their hands. Taking their cue perhaps from the online endurance tests to which Spam and Twinkies have been subjected, hundreds of Peeps are tortured and destroyed each year, and the results are publicized on Internet "snuff sites." Though the sites come and go, and many colorful and vicious methods are discussed (including fire, boiling, and some exotic tricks with lasers and liquid nitrogen), the classic method of Peep disposal is the microwave.

Nuking Peeps produces satisfyingly consistent results: Grimly awaiting the inevitable, the little Easter martyr will at first exhibit no reaction to the radiation streaming through its fluffy form. But slowly a subtle trembling overtakes its body, followed by convulsive spasms of growth as the baby chick balloons into a monstrous molten amoeba of sweetened goo. Its split-second supernova is followed by quick collapse, as the creature deflates into a difficult-to-clean puddle of sugary cornstarch and gelatin.

While it might be easy to blame these evils on the soulessness of a generation of technophiles caught up in the mechanistic world of computers and microwaves, the root of the problem seems to go deeper than this. The need to torture

marshmallows can clearly be traced back to the days when man first crouched around a fire (with marshmallows).

The tradition of the marshmallow roast probably dates back to the 1940s or earlier, and only recently has any individual stepped in to question or altar this barbaric ritual. Today, a small mail-order company, Lenhart Associates, markets MallowMate, a "no flame, no burn marshmallow pretoasting spray." One aerosol squirt to your little cornstarch friend before warming him over the fire will not only protect him from disfiguring burns but will add a "delicious vanilla, strawberry, or coconut flavor" to your cruelty-free campfire treat.

"America's Most Famous Dessert"

If offered the choice between a bowl of Jell-O or an experimental laxative concocted by a male carpenter named Pearl, chances are most people would go with the Jell-O. Yet a little over a hundred years ago there would be no choice

in the matter, as the former and the latter were one in the same.

In 1887, in the upstate New York town of LeRoy, Pearl Wait was attempting to create laxative teas and cough remedies, using gelatin as a thickening agent. Wait was refining the taste of his cure-all, adding fruit flavors to the gelatin-based mixture to mask the medicinal taste, when he realized that this fruity gelatinous stuff might actually sell on flavor and novelty alone. He asked his wife, May, to try some, she agreed, and suggested a name for this wobbly wonder: Jell-O.

After, presumably, removing whatever bowel-loosening agents he'd originally included, Wait tried to market the recipe around town for a while. But, as it turned out, he was better at concocting and carpentry than at sales. Discouraged, he sold the patent in 1899 to another man with an odd first name: Orator Frank Woodward. Woodward owned the Genesee Pure Food Company, a company built on his skills at marketing items like a surrogate cereal-based coffee ("Grain-O") and egg-shaped balls of insecticide with "miraculous power to kill lice on hens when hatching." After pushing these, a tasty gelatin dessert was a cinch to promote, and it soon became his leading product. By 1925, Genesee Pure Food had become the Jell-O Company.

Long before Bill Cosby began surveying your digestive system, insisting there was "always room for Jell-O," the company was hiring top talent to push the jiggly stuff. Maxfield Parrish and Norman Rockwell both illustrated Jell-O ads, and Frank L. Baum was commissioned to write several books in his "Wizard of Oz" series published with Jell-O recipes in the back.

The '60s were a time of upheaval for Jell-O, as it left its home in LeRoy in 1964, and moved to a new production center in Dover, Delaware. Jell-O consciousness was expanded with a new product line of Jell-O gelatin for salads, with flavors like celery, seasoned tomato, mixed vegetable, and Italian. Oddly enough, lime Jell-O—perhaps the most startlingly psychedelic color offered—was not introduced during this decade but had been around since the '30s when it was promoted as a citrus flavor ideally suited to Depression-era recipes using Jell-O in tangy or salty salads. While it may have worked in the '30s, Jell-O and tomatoes never really hit it off in the '60s, and the salad gelatins went the way of chocolate Jell-O (deceased 1927) and Cola Jell-O (deceased 1943).

Wrestling with Jell-O

By 1991, the cultural significance of Jell-O had risen so much in status that even the gray-beards at the venerable Smithsonian Institution felt compelled to announce a conference on the topic. Press releases for their national symposium on "Jell-O in History" listed seminars such as "American History is Jell-O History," "The Semiotics of Jell-O," "The Dialectics of Jell-O in Peasant Culture," and "Jell-O Salad or Just Desserts: The Poetics of an American Food." The date of this conference, it should be noted, was April 1.

By 1996, Jell-O had made its way into space aboard the Russian *Mir* space station at the request of American astronaut Shannon Lucid. Prepared by adding boiled water to drinking bags containing the powdered treat, these bags were refrigerated and then removed with great ceremony on Easter Sunday. After experiencing their first mouthful of Jell-O, Lucid's Russian colleagues began wheedling her weekly to conjure up some more of the stuff as a regular Sunday treat.

"It is the greatest improvement in space flight since my first flight over 10 years ago," Lucid told Reuters. "Every once in awhile, Yuri will come up to me and say, 'Isn't today Sunday?'"

Jell-O's adaptability in the kitchen is mirrored by its adaptability in our culture. It's played a role not only in man's highest achievements but also in many episodes he might rather forget. Jell-O shots, using vodka in place of the cold water, have for several decades produced painful morning-after recollections, while Jell-O wrestling, popularized in the late '70s, has surely left Jell-O in places God never intended. For those whose lust for Jell-O lubricated sin is not satisfied by any of the above, there's even an online newsgroup for discussing "sexual stimulation from gelatin": alt.jell-o.fetish.

■ SNACKIN' USA ■

That's a Cracker Jack!

In the late 1800s, F.W. Rueckheim, a German-American popcorn vendor in Chicago, began experiments destined to create a new breed of popcorn—a sugary fusion of popcorn and peanut brittle. His earliest efforts produced nothing

In a Jiffy...

They Didn't Have Microwaves

French explorers in the Great Lakes Region found the Iroquois popping corn in clay pots filled with heated sand in 1612. Not only were the popped kernels eaten, but they were also made into a soup and used decoratively. The Winnebago popped their corn right on the cob, skewered over a bonfire, weenie-roast style. In Arizona, the Papagos were even more serious about their popcorn, preparing it in immense clay ollas (earthenware pans as much as eight feet across).

Archeological evidence suggests that popcorn originated in Mexico and then spread to what is now the United States. Carbon dating of kernels discovered in Chiricahua cave dwellings of New Mexico indicate the early Americans were eating the stuff as far back as 3600 B.C.E.

In 1519, Cortes encountered this form of corn being used by the Aztecs as an important food source and to decorate ritual clothing and implements associated with Tlaloc, the god of maize. Before this, Columbus, on his misguided journey to Asia, found popcorn popping up in the West Indies and is said to have brought a sample back to Spain.

For the most part, however, popcorn remained unknown to Europeans and was regarded as a great curiosity as late as the 1700s, as in this description of the fluffy novelty encountered by the Portuguese explorer Felix de Azara in Paraguay. "It is boiled in fat or oil, the grains burst without becoming detached," he wrote. "There results a superb bouquet fit to adorn a lady's hair at night without anyone knowing what it was. I have often eaten these burst grains and found them very good."

but treacly, unwieldy conglomerations, but soon he devised a method that would caramelize the corn and nuts without gluing it all together. In 1896, a gleeful customer tasted the stuff, and

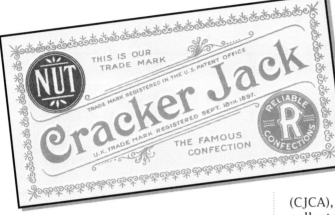

Turn-of-the-century Cracker Jack box.

expressed his delight in the slang of the day, saying, "That's a cracker jack!" and the phrase stuck to the caramel-coated corn for over a century.

In 1908, Cracker Jack was mentioned in the hit song "Take Me Out to the Ball Game," fixing it forever in the public consciousness as an All-American standard. (Oddly enough Jack Norworth, who wrote the lyrics, didn't see a game until 34 years later; no one knows if or when he sampled Cracker Jack.) This song, however, wasn't the first to have mentioned Cracker Jack. Already by 1896— the same year the product was named— "The Cracker Jack Two-Step" was published as music for a "Cracker Jack Party"— a concept depicted on the sheet music by an illustration of children seated around a Cracker Jack-laden table surrounded by emptied cartons of the snack discarded on the floor.

Since 1912, the year prizes were first stashed in the boxes, over ten thousand varieties of tin, plastic, and pasteboard surprises have been excavated from amidst the nuts and kernels. Some, such as the first set of baseball cards ever printed, are worth as much as $100,000.

The patriotic red, white, and blue packaging with the Sailor Boy and dog was the last element of the familiar treat to fall into place. It showed up immediately after World War I. Should you ever be asked, the dog's name is "Bingo." The boy's name you can probably guess.

Answers to more esoteric Cracker Jack questions can be directed to the editor of *The Prize Insider*, the monthly newsletter of the Cracker Jack Collectors Association (CJCA), a group of around two hundred collectors in the U.S., Canada, and France who take candy-coated popcorn products very seriously. CJCA also holds an annual convention in Kansas City featuring a swap meet, auctions, speakers, contests, and exhibits of CJ memorabilia.

Crunch Potato Slices

Across the North Sea from these quibbling nations, the English defy their American cousins by consistently referring to fries as "chips," while reserving the word "crisps" for those more thinly cut potatoes commonly sold in plastic bags.

Miscommunications regarding crispness as well as the manner in which potatoes are to be sliced for frying, however, can have positive results, as demonstrated during vacationing railroad magnate Commodore Cornelius Vanderbilt's 1853 visit to the Saratoga Springs resort in New York.

While dining at the resort, it's said that Vanderbilt was served a plate of fried potatoes sliced much thicker than he preferred. After sending them back, he was surprised when a bit later the waiter returned with another plateful

Commodore Cornelius Vanderbilt (circled) relaxing at Saratoga Springs, where his demands for "thinness" resulted in the invention of the potato chip.

enjoyed what he called "crunch potato slices," setting an example for the other social climbers patronizing the resort.

A taste for the trendy "Saratoga Chips" gradually spread from the East Coast throughout the country, and by 1933, the National Potato Chip Institute (NPCI) was founded to assist with distribution and proselytize outlying regions, where more provincial store owners were occasionally found marketing the chips as newfangled soap flakes or a breakfast cereal to be enjoyed with cream and sugar.

The Man Who Invented Nothing

In Camden, Maine, stands a 28-foot statue of one Captain Hanson Gregory—a man who invented something only present when it's absent. In 1847, Camden residents believe, this sea captain invented the doughnut hole. Legend stages the discovery during a violent storm on the high seas. For some reason, the Captain chose this tempestuous interlude to begin munching on a bit of cake and was forthwith hurled by a powerful wave against the ship's wheel, skewering his cake in the process on one of the wheel's handles. Recognizing the advantage of keeping

more thinly sliced, yet still wholly unsatisfactory. Sending them back yet again, Vanderbilt stressed the extreme importance of thinness in his enjoyment of potatoes. Thinly sliced potatoes, he explained peevishly, were essential to his enjoyment of the meal and indeed his entire stay at the resort.

When they arrived in the kitchen yet again, George Crum, the exasperated cook on duty at the time, took the rather large risk of putting the tycoon's sense of humor to the test. He prepared Vanderbilt a plate of deep fried potatoes sliced to near transparent thinness. Luckily for Crum and lovers of potato chips, Vanderbilt

> **I**n Camden, Maine, stands a 28-foot statue of one Captain Hanson Gregory—a man who invented something only present when it's absent. In 1847, Camden residents believe, this sea captain invented the doughnut hole.

both hands on a wheel, yet unable to give up on the sweets, Captain Gregory decided it would be necessary in the future to have all his cakes baked with prepunched holes so that they might be more easily spindled on what undoubtedly became an unpleasantly sticky wheel.

Complex geometry or simple intuition has led less colorful characters to punch a hole in similar cakes before deep frying in order to increases surface area exposed to the hot oil (and thereby eliminate an uncooked center).

The Dutch didn't need to be told about any of this. They'd been deep frying balls of dough or *oliebollen* (oil balls) and *olykoeks* (oil cakes) since the sixteenth century. Their solution was to merely to keep them small so they would easily cook all the way through.

The English pilgrims who swung by the Netherlands for a layover on their voyage to Plymouth probably picked up some oily cakes on their way. In 1809, Washington Irving in his "Knickerbocker History of New York," a satiric account of the Dutch traditions of "New Amsterdam," provided the first description of "dough nuts" as "balls of sweetened dough, fried in hog fat."

The Embarrassing History of Doughnuts

Dutch *oliebollen* were originally a food for Carnival. Because this pre-Lenten festival is traditionally a time when normal social rules are suspended, the foods associated with the celebration sometimes have fairly naughty names. Schoolboys snickering over the "nuts" in doughnuts are actually sharing in a centuries-old joke. The "oil balls" of the Protestant Dutch may not be particularly rude in name, but they are probably related to

more explicit testicular analogies such as the Spanish *bolas de fraile* or "friar's balls" still eaten in South America.

Throughout Christendom there is something about Carnival that seems to call for snacks that are both deep fried and dirty. Many of these have adapted themselves to year-round use, like the nut-sized sugar-dusted fritters enjoyed by the French and Swiss as *pets de nonne* (nun's farts). When Bavarians speak of a *Nonnafuerzla* or "nun's fart," however, they're referring to a doughier fried and sugar-covered dumpling (if not the flatulence of an actual Bride of Christ). And the name of the deep-fried Spanish cakes, *suspiro de monja* ("nun's sighs") has an erotic suggestiveness to it that probably was permitted into the language thanks to Carnival.

Even in our secular age, this irreverent association between fried pastries and authority continues. The popularity of doughnut stands as one of the few 24-hour establishments that law enforcement officers can break for a bit of caffeine and cholesterol is widely known and widely parodied. At the height of animosity toward the Los Angeles Police Department during the 1992 Rodney King trial and subsequent riots, the phrase "Bad Cop! No Doughnut!" became, for instance, a popular expression of dissatisfaction. Donut Cologne, a gag item marketed in the late '90s by three California firemen clearly played off this theme, offering three ounces of sickeningly sweet "essence of cinnamon crumb" bottled in a doughnut-shaped vial emblazoned with a gold badge.

Perhaps the most irreverent anti-authoritarian doughnut slur of the century was self-inflicted—against the president of the United States, no less. It occurred on June 26, 1963, as John F. Kennedy

> **A**t the height of animosity toward the Los Angeles Police Department during the 1992 Rodney King trial and subsequent riots, the phrase "Bad Cop! No Doughnut!" became, for instance, a popular expression of dissatisfaction.

BAD COP NO DONUT!

A popular slogan in Los Angeles during the 1992 Rodney King trial.

was addressing the citizens confined on the Western side of the Berlin Wall. Kennedy concluded his speech in grand style, with the observation, "All free men, wherever they may live, are citizens of Berlin, and, therefore, as a free man, I take pride in the words *Ich bin ein Berliner.*" Unfortunately, the words in which he took such pride actually translate into "I am a jelly doughnut." It would also imply that the 35th U.S. president was dusted with powdered sugar. *Ein Berliner Pfannkuchen* is a local pastry known universally as *ein Berliner.* "*Ich bin Berliner*" would've worked fine, however, since German never uses the indefinite article before citizenships, nationalities, religious, or ethnic groups.

JFK got a rousing response anyway. Even during their former isolation, Berliners remained worldly and aware of foreign ways, including bungling of the language. As the citizens of Berlin have been known to say, "Not every Berliner is filled with marmalade."

■ ROT YOUR TEETH ■

Killer Kandy

In 1956, General Foods chemist William Mitchell was working on a new wonder product designed to capture the fizz from Coke and reduce it down into the powdery portable form of Kool-Aid. Unfortunately, Mitchell's "just add water" miracle never had the chance to make it to the market, as that niche had already been filled by Fizzies, a novelty soft drink of the early '60s that came in the form of Alka-Seltzer-like tablets. After languishing in the lab for over 20 years, General Foods decided to take Mitchell's fizz-powder and reconstitute it into something nearly identical to fluorescent aquarium gravel and market it as a candy: "Pop Rocks" exploded onto the market in 1975, and during the next 5 years more than 5 million foil packets of these little globules were snatched off the shelves, making Pop Rocks the best-selling candy in history.

Regional Delicacies

We Don't Eat That Here

Fried Pickles
A specialty of Southern States. Akin to fried green tomatoes, these are deep fried dills.

Frito Pie
A recent, primarily Texan, addition to the white trash menu. Originally served in the corn chip bag, the dish consists of a mess of Fritos, smothered in chili, cheese, and onions. Similar to Poutine, a truck stop favorite in Quebec, consisting of brown gravy ladled over a few handfuls of fries and melted cheese.

Red Flannel Hash
An eccentric New England desire to combine beets and bacon is realized in this minced and mashed bright red mush of corned beef, potatoes, chopped eggs, and seasonings.

Scrapple
Specialty of Eastern Pennsylvania. Odds and ends of a pig otherwise unusable, swept up from the butcher's floor, mixed with cornmeal and spices and rolled into a sort of sausage intended to be sliced and fried for breakfast. More or less the same as "pork loaf" from the same region and somewhat like "mush" served in the northern Midwest except for the addition of meat. Mush and scrapple are both sometimes eaten with maple syrup.

Moon Pie
As in "RC Cola and a Moon Pie" (the low-budget Southern equivalent of "pie and coffee"). A marshmallow and Graham Cracker sandwich encased in chocolate. Baked by Tennessee's Chattanooga Bakery since 1917, the pie is said to have been created by Baker Earl Mitchell, Sr. after visiting an Appalachian mining town's company store. Taking an impromptu market survey, Mitchell found a miner just off from his evening shift, cornered him in

the store, and questioned him as to his preferences in baked goods.

When asked what kind of dessert he'd most like to pack in his lunch box, the miner thought for a moment and then described something solid, sweet, and filling.

Inspecting Moon Pies in the early 1950s.

"About how big?" Mitchell asked.

The miner glanced up at the rising moon, framing it with his hands. "About that big," he said.

By the 1950s, the treat was so popular that the Chattanooga Bakery produced nothing else.

Cheese Steak
First of all, don't think about calling it a "cheese steak sandwich." Call it a "cheese steak." That's what they call it in Philly. This is beef, shredded and grilled. It's fairly tasty, but it's probably from a part of the animal that never even shook hands with the steak-bearing anatomy.

Just to be safe, most people like to cover any potential problems with a layer of blistering hot cheese and, usually, some roasted green peppers. This is no longer merely a "steak" (shredded beef sandwich). It is now a "cheese steak." White American cheese, provolone, mozzarella, and, yes, even Cheez Whiz are all considered perfectly acceptable cheeses.

Somehow, during its rise far above the competition, Pop Rocks appears to have attracted the jealous attention of the gods. The candy that dared to be different was suddenly smeared as the candy that could kill when rumors about Pop Rocks-related deaths began to spread some-time around 1979.

A package of Pop Rocks, a can of soda, and a child actor were the key players in this tragic and untrue tale of overindulgence. The thrill-seeking celebrity in this legend was John Gilchrist, the kid who played "Mikey" in the 1970's "Mikey Likes It" advertising campaign for Life cereal, and his fatal mistake was downing a package of Pop Rocks along with a can of soda (or several cans and/or several packages, depending on the version transmitted). This infernal combination supposedly produced a ferocious buildup of gasses and ruptured the young juggernaut's insides, putting an end to the nearly forgotten celebrity and providing a cautionary example for Pop Rocks abusers nationwide.

> **S**omehow, during its rise far above the competition, Pop Rocks appears to have attracted the jealous attention of the gods. The candy that dared to be different was suddenly smeared as the candy that could kill when rumors about Pop Rocks-related deaths began to spread sometime around 1979.

denying the rumors by taking out full page ads in 45 major publications and sending 50,000 letters to high school principals around the country.

The company even bankrolled a nationwide speaking tour by the candy's inventor, where he explained in hundreds of cities across the country that his creation actually produced less gas than that found in half a can of carbonated soda.

Despite these measures, public reaction was so hysterical that General Foods chose to withdraw the controversial candy rather than combat the wildfire of rumors. The company unloaded the rights to the product to Kraft Foods, who reintroduced it in 1985 as "Action Candy," sold through a custom-named subsidiary, Carbonated Candy. Around the same time, a competitor candy, Zotz, appeared on the market—in two forms: first as a sort of jawbreaker with a candy shell shielding an effervescent interior and, in unadulterated form, as *Power* Zotz, an uncut powder to be consumed full strength by hardcore addicts.

The panic caused by this rumor actually necessitated intercession by the Food and Drug Administration, particularly in Seattle where a 24-hour hotline was set up to accept calls from panicking parents. Meanwhile, General Foods went to work

Once tabooed, the candy took on the sexual appeal of anything forbidden. A new set of rumors regarding the candy's use as a tactile stimulant employed in a sex play began circulating. While most denied firsthand knowledge of this application, there can be little doubt these stories had a much more factual foundation.

In 1979, the film *The Tin Drum* provided "documentation" of a sexual episode in which the protagonist licks fizzy soft drink powder out of the hand of his nanny. The 1997 decision by an Oklahoma City judge to send police out to seize video copies of this Academy Award winner from local video retailers and customer homes was related to such "pornographic" interactions between these two characters.

Melts in Your Mouth, Not on Your Trigger Finger

While the Spanish Civil War annihilated nearly 1 million lives, did grave injury to the idealism of leftist internationalists, and ended in 36 years of fascist dictatorship, it did—at least—give us M&Ms.

According to legend, chocolate mogul Forrest Mars Sr. spent enough time among Spanish soldiers during a trip to the Iberian peninsula in 1936 to observe them eating small bean-shaped chocolates protected by a sugary shell.

A few years later, the entrepreneur had his own version of the candy armored with sugar shell and at the ready for U.S. entry into World War II. This rugged candy packaged in rugged cardboard tubes was eagerly purchased in great quantity by the U.S. military as an easy-to-transport morale builder for GIs overseas.

After the war, the candy continued to grow in popularity through the late '40s

> While the Spanish Civil War annihilated nearly 1 million lives, did grave injury to the idealism of leftist internationalists, and ended in 36 years of fascist dictatorship, it did—at least—give us M&Ms.

and into the '50s. Yet the veteran war-horse was still not quite the candy we know today. While engineering this candy for frontline duty, no attention had been paid to frivolous details such as color, and all M&Ms at this time came in standard-issue brown.

Regardless of the Color of His Shell

It wasn't until the dawning of the Age of Aquarius that Mars turned to the rainbow for inspiration and, in 1960, began manufacturing red, green, and yellow M&Ms. Through the '70s and '80s some color shuffling went on, with a few significant additions and switches, but in 1995, the company threw open the doors to democracy by putting the color issue to the public.

Invited to vote on a new color addition, consumers were asked to choose between pink, purple, blue, or no change. An astounding number felt compelled to make their voice known, and of the 10,234,142 votes, well over half (54 percent) demanded that the color blue finally be assigned its rightful place in the candy kingdom.

Blue food, however, is a crime against the conventional wisdom of pop psychologists everywhere. Denounced as psychologically relaxing, unstimulating to the senses and the appetite, blue is taboo when it comes to food.

Yet as early as 1992, there were subversive rumblings. At a national confectioners' convention that year in Washington, DC, hundreds of companies simultaneously debuted products

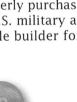

colored with the forbidden color. Fulminating for three full years, the blue revolution was already in full sway by 1995 when this sham "election" was held to create the impression that Mars was graciously allowing choice

where in fact *no choice existed!* Blue was a mandate from the masses! The oligarchy of experts was toppled, and humbled Mars executives regrouped and began listening earnestly to the voice of the people, to their yearnings, their folklore, and myths. In this, they believe, lay the key to successfully manipulating the chocolate buying masses, and their hopes were not in vain.

The Birds, the Bees, and the Green Ones

Ever since the early '70s, there has existed a powerful mythology associating green M&Ms with sex. One version has the green candies acting directly as an aphrodisiac; in another, the selection of a green candy from a mixed bowl merely implies sexual readiness. Combining the two beliefs, making a gift of a green

candy to a potential partner can imply sexual readiness of the benefactor as well as hopes that the candy ingested will affect the recipient as an aphrodisiac. Similar associations have been made with green jellybeans and Gummi Bears.

One possible explanation of the belief lies in the candy's use by the military. Some say that soldiers longing for their wives and children would make it a habit to selectively pocket green M&Ms from their K-rations in anticipation of their homecoming. Upon their

discharge and return, they would greet their children with a gift—several handfuls of candy—and a game—the candy would be scattered into the lawn for the children to hunt. With the children thus engaged outdoors, the soldier would then bring his wife inside to enjoy a game of another sort. Offering better camouflage against the grass, green candies would be the obvious choice to ensure a longer interlude of privacy.

While it makes for a nice anecdote, this explanation seems as unlikely as the claim that the sexual association with green dates back to its symbolic role in ancient pagan fertility cults.

> **E**ver since the early '70s, there has existed a powerful mythology associating green M&Ms with sex.

Even as attention focused on green and blue M&Ms throughout the '90s, Mars had an eye toward the next millennium. Currently, the company is test marketing M&M Colorworks, a bold new color-set that will make the rainbow of 1960 look

like a traffic light. Available exclusively via mail order and a few select retailers, M&Ms Colorworks are sold like cement in 40 pound bags costing around $200 each and filled with custom mixes of 1 to 5 colors chosen by the consumer from a selection of 21 designer hues. The range includes some surprising new choices,

such as teal, maroon, aqua, and even candy purposefully colored gray.

Pez—America's Sweetheart

While the taste may be a little more enticing than chewable vitamins and while there may be some inherent indignity in gobbling pellets from a dispenser like a lab monkey, Pez candies and, more

Over one hundred web sites currently obsess over these plastic contrivances.

importantly, Pez candy *dispensers* have charmed their way into the hearts of consumers all over the world.

But for a select few of these Pez-hungry consumers, regarding these plastic gizmos as mere candy dispensers would be akin to calling a Rolls Royce a thing that holds gasoline. These are the Pez collectors, and the fanatical among them will part with rather large piles of green in order to obtain coveted dispensers. Whereas new Pez with candy go for about $1.50, a vintage clown dispenser can command up to $70; Santa Claus can relieve you of $300, and certain versions of the "Alpine Boy" fetch up to $900. The discontinued bride and groom dispensers

> **O**ne of the most expensive varieties, the notorious "Make-a-Face," was the Mr. Potato Head of the Pez kingdom. The character atop this dispenser consisted of a featureless head that came with 17 tiny plastic accessories that could either be plugged into the face to build up to 150 unique visages or put in the mouth and choked back into a child's windpipe. Withdrawn in 1972, the same year it appeared, the Make-a-Face dispenser now is worth about $3,200.

are rather pricey, but the groom ($500) seems to have married out of his class with the bride price hovering between $1,500 and $2,600.

If all this strikes you as a little unhealthy, you'll be even more alarmed at the high-price Pez collectors place on dispensers that can kill a toddler. One of the most expensive varieties, the notorious "Make-a-Face," was the Mr. Potato Head of the Pez kingdom. The character atop this dispenser consisted of a featureless head that came with 17 tiny plastic accessories that could either be plugged into the face to build up to 150 unique visages or put in the mouth and choked back into a child's windpipe. Withdrawn in 1972, the same year it appeared, the Make-a-Face dispenser now is worth about $3,200.

Even more terrifying was one of the few Pez dispensers to break from the traditional flip-top form. In the 1950s, Pez designers came up with a neato and reloadable Space Gun that actually used candies as projectiles. It's not clear

As seen in **"Ripley's Believe It or Not!"**

Gary Doss' Burlingame Museum of Pez Memorabilia (Burlingame, CA) is a shrine to America's favorite candy dispenser.

whether a child actually misfired a candy into his own trachea or whether a few parents with a modicum of common sense objected to a toy that trained their kids to place the barrel of a gun in their mouths and pull the trigger for a yummy treat. Either way, it didn't take long for this thing to get yanked. Today the Pez Space gun, the most expensive dispenser of all, is worth nearly $6,000.

Pezervationists

These are the sorts of items drawing well-heeled Pez enthusiasts to one of the many collector conventions around the country. St. Louis has been hosting an annual event since 1992, with major gatherings also taking place in Cleveland, Ohio, and Orange, Connecticut (the city in which the candies, though not the dispensers, are made). Los Angeles also hosts a convention, where, in addition to the usual exhibits, auctions, and collecting seminars, fanatics have had a chance to admire the Pez car, a 1977 Dodge Aspen transformed with glue and 1,400 dispensers into a roving Pez museum.

Pez goes psychedelic.

In between conventions, Pez pilgrims can drop by the Museum of Pez Memorabilia hidden away in a computer store in Burlingame, California. There, in addition to the 280 Pez dispensers mounted on toothbrush racks, curator Gary Doss

Sticky Business

Congratulations! It's a Cigar!

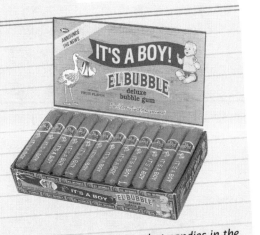

While the gun that shoots Pez into kids' mouths was snatched off the market in the 1950s, activists today still fight battles against candies they believe teach kids other ways to kill themselves. The activists' oldest enemy: the candy cigarette.

These chalky sugar sticks, tinted at either end to indicate glowing ash and filter and packaged in dead-ringer imitations of brand-name cigarette packs, are regarded by critics like pediatrician Jonathan Klein of the University of Rochester, as nothing less than "smoking toys." Illegal in many school districts and whisked from the shelves of two thousand 7-Elevens more than a decade ago, these confectionary cancer sticks are now, like cigarette-smoking camels, an endangered species.

Though there are some holdouts, like World Candies Inc., who still manufactures "real" fake cigarettes ("Kings," "Triumph," "Round Up," "Stallion," and "Victory"), others have discontinued the item or mollified critics with significant alterations. New England Confectionery Company, producers of Necco wafers, recently did away with the red "ash" tip, euphemistically renamed the product "Candy Stix," and repackaged them in a box of more innocuous proportions with the "tax stamp" removed.

While candy cigarettes are now more or less a dead-dog issue, critics eager to beat on something can now whale away at Big League Chew (although manufacturer Amurol Confections now market the product as "the healthy alternative"), a popular shredded bubble gum masquerading as chewing tobacco, while others wring their hands over the possibility that candies in the shape of lipstick, bar soap, CD ROMs, floppies, or sidewalk chalk will entice kids to gnaw on their real-life equivalents, or that candies housed in elaborate plastic dispensers shaped like beepers, cell phones, Game Boys, and boom boxes will encourage children to dismantle these devises to get at the tasty windpipe-jamming components inside.

Other activists point to the dangerous and recent trendiness of cigars, which they correlate with an upswing in sales of bubblegum impostors. Bubblegum or chocolate cigars, however, have long been on the market, sold not only as a children's candy, but also—thanks to their symbolic role as a celebratory luxury—as a gift given to nonsmoking adults at the occasion of a baby's birth. Similarly, bubblegum cigars, as a politically correct replacement for the genuine carcinogen, have frequently been handed out by politicians on the campaign trail. Nixon and Bush both handed out candy cigars as a symbol of anticipated victory. Bill Clinton also dispensed bubblegum cigars as a symbol of political victory, and Lord knows what else.

Big League Chew—preparing little leaguers for tobacco road, or the "healthy alternative"? You make the call!

exhibits Pez ads, packaging, store displays, and mail-in premiums such as Pez T-shirts, puzzles, neckties, banks, and magnets. One of the highlights of Doss' collection is the 1960's "Love Pez," topped not by the usual character head, but by a psychedelic eyeball perched in the palm of a hand. "It is very odd," remarks Doss. "It did not sell well because it sold originally with flower-flavored candy."

The worldwide web also offers a number of virtual museums featuring photos of various private collections as well as newsgroup forums like alt.food.Pez for the discussion of Pez rarities, rumors, pricing, and collection strategies. Online collectors markets regularly update prices according to demand. All in all, more than one hundred web sites currently obsess over these little plastic contrivances.

Even the general public can't escape contact with these little plastic pellet pushers as they crop up in movies such as *Stand By Me*, *ET: The Extraterrestrial*, *The Client*, and *Toy Story*. Fans clamoring for the Elvis dispenser featured in *The Client*, however, were gravely disappointed to learn that such an item was never in fact on the market but, rather, a unique creation fabricated for the movie.

These customized dispensers, usually created by decapitating a doll or other toy and grafting it to a dispenser, are known to collectors as "fantasy Pez," and their construction is another pastime of the truly addicted who can't content themselves with the four hundred or so models actually manufactured by the company. In 1961, a legendary set of custom dispensers was even given to the First Family, including a Democratic Donkey-headed model handcrafted for JFK.

It's a Pez World, After All

Certainly Pez inventor Eduard Haas never would have imagined his invention presented as a gift to the President

Pez, Pez, and more Pez!

Pezervation Society, would like to see conquered by Pez.

"I have one dispenser I have nicknamed Pedro," says Martin. "I mail him to other collectors, and they take him on trips all over the world and then return him with photos of his trip. That one dispenser has met famous people, has been to every Disney park, and sunned on the beaches of Mexico. He's been to the Pez factory, been scuba diving, been to practically every big city and landmark in the U.S., and traveled to many countries around the world. My goal is to have him be the first Pez to orbit the earth in the space shuttle!"

of the United States when he came up with it back in 1927. The United States was far away across the Atlantic, and the Austrian inventor was more concerned at the time with helping people stop smoking than with making whimsical candy dispensers for American Presidents or children. Haas' original concept was to give smokers conditioned to reaching for their lighters a satisfying breath mint rather than a smoke—hence the flip-top design adapted to dispense candy instead of butane flames.

Cartoon heads were never part of the plan, and today's fruity flavors probably would have disgusted Haas, whose original candies were strictly peppermint. The name, Pez—one of the few things unchanged since Haas' conception—is in fact a contraction of the German word for peppermint (*Pfefferminz*). It wasn't until Haas tried to market the product in the U.S. in 1952 that the unsuccessful adult version was re-tooled into the kiddy candy beloved today.

Pez has been successfully marketed in 60 countries all over the world. But there is one final frontier Dennis Martin, publisher of the bimonthly newsletter *The Fliptop*

Chewing Gum

In much of the world, chewing a stick of gum is akin to flashing your American passport. Though gum is chewed abroad, this great American signifier is not chewed with quite as much gusto anywhere else. Even the sound of our speech is identified with it, as some foreigners in attempting to describe the sound of American English will tell you it sounds like we're "chewing our words." Noisy chewers and gum smackers particularly fit the stereotype of Americans as vulgar savages, and the notion of gum-chewing as a somewhat subhuman trait is endemic to European culture, as in the Czech Republic, where the same word (*zvykacka*) is used for gum and the cud chewed by a cow.

While most Americans probably share few genes with a cow, it's true that this habit is something truly American. Our colonial ancestors picked it up from the Indians of New England who were fond of masticating the gummy resin of spruce trees. (In Europe, gum chewing was a lost art once practiced by the ancient

Greeks who chewed resinous bark from the mastic tree as a means of cleaning their teeth and freshening their breath, but during the Dark Ages, this, along with so many other achievements of higher civilization, slipped into oblivion.) It was an American entrepreneur, John B. Curtis, who in 1850 gave the world its first commercially produced chewing gum, "State of Maine Pure Spruce Gum," made with tree sap and paraffin, with the same evergreen flavor the Indians had taught the colonists to enjoy.

Curtis' sap and wax approach, however, didn't last long and, less than 20 years later, inspiration for a new kind of gum came not from the native people of New England but those south of the U.S. border. The Mayan Indians had long made use of *chicle*, the rubbery sap of the sapodilla tree, not only as gum, but also to create a sort of rubber sandal by repeatedly dipping the soles of their feet in the liquid latex.

Mexican General Antonio Lopez de Santa Anna, while remembering the Alamo during his exile on Staten Island, also remembered this use of *chicle* in discussions with photographer and chemist Thomas Adams. Interested in possible industrial applications, Adams asked the former General to get him some of this substance to test, which he did in 1869.

While these experiments failed, Adams did find that, with a bit of flavoring, small grayish balls of the stuff could be chewed much like the paraffin chewing gum of the day. After a bit of test marketing, Adams eventually went on to mass produce Blackjack licorice-flavored gum— the oldest variety of gum still sold today. By the late-1890s, William Wrigley, a former soap and baking powder salesman, turned his attention to this gummy commodity, and within a decade, chewing gum was stuck permanently on the American scene.

Wads of Glory, Wads of Sin

Today, roughly one hundred thousand tons of gum are chewed annually, enough to model a full-scale cruise ship should you be so inclined. What becomes of this one hundred thousand tons of masticated gum once it's lost its flavor is a source of great vexation to many, while in San Luis Obispo, California, they've taken a nasty problem and created from it a tourist attraction, (albeit a somewhat distasteful one). Bubblegum Alley, a six-foot-wide passageway between a couple of two-story brick buildings, takes its name from the deposits of chewed stuff encrusting the walls on either side. This ever-changing interactive work of public art begun sometime back in the 1950s, features not only wads haphazardly smashed into place but also some rather intricate collages and spontaneous sculptures crafted from gum.

In Singapore, however, the attitude toward disposal of the sticky stuff is quite a bit less easygoing. In fact, the import, sale, and even possession of chewing gum in this country is strictly illegal. Importers wishing to travel with gum through the country must be sure that it is "conveyed in a container or in completely covered vehicles or wagons which are capable of being locked, sealed, or otherwise secured." Those in violation risk fines of $10,000 to $20,000 and 10 months to 2 years in prison. While some see these restrictions as an extension of the government's extremely zealous anti-littering laws, the motivation for passing this bit of legislation in 1992 is supposedly not just aesthetic. Earlier that year, a single piece of gum, discarded in a manner that blocked electrically activated doors on a mass rapid transport train, is supposed to have done devastating financial damage by delaying the departure of the gummed-up train, backing up trains all over the island, and causing thousands of commuters to arrive late for work.

> In 1997, Palestinians alleged that the Israelis were seeding the West Bank and Gaza Strip with packs of strawberry chewing gum laced with the female hormone progesterone. The hormone was supposed to turn women into merciless sex machines, rot Islamic morals to the core, and ultimately sterilize the population by burning out young hormonal systems with overdoses of progesterone.

Not far away in Korea, chewing gum is a friend of management. There, work efficiency is believed to be improved by chewing gum spiked with coffee flavoring and caffeine. Popular brands include Buzz Gum and Coffee Jazz ("Instant Coffee for the 21st Century"). Ginseng gum is also sold in Korea and elsewhere as an overall tonic and aphrodisiac intended to improve efficiency of another sort. In the United States, "aphrodisiac" gums occasionally appear, such as Love Gum ("a full-potency gum to increase romantic power") and Frenchie's Spanish Fly Chewing Gum marketed by Swingers, Inc., of Gary, Indiana. At $1 a stick, consumers might be disappointed to learn that the only unusual ingredient listed on Frenchie's package is cayenne pepper.

In the Middle East, on the other hand, aphrodisiac gum has been considered a peril. In 1997, Palestinians alleged that the Israelis were seeding the West Bank and Gaza Strip with packs of strawberry chewing gum laced with the female hormone progesterone. The hormone was supposed to turn women into merciless sex machines, rot Islamic morals to the core, and ultimately sterilize the population by burning out young hormonal systems with overdoses of progesterone. Perpetrators of this fiendish plot were said to focus particularly on areas around schoolyards, enticing children with prices scaled to the prepubescent budget and seducing them further by including with the gum provocative stickers depicting "The Legend of Pocahontas" and "Aladdin and the Magic Lamp." After extensive "laboratory testing," Salah Waheedi, a Palistinan Supply Ministry official, declared to the international press, "This chewing gum causes sterility and stimulates sex. This is proved. This is scientifically proved."

For a small minority, the aphrodisiac effectiveness of a gum has less to do with the ingredients than the bubbles and bubble-blower. Documented primarily by a handful of sites on the worldwide web, these are the bubble-blowing fetishists who collect and post for erotic

"The gum that puts you in the mood for love!"

Big Things Come In Little Packages

enjoyment photos of bubble gum blowers as well as real-life anecdotes of bubble blowing encounters.

At the other end of the spectrum, Life Lines Inc. of Homer, Arkansas, does the Lord's work by distributing a novelty known as Bible Gum. Packaged by developmentally disabled workers in Southern Missouri, these tiny folded cartons open to reveal two tabs of gum and a miniaturized passage from the *King James Bible*. Marketed through nationwide mail-order primarily to Sunday school teachers, the gum is promoted as a surefire way to make those Bible lessons "stick."

■ ICE CREAM SHOP ■

32 Flavors and Counting

By all accounts, chocolate mogul Milton Snavely Hershey is said to have become a wee bit eccentric in his later years. Known as a political progressive and even something of a visionary, the millionaire was used to doing things his way, and this extended to the menu of his fabulous resort, Hotel Hershey, which for a time served some fairly visionary sherbets made according to the old man's own instructions. Two of the more innovative flavors, in this case, were *beet* and *onion*.

Bizarre as this may sound, Hershey was not alone in his love of vegetable flavored iced desserts. Onion ice cream is regularly served at California's Imperial County Sweet Onion Festival, as is garlic

shiso (Japanese "basil") ice cream, *nozawana* (Japanese pickle) ice cream, and the fiery *wasabi* (green horseradish) ice cream.

How'd it Get in the Freezer?

The spirit of experimentation that pervades these frozen creations must've been present back around 200 B.C.E. when, in the mountains of ancient China, someone got the notion to mix up snow with sweetened ground rice. In India, too, there are very early references to frozen sweets, and the Turks and Persians enjoyed sherbet (from the Arabic *sharbah*), which for them meant a combo of snow, honey, fruit, rosewater, or other flavorings.

A number of ancient rulers screamed for ice cream. King Solomon reportedly enjoyed iced desserts, as did Alexander the Great, who had 15 trenches dug and filled with snow from the mountains shortly after conquering Egypt in 345 B.C.E. so that he could celebrate with a constant supply of sherbets. The Roman Emperor Nero was said

ice cream at the Garlic Festival in Gilroy, California. Tomato ice cream was a favorite in Philadelphia during the late nineteenth century, while black and white pepper ice cream is trendy on more sophisticated urban menus of today.

Basil, sage, pansy, geranium, and cactus pear are some of the ingredients among the 54 flavors offered at "Out of the Flower," a Dallas-based ice cream and sorbet shop opened by French-trained culinary progressive Michel Platz. With recipes developed from soups and sauces he prepared as a chef, Platz's highly acclaimed herbal and floral concoctions have even been blessed by Pope John Paul, who enjoyed a few frosty mouthfuls during his 1995 U.S. tour.

But some of the world's most startling ice cream innovations are those created in Asia, where red bean along with green tea are particularly popular flavors. The Japanese have probably done more than anyone else to stretch the envelope with *miso* (fermented bean paste) ice cream,

> **O**nion ice cream is regularly served at California's Imperial County Sweet Onion Festival, as is garlic ice cream at the Garlic Festival in Gilroy, California.
> Tomato ice cream was a favorite in Philadelphia during the late nineteenth century, while black and white pepper ice cream is trendy on more sophisticated urban menus of today.

MONITOR
Ice Cream Freezer
(Double-Geared)

Size	Copper Can	Steel Can
40 quarts	$125 00	$119.00
30 "	120.00	115.00

Smaller Apparatus. See page 7

Pulleys, 16 in. diameter, 4 in. Face.

Speed, 200 Revolutions.

Floor space, 26 in. wide, 36 in. long.

Weight, about 650 Pounds.

This machine can be operated either by steam or horse-power, gas engine, electric or water motor. The gears which operate the can and dasher are enclosed in an iron housing, which covers them and prevents any accident to the workman while in operation. There are no parts to become disengaged and the **apparatus** can be removed and replaced in less than half a minute. Our **patent spiral dasher** is used in this machine.

to frequently send slaves to the Apennines to haul back mountain snow and ice so that he could indulge at whim in an imperial snow cone.

Though the glories of classical ice cream melted away into the Dark Ages, it was rediscovered during the Renaissance through trade with the East. Possibly thanks to Marco Polo's fancy Chinese

> **The Roman Emperor Nero was said to frequently send slaves to the Apennines to haul back mountain snow and ice so that he could indulge at whim in an imperial snow cone.**

retained as an exclusive privilege of Charles' court, until the monarch lost his head to the executioner's ax in 1649. As the king's head hit the ground, Tissain's secret hit the streets. By 1768, Brits everywhere were clamoring for a taste of this royal treat, and in response, English author M. Emy published *The Art of Making*

This amazing roadside ice cream joint was located near Berlin, CT.

notions about frozen desserts, the Italians ended up bearing the gospel of ice cream to the rest of Europe. With the marriage of the Italian Mary de Medicis to the Henry IV of France, Italian *gelati* became trendy among the French and, from there, passed to England via a French chef, Gerard Tissain, employed by the court of Charles I. "Cream ice," as it was called in seventeenth century England, was

Frozen Desserts, in which ice cream was characterized as "food fit for the gods."

Within the next few decades, common people were even getting a taste of the stuff as Italian ice cream vendors took to the streets, crying *"Gelati Ecco uno poco,"* which the English obligingly reduced to "Hokey Pokey," a name still used by New Zealanders to designate vanilla ice cream with crunchy, flavored bits.

A typical turn-of-the-century pharmacy with requisite soda fountain and soda jerk.

Naturally, American colonialists weren't about to be left out of the game. Bookkeeper's records show that George Washington blew about $200 on ice cream in the summer of 1790. Thomas Jefferson learned a thing or two about the stuff while serving as minister to France and is known to have served a dish resembling Baked Alaska at Monticello, and Dolly Madison is said to have insisted on ice cream at the inaugural ball celebrating her husband's election in 1813.

> **Bookkeeper's records show that George Washington blew about $200 on ice cream in the summer of 1790.**

Sodas, Sundaes, and Epsicles

Once ice cream was firmly established on this continent, American ingenuity, along with friendly forces of happenstance, went to work on finding new ways to use it.

Soda fountains serving seltzer flavored with a variety of syrups were already doing brisk business in the 1870s. At the 1874 Franklin Institute Celebration in Philadelphia, sodas flavored with chocolate syrup were said to have been a major attraction. According to legend, the frazzled soda jerk ran out of chocolate syrup and resorted to melting down and mixing in some more readily available chocolate ice cream.

Not only did he manage to avert a riot, but his customers actually liked the new taste, crowding around the stand even thicker than before. In the ensuing rush, a few dollops of unmelted ice cream ended up in these fizzy chocolate solutions. This was an even bigger hit, and pretty soon the vendor was bypassing the melting process altogether, merely spalshing the ice cream with a little seltzer before shoving it across the counter. Before anyone had time to think about it, the ice cream soda had been born.

The way in which the masses embraced the ice cream soda struck many as unseemly. Being a new phenomenon, it was assumed to be sinful. Observing the giddy joy with which sinners consumed this novelty, some concluded that the combination might have intoxicating effects. This was the attitude in Evanston, Illinois, when, amidst great misunderstanding, city fathers passed a law decreeing that if citizens were to indulge in this vice they should at least not defile the Sabbath with their activities. Weekends were big sales days for ice cream, and vendors began a frenzied search for a substitute. The soda-free result they dubbed the "Sunday." Old timers sniffed at this impertinence and demanded that at least the spelling be changed to "sundae" so as not associate the Lord's day with this particular form of decadence.

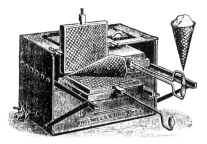

ICE CREAM CONE OVENS.

FOR GAS OR CHARCOAL.

These Ovens are used for baking a crisp cake, which is folded cone-shape and filled with ice-cream, making a most refreshing novelty and a good seller. Full information with each oven.

Price $35.00

Forget the Spoon

The story of the ice cream cone's invention is yet another miniature three-part drama of crowds, compromise, and delicious resolution. In 1904, an ice cream vendor was doing a brisk business selling dishes of ice cream at the St. Louis World's Fair. But 5 or 10 cent dishes kept strolling off as souvenirs. Down the midway, E.A. Hamwi, a Syrian concessionaire selling a waffle-like fritter, *zalabia*, heard of the vendor's troubles and suggested the ice cream be scooped into an edible container—one of his *zalabia* rolled into a cone.

True? Probably not. For the first ice cream cone was patented by Italian immigrant Italo Marchiony a year earlier. We might suspect a little journalist creativity

soda Fountain

Frank Epperson, inventor of the Epsicle, er, Popsicle, and happy customers.

was involved as this account resembles too closely the story of the hot dog bun's origin, in which fairgoers are walking off with cotton gloves instead of ice cream dishes. But both vendors persevere in their optimism and turn to their neighbor for a history-making solution.

And yet one more fortuitous accident with frozen desserts: In 1905, one year after St. Louis fairgoers were eating ice cream out of rolled Syrian fritters, Frank Epperson, an 11-year-old California boy, experienced a very productive lapse of attention. After stirring some powdered fruit drink mix into a glass, Epperson became somehow distracted and forgot about the drink all together. Maybe it was the unusually cold weather that made the boy lose interest in this summery beverage. California was experiencing record lows that year—so cold, in fact, that the drink, forgotten overnight on the back porch, froze solid.

Discovering it the next morning, Frank was intrigued. Though lackluster in its liquid state, the drink took on a whole new appeal when frozen. Grasping the mixing spoon embedded in the ice, he tried to pry out a piece to sample, but the handle stayed stuck, and the glass slid away, leaving Frank holding a sort of frozen lollipop, which proved to be quite tasty.

Working as a concessionaire at a beachfront park 18 years later, Epperson decided to duplicate this icy treat, substituting a normal freezer for an abnormally cold porch. And the name he chose for this new concession? The Epsicle. You can call it the "Popsicle." Epperson did, though it took him a few years to give in.

Right: Popsicle poster, 1932.

Too Good To Eat

This chapter's full of food to be eaten with the eyes. Some are edible dainties, some are harder to swallow. It's about food playing make-believe— sugar cubes as architectural building blocks; mouth-watering latex counterfeits; culinary creativity in wax, ivory, inflatable vinyl, and ferrous concrete. It's about foods transformed from pasty chunks or boiled slabs into wild spirals, plumes, rosette, towers, telephones, clothing, and cars. Half-baked or perfectly rigged to explode in the diner's imagination, these creations are a sort of unruly blend of cookery, toy-making, practical jokes, poetry, and puns.

Details aside, this survey should suggest the spirit of these undertakings, convincing the reader, at the very least, that whoever first rammed an apple into the mouth of a roasted boar must've chuckled at the pretty picture he'd created.

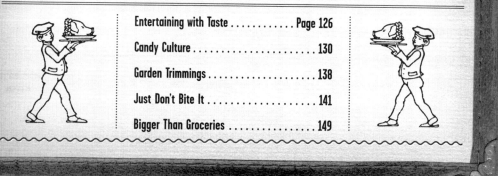

■ ENTERTAINING WITH TASTE ■

"Excuse Me . . . Where's the Vomitorium?"

"They vomit so that they may eat and eat so that they may vomit."

The great stoic philosopher Seneca thus described the wealthy Romans and their use of the notorious *vomitorium*, where gluttons purged themselves to make room for further gluttony. Yet somewhere in this vicious gastric cycle, even the most decadent Romans must've stopped eating and stopped spewing long enough to look at their food.

"Visual feast" is a term used loosely today, but the banquet tables of wealthy Romans offered the eye a feast every bit as excessive as that offered the belly. Before these elaborate presentations could be torn apart by greedy diners, some less hedonistically inclined diners, such as the Latin poet Petronius, would preserve for all time these fantastic landscapes of the patrician table. In the *Satyricon*, he describes a fictional feast based upon his experience among Rome's nouveau riche. Although a writer of fiction, Petronius was more than expert on luxury as Emperor Nero's *arbiter elegantiae,* or advisor in matters of living it up. The lengthy feast sequence in the *Satyricon* includes quite a few noteworthy tidbits, such as:

- An edible representation of Pegasus consisting of a roasted hare outfitted with wings.
- Roasted fowl created from pastry stuffed with walnuts and raisins.
- Honeyed dormice

perched atop miniature archways and bridges constructed over a table of hors d'oeuvres.

- A wooden hen giving birth to pastry shell eggs containing roasted songbirds floating in peppered yolk.
- A genuine roasted pig with piglets of pastry suckling at each teat. Inside the cavity of the pig was a stowaway flock of birds that fluttered out into the banquet hall when the roast was sliced open.

The Spread and the Show

This sort of culinary showmanship by no means died with the Roman Empire. The show did go on—in grand style. Royal banquets of the Middle Ages and Renaissance, for instance, made use of the old Roman bird routine, concealing live birds not only in hollowed roasts and pies but also folding them in napkins to either rattle or delight unwary dinner guests.

Jaded bachelor party types, who've seen strippers pop out of a cake or two, may not think much of a few birds escaping a pastry shell, but these sorry boys-only affairs don't hold a candle to the royal celebration that honored the Duke of Burgundy in 1454. Rather than just one lap-dancing hip-wiggler crouched inside a cardboard cake, the Duke was surprised by 28 musicians exploding out of an immense pie and then bursting into song. This memorable moment is said to be the basis for the Mother Goose rhyme:

> **J**aded bachelor party types, who've seen strippers pop out of a cake or two, may not think much of a few birds escaping a pastry shell, but these sorry boys-only affairs don't hold a candle to the royal celebration that honored the Duke of Burgundy in 1454. Rather than just one lap-dancing hip-wiggler crouched inside a cardboard cake, the Duke was surprised by 28 musicians exploding out of an immense pie and then bursting into song.

A royal Roman banquet. Or Hollywood's version of it, anyway.

"Four and twenty blackbirds
Baked in a pie.
When the pie was opened
The birds began to sing
Wasn't that a dainty dish
To set before the king?"

Whereas today we might throw a few lousy CDs on the player for a dinner party or at best hire a pianist for a truly swank affair, aristocratic hosts in centuries gone by staged entire variety shows for their dinner guests with poets, singers, magicians, or acrobats performing between courses. Sometimes, the act might consist of the theatrical presentation of the next item to be served, such as in Petronius' account of a brawl staged between two servants who in simulated rage end up smashing clay vessels containing mussels and scallops prepared for the guests.

Returning to that 1454 banquet held in honor of Philip the Good, Duke of Burgundy, we find that the orchestra in a pie trick was merely an appetizer for greater stunts to come. Not only was a dragon flown on cables across the banquet hall, but the feast culminated in the arrival of a "giant" outfitted as a Turk. On a leash he held an elephant, and atop this beast was a castle in which rode a woman costumed as a nun representing the Holy Church. (Christendom was at the time distressed by Turkish sovereignty over Constantinople,

and the nun had been scripted to beseech the Duke to embark upon the crusade he had already prepared against the infidels.)

Such diversions offered between the main courses were called *entremes* in Old French and Old English because they came between (*entre*) the main dishes (*mes*), and this word is similar to the word used for side dishes in many Romance languages. Ultimately, the word comes from the Latin *intermissus*, the same word from which we get "intermission," and that's exactly what these were—elaborate halftime shows.

Sometimes the entertainment would have less to do with performance than with the dramatic presentation of a striking and edible work of visual art. Meat pies might be gilded with thin gold leaf; other times, entire feasts might be "gilded" with a paint of egg yolk and saffron or colored to indulge a royal whim. (A peacock entirely sheathed in gold leaf is said to have appeared on the table of King Richard II in 1398.) Edible collages assembled from variously colored slivers of meat set in aspic might, for instance, be used to represent the family coat of arms—a medieval equivalent of today's fruit-n-Jell-O masterpieces.

Meat of wild game was often ground to squishy meat pâté and then used to re-stuff the animal's skin so the beast could attend the feast in its entirety, naturalistically posed with, say, an apple between its teeth, its bristly hide concealing

> **W**hereas today we might throw a few lousy CDs on the player for a dinner party or at best hire a pianist for a truly swank affair, aristocratic hosts in centuries gone by staged entire variety shows for their dinner guests with poets, singers, magicians, or acrobats performing between courses.

Exotic wild game was a favorite dish of the fifteenth century French aristocracy.

the daintily prepared meat beneath. This stuffing is actually called forcemeat or farcemeat (the word "farce," designating a broad and absurd comedy, derives from this associated verb "farce," meaning "to stuff or render pompous"). Among these comically grotesque creations would sometimes appear mythical beasts—kitchen monsters created by medieval cooks who'd stitch parts of one animal onto another (a cockatrice, for instance, composed of a rooster body trailing the tail of an eel). These entertaining counterfeits executed in edible materials were generally known as "solteties" (Middle English) or "subtleties." "Subtle" here is used in the old sense of "crafty."

Returning again to Duke Philip's Burgundian blowout, we find some tasty examples of foodstuff figurines: a tiger battling a giant snake, a jester riding a bear, a wild man atop a camel, and various model ships and buildings. Some of these ornaments, though not entirely edible, included clockwork components,

such as a miniature forest with wild animals that "moved as if alive," a ship sailing from shore to shore, a castle tower squirting orange punch into a moat, a cathedral with functional pipe organ and musical "choir," and a figurine of a young boy pissing rosewater into a silver model ship.

This emphasis on the art of culinary presentation led to each royal family promoting particular cooks gifted in the field. Just as certain chefs might specialize in the preparation of meats or sauces, the *Garde Manger* was the chef in charge of presentation and finishing touches executed not in the palace kitchens but in the cold holding room adjoining the banquet hall.

Today's *Garde Manger* generally arranges buffets and creates garnishes, but he may still create mosaics of fruits or nuts, wield a die-grinder to carve an ice-sculpture swan, chisel corporate logos out of cheese, or carry on the tradition of these medieval subtleties.

■ CANDY CULTURE ■

The Mosque Was Delicious, but the Pagoda Was Too Sweet

In most of Europe up through the fifteenth century, it was the upper crust that enjoyed the privilege of rotting their teeth with sugar. While peasants contented themselves with honey from the nearest hive, the nobility preferred sugar shipped from far-off Southern lands. The cost of transportation made it such a scarce commodity that, in 1226, King Henry III of England had to scrabble just to scratch together a scant three pounds of the stuff. Because of its snob appeal, and because it could easily be worked with a little heat and water, sugar was of primary importance in crafting subtleties for lavish banquets.

While, at first, bluebloods had to content themselves with decorative figurines that looked as if they'd been sculpted from oversized sugar cubes, at some point in the eighteenth century this began to change as more progressive confectioners—tired of these crumbly sugar paste novelties—went to work on a new technique for boiling sugar so that it could be cast like resin into smooth rigid forms.

> **B**ringing a fascination with classical architecture to his culinary presentations, Carême and his followers transformed mere desserts into grandiose and fantastic landscapes replete with edible Greek temples, romantic ruins, exotic pagodas, Turkish mosques, mysterious grottoes, hunting scenes, and hermit's caves— all fabricated from elements cast in sugar, molded in marzipan, or carved out of butter and lard.

As a result, increasingly elaborate reproductions of classical sculpture, heraldic symbols, baroque architecture, mythological creatures, and exotic images from the New World were cast in molten sugar, sometimes in separate pieces, which were adhered together using more melted sugar, like some haute-cuisine version of a kid's plastic model kit.

Toward the end of the 1700s, critics had begun sniggering at these ponderously baroque constructions until the practice was resurrected by the prestigious Antonin Carême. Generally regarded as the father of haute cuisine, and dubbed the "cook of kings and the king of cooks" by renowned nineteenth-century gastronome Brillat-Savarin, Carême became famous for desserts presented as extravagant set pieces (*pièces montées*) at banquets in honor of Napoleon, England's King George IV, Czar Alexander, and Baron de Rothschild.

Bringing a fascination with classical architecture to his culinary presentations, Carême and his followers transformed mere desserts into grandiose and fantastic landscapes replete with edible Greek temples, romantic ruins, exotic pagodas, Turkish mosques, mysterious grottoes, hunting scenes, and hermit's

Antonin Carême.

Let Them Eat Croquembouche

Pyramids and Cakes

If chocolates are for courting, then the next edible milestone along that path should be the wedding cake. Ceremonial foods have always been important in weddings, and the first English wedding celebrations were inseparable from the aspect of feasting. The word "bridal," in fact, comes from "bride" and "ale," an old English word designating not only the drink but also any country festival at which ale might be consumed.

The first "wedding cakes" in Anglo-Saxon tradition were actually pies. Along with those pies went a tradition similar to throwing out the bouquet. In this case, it was a glass ring baked into the pie; the recipient of the ring-bearing slice would be the next to marry (assuming they didn't choke on it by mistake).

The familiar multitiered wedding cake, despite all the hullabaloo about this being "traditional," is a surprisingly modern innovation, dating back only to around the turn of the century. While history records many elaborate wedding feasts often featuring noteworthy cakes, such cakes were inevitably looked upon as something innovative rather than something traditional. It wasn't until royal English bakers served up an outstandingly elaborate multitiered cake for the wedding of Queen Victoria's granddaughter in 1859, that fashionably unoriginal people began copying this as the prototype of all wedding cakes. And it wasn't until several years into the twentieth century that this prototype had really solidified into today's prototype—that is white with three tiers separated by columns.

None of this is to say that there were no precedents to this idea of stacked conglomerations of cake. There were—just very different ones. The French have been known to stack cakes, and did so long before Queen Victoria's bakers decided it was a nice idea. They've also been known to have had a dispute or two with the English, as with the claim of who created the modern wedding cake.

The French say that their traditional croquembouche, a pyramidal confection formed of many small cream puffs piled up and glued together with hot caramel, is the original. Since the eighteenth century, aristocratic French have made a habit of stacking pastries and sweets in a variety of symmetrical arrangements such as pyramids, sometimes as elements in even larger dessert tableaux including numerous similar arrangements, some on special frameworks and some interspersed with edible figurines. While the croquembouche is regarded as the traditional French wedding cake, stacked sponge cakes of the sort more familiar to American wedding guests are now also served in France.

Unimpressed by this eighteenth century precedent, the English point to an even earlier forerunner among the Anglo-Saxons who would also pile sweet buns or cookies in a tower as part of their wedding celebrations. The point here was to invite the newlyweds to lean together to kiss over the tower each time more sweets were added. The higher the tower was piled without being disturbed by the couple's kiss, the more children that marriage would produce.

The French, however, believing that there are better ways to come up with offspring, claim that it was a French chef touring England who hit upon the idea of taking this unstable pile of sweets and cementing the whole thing together with white sugar icing. The English point out that this ruins the game altogether.

caves—all fabricated from elements cast in sugar, molded in marzipan, or carved out of butter and lard.

In 1833, Carême moved on to that great pastry shop in the sky, though his followers and rivals continued to crank out these precisely modeled fantasies right through the end of World War I. But with the appearance of softer fondants of gum Arabic and sugar, cakes and confections casually draped with "garlands" of icing began to replace those persnickety creations inspired by Monsieur Haute Cuisine. But even today, on more formal occasions, where inflexible tradition reigns, we still see traces of Carême's architectural mannerism in the classical columns typically adorning wedding cakes.

This same mania for precision manifests itself with more high-handed techiness in the cake decorator's use of airbrush for precise renderings of custom imagery. Thus, edible colors misted onto white icing canvases can create photo-real portraits of the cake's recipient, favorite pet, or other image of choice. Cake consumers less tolerant of human error can even resort to digital scanning and ink-jet printing technologies to transfer treasured family photos onto superhumanly smooth sheets of white icing that are later mechanically transferred to ma-made cakes. This special-order service is offered today by many forward-thinking bakeries.

A piece of Babs with your coffee?

Cakes that Sprout Trees and Shoot Steam

The traditional English cake, though covered in white icing, is a fruitcake base. In Ireland, the cake served is an even richer variation drenched in brandy or whiskey.

In the Caribbean, fruitcake is also used, though here it's drenched in the native rum. In the West Indies, it's considered good luck to see the cake before the bride and groom do, and guests will donate money for the privilege of taking a peak. In Jamaica, guests who can't make it to the festivities are mailed preserved slices of the rum-pickled cake. In Bermuda, the couple takes home a different kind of souvenir: the tiny seedling used to decorate the top of the cake is planted in their new home as a symbol of their growing love.

The Icelandic wedding cake is called a *kransakaka* and is a basket-like structure composed of stacked rings of almond cake decorated with swirls of icing and filled with chocolates and assorted sweets. In Denmark, a similar cornucopia built of rings is sometimes decorated with the likeness of the bride and groom modeled from marzipan.

In Yemen, it's not a cake at all that's featured but deep-fried fritters, and in the Ukraine it's a bread, blessed and decorated for the occasion with religious and folkloric themes.

Unquestionably a Western import,

wedding cakes in Asia are appreciated less for their culinary merit than for the decorative qualities. In Japan, a compromise between the high cost of producing cakes, which otherwise hold no place in the Japanese diet, and the desire to create an impressive display have given birth to elaborate artificial cakes. These towering showpieces are generally cast from fiberglass and iced and detailed with wax, though, to facilitate the ritual of cutting a slice, they will contain a minimal amount of actual cake or at very least a

> In Japan, a compromise between the high cost of producing cakes, which otherwise hold no place in the Japanese diet, and the desire to create an impressive display have given birth to elaborate artificial cakes. These towering showpieces are generally cast from fiberglass and iced and detailed with wax.

slot into which a knife can be inserted. Another gimmick gaining in popularity is a lever concealed within the cake so that at the moment of insertion, the cake emits a blast of steam or dry ice, though what exactly this might symbolize remains an interesting subject of debate.

Make That One Dozen Marzipan Geese—Life Size, Please

While classical columns continue to adorn modern wedding cakes, during the 1800s a less grandiose expression of this architectural impulse cropped up in Germany's gingerbread houses (*knusperhaüschen*). In France, a like-minded holiday attempt at edible model-making was the Yule Log (*bûche de noël*), a layered sponge cake rolled logwise, dressed with simulated bark icing, and planted round with candy mushrooms. Instead of carved, cast, and reassembled sugar components, these projects take a simpler, more folksy approach, using flat cookies, icing, cake, and marzipan.

Marzipan, a mixture of ground almonds and sugar, is particularly versatile. Its light, neutral color is easy to tint, and its putty-like consistency is a cinch to work—basically a tasty version of Play-Doh. The stuff was employed centuries ago to model the subtleties of medieval banquets and continues to be used to make marzipan fruits (*frutti di martorana*)—beloved by the Sicilians or the diminutive New Year's pigs Germans exchange for good luck.

Originally arriving in Europe via crusaders who'd been rubbing shoulders with the Arabs and Venetian and Hanseatic traders who knew a good sweet when they saw one, the marzipan originated in Persia as the crowning delight at the banquets of sultans. One of the earlier references to this sweet paste dates from around 965 A.D. and refers to a marzipan fish swimming in a dish of honey given as a reward to the Persian poet, Al

Mutanabbi, whose pen had produced verse equally sweet. Because the importation costs were steep, only the better lords and ladies got to nibble at the stuff. Its value was so great, in fact, that the city of Sienna saw fit to present the Holy Roman Emperor Charles IV with loaves of gilded marzipan as a tribute in 1368.

Though most often used in royal kitchens, marzipan was also ground and mixed in the mortars of pharmacies, prescribed through the eighteenth century by physicians who would have the stuff rolled into pills and combined with healing herbs, ground pearls, and even crushed gemstones.

By the early 1800s, love for this royal treat had extended beyond Europe and Islamic countries. Around that time, Germany's leading marzipan manufacturer would annually receive orders from the Tsar of Russia requesting one dozen life-size marzipan geese (for reasons not fully disclosed).

> **T**hough most often used in royal kitchens, marzipan was also ground and mixed in the mortars of pharmacies, prescribed through the eighteenth century by physicians who would have the stuff rolled into pills and combined with healing herbs, ground pearls, and even crushed gemstones.

an expensive perfume. An only slightly less extravagant version of this sweet-smelling trinket, often exchanged by Elizabethans, was an apple or orange "stikt round about with cloaves."

While native fruits might often be preserved through the winter in honey, then removed and later eaten along with the crystallized "sugar" by sweet-toothed medieval types, real fruit-flavored candy didn't show until a particularly clever eighteenth-century confectioner devised a system of boiling fruit with sugar and clarifying the result to produce a brilliantly translucent hard candy retaining some of the flavor and color of the fruit used.

This is the stuff Americans generally call "hard candy" or "sugar candy," and though you'd be hard-pressed today to find an adult who'd prefer this cloying confection to a decent chocolate, at least it makes for a cheap sugar fix.

It All Crystallizes

If Northern Europeans found ground and sugared almonds from the South marvelous enough to buddy up with gemstones and pearls or to dress up in gold and present to an Emperor, it should come as no surprise that other nuts, spices, and fruits from foreign lands would also get the royal treatment. Gilt nutmegs were another trendy medieval gift, as wa the pomander, a word originally designating a precious silver case containing an equally valuable stash of spices. Carrie to mask the abundant and unpleasant odors of those days—and supposedly ward off infection—the pomander was a popular gift in courtship, equivalent to

Just pop 'em on your eraserhead and start lickin'!

But that's not what they were thinking in the eighteenth century. For them, this jewel-like substance was some sort of marvelous amber, preserving year-round the very essence of summer's freshest fruits. Its highly refined clarity made it a natural for aristocratic tables, where it functioned as an edible stand-in for blown glass or crystal centerpieces. Its luminescent color also influenced many confectioners to cast it in faceted shapes resembling gemstones.

Of course, children were just dying to put these tasty little baubles into their mouths, and within a century, this stuff had moved from the tables of the aristocracy to the sticky hands of working-class children, who were buying it for a penny a pop and enjoying it as both play thing and sweet. Molded in the shape of tiny animals, people, trains, guns, ships, and wagons, these fanciful tidbits were in fact marketed as "sugar toys" up through the 1900s.

The candy cane is one of the first forms of hard candy recorded. Supposedly devised by a choirmaster of the Cologne Cathedral, its shape was intended to mimic the crooked staffs carried by the shepherds of the Nativity. Its benevolent creator is said to have given these treats as a reward to choirboys exhibiting good behavior during a mind-numbingly long reenactment of the first Christmas staged in the church.

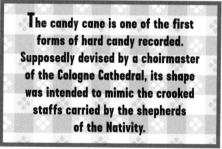

The candy cane is one of the first forms of hard candy recorded. Supposedly devised by a choirmaster of the Cologne Cathedral, its shape was intended to mimic the crooked staffs carried by the shepherds of the Nativity.

In Palermo, Sicily, the pious celebration of All Soul's Day is made more appealing for children with surprise gifts of candy. In this case, however, it's not St. Nick who delivers the goods but, rather, the deceased who come shambling in from the Great Beyond to leave marzipan fruits and dolls made of sugar.

Edible Art for Ghosts and Gods

If you're talking about candy and talking about the dead, you're bound to end up discussing Mexican *calaveras de dulces* or sugar skulls. Given to children as a treat on the Day of the Dead (*Dia de los Muertos*), and also left as a tribute on the graves of the recently departed, these delectable death's heads are made of sugar, egg white, lemon juice, and cream of tartar. Also called *alfeniques,* such candies are found throughout Mexico but are most visible in the towns of San Miguel de Allende, Guanajato, and Toluca. Since 1630, Toluca has hosted the annual *Feria de Alfenique*, showcasing the work of nearly a hundred families for which the handcrafting of *alfeniques* is an art handed down through generations.

Besides the traditional skulls, bones, and coffins created from either sugar, marzipan, or chocolate, other items, such as candy letters (representing personal initials), candy shoes, umbrellas, and little bottles filled with liquor are also made by local craftsmen. Special breads baked for the day are decorated with tiny crossed bones modeled in dough. In Ecuador, artisans also create small ornaments representing people, flowers, or special animals that are likewise placed on graves of relatives. Common from Mexico through South America, the practice of modeling with dough dates back to the time of the ancient Aztecs.

Long before pre-Columbians were rolling out dough for either art or food, the priests of Zeus over in Diasias, Greece, were modeling bread offerings in the shape of pigs, sheep, or fruits. Stag-shaped cakes were what Diana, goddess of the

A Day of the Dead altar featuring a deceased soul's favorite foods.

Children love to eat calaveras de dulces *(sugar skulls) on the Day of the Dead.*

offerings to be burned on the Tibetan New Year's (*Lu Yugpa*). But the real show comes 15 days later on *Chogna Choeba*, the first new moon of the Tibetan year. It's then that Buddhist monks begin constructing colorful and ornate dioramas populated by countless mythological and legendary beings and surmounted by palaces and mountains towering as high as 20 feet. And it's not dough, wax, or clay from which they create these intricate scenes, rather, the medium of choice is . . . yak butter.

If you can imagine the smell of a yak, and if you can imagine the smell of butter in a land where refrigeration is a rarity, you can probably get a mental whiff of the weird spectacle these sculptures present. Nonetheless, this pungent substance is omnipresent throughout the Himalayas and is used in tea and as a fuel for lamps as well as these devotional carvings. Because it easily liquefies on contact with a warm hand, it's often submerged in ice cold water while being carved.

Monks specializing in the art spend years studying up on underwater carving technique, along with contemplation of the holy texts from which every detail of their compositions are drawn. Though interrupted briefly by Chinese rule, the recently resurrected tradition of yak butter sculpting dates to the fifteenth century. The creation of these highly perishable works of art serves the monks as a form of meditation upon earthly transience. After modeling and coloring these elaborate dioramas, their ephemeral nature is emphasized as the sculptures are carried in torchlight processions down to a nearby river, where they are hacked to pieces and chucked into the flowing stream.

hunt, liked to see on her altars, and phallus-shaped loaves were eaten in many a Dionysian ritual. In *Skiraphoria*, a rite celebrated exclusively by females, bread-dough figures of snakes, suckling pigs, and penises were thrown into a cave sacred to the goddess Demeter. The priests of the Eleusinian cults prepared not only breads shaped like male members, but also female genitalia for banquets of initiation. And before all this, over in Egypt, some worshippers would occasionally play it cheap by sacrificing counterfeit swine made out of wheat paste instead of the pricey flesh and blood models.

For centuries, the Chinese have also crafted small dolls of rice flour and water for use in weddings, funerals, and other ceremonies. Lacy figurines made from boiled sugar are also produced there— butterflies, dragons, and human figures created by craftsmen working the molten sugar with many of the techniques used by glass blowers.

In Tibet, it's barley dough (*tsampa*) they use today, pressing it into a variety of molds or modeling by hand symbolic

■ GARDEN TRIMMINGS ■

Vegetable Carving Saves the Day

While puttering around with yak butter in Tibet may seem a bit remote to most readers, other aspects of Eastern creativity in the kitchen have more direct influence on the way food shows up on our plates. The development of nouvelle cuisine in the '70s and '80s owes much to the Asian appreciation for lighter ingredients and more dynamic colors and compositions.

Take, for instance, the influence of Chef Alfred Portale's presentation of salads in colorful and precarious pyramids in the kitchen of New York's Gotham Bar and Grill. In Japan, you can find a clear precedent in similar arrangements, where beyond eye-catching effect such displays strive for metaphor—mountains of chopped tuna, for example, rise over a forest of daikon sprouts and are dusted with a snowy (and punning) cap of grated yam (*yamaimo*).

In many regions of Asia, chefs traditionally engage in such culinary counterfeiting, particularly in Thailand, where master fruit and vegetable carvers deftly transform cucumbers into lotuses, melons into delicate roses, and radishes into fish. Considered a mark of aristocratic upbringing and a matter of national pride, exhibitions of fruit and vegetable carving draw Thais to seasonal festivals in Songkhla, Nakhom Pathom, and Kamphaeng Phet, where competitive displays of this skill take place amid parades of fruit and flower bedecked floats.

There is even a classic Thai poem composed by King Rama II in which the art of vegetable carving saves the day. Rama's narrative tells of a queen wrongfully banished from her throne and forced to work in the kitchen of her rival. One day, the queen's son shows up for dinner in the palace where she is secretly held. Skilled in the art of fruit carving, she spends her time carving scenes from the young prince's life in a squash that is slipped into the soup the prince is served. Naturally, the son recognizes the biographical renderings embellishing the squash and thereby grasps the nature and location of her

Chef Alfred Portale's lobster salad as presented at New York's Gotham Bar & Grill.

captivity. All is righted, and the usefulness of fruit carving is reaffirmed.

A Rose by any Other Name Would Taste as Sweet

It's not just fruits and vegetables from the garden, but also flowers which can be used decoratively at the table. But arranging a bouquet for the kitchen can be such a problem! There are just so many considerations to take into account—nasturtiums are peppery and might nicely off-set the beanlike taste of your tulips, but what about those chrysanthe-mums? Their sharp taste really calls for ginger, and that's not going to blend with those earthy tulip flavors. Both the yellow and purple johnny-jump-ups look good in there, and their minty zest might go with the nasturtium, but it'll just fight the chrys-anthemum's tang . . . .

Edible flowers may have just blossomed on some trendy menus, but those stuffed squash flowerets you're about to bravely devour have been served in Italian and Hispanic countries for centuries. Day

lily buds were being munched as early as 140 B.C.E. in Asia, and the ancient Romans sprinkled violets, roses, and marrow flowers throughout their cuisine.

Of all the flowers, the rose is perhaps closest to the gastronome's heart (and stomach). In Morocco, the flower is used to flavor chicken stews (along with yellow calendula petals, the "poor man's saffron"). In India, throughout the Near East, and in North Africa, rosewater lends a distinctive sweetness to desserts like baklava. Cooks of medieval Europe used rosewater in much the same way to sweeten puddings and pastries, as well as fish and game. One medieval dinner guest happens to have recorded quite a diverse bouquet of flavors at his table, writing, "Marigolds seasoned the venison; roses graced the stew, and violets mingled with wild onion in the salad."

Many cultures have preserved roses, violets, and lavender dipped in sugar and egg white to be eaten as crystallized candy or used as edible decoration on other dishes. In the seventeenth century, carnation petals became one of the many closely guarded ingredients

> **E**dible flowers may have just blossomed on some trendy menus, but those stuffed squash flowerets you're about to bravely devour have been served in Italian and Hispanic countries for centuries.

used by Carthusian monks to concoct Chartreuse liqueur. Romantic Victorians were particularly fond of roses, brewing the dried petals into a tea, and using them to infuse honeys, jams, oils, vinegars, and syrups. Even thoroughly unromantic types prize rose hips (the fleshy base below the petals) for its high level of vitamin C and purported effectiveness against many an unromantic ailment such as diarrhea or scurvy.

> **While Americans may find overgrown radishes a curious medium for pious renderings of biblical scenes, we tend to take for granted our own desire to annually hollow out vegetables, carve in some human features, and plant a candle in the cavity.**

I Saw Jesus in a Radish

The Indian artisans of Oaxaca, Mexico, also know a thing or two about carving up veggies. This time it's a large local species of radish that's the object of artistic endeavor. The large size and grotesquely evocative shapes assumed by the root easily suggests all sorts of images to those handy with a knife. Colonial priests are also said to have done some suggesting, as  it was the local Spanish padres who originally encouraged the natives to go ahead and whittle away on these yam sized vegetables, setting up an annual competition that's been held each December 23 since 1693.

Known as *Noché del Rábano,* the event draws hundreds of competitors (including children) trying to outdo each other in intricacy of tableaux rendered. Proximity to Christmas makes Nativity scenes a natural, but other religious and historical depictions turn up, including quite a few Virgins of Guadelupe and a smattering of Aztec gods and heroes. Still-lives assembled from dried cornhusks and chrysanthemums are also created. Mariachis circulate about the plaza providing musical ambiance from afternoon till evening when the winner is selected and fireworks cap it all off.

You have your pick of explanations for the festival's origin. The diplomatic version describes it all as a celebration of the European's introduction of the radish into Indian agriculture.

The more provocative theory begins with the Spanish priests frustrated in their attempts to get the newly baptized Indians to honor the Christmas Eve fast. They then conceive the carving competition as a scheme to get their stubborn parishioners to harvest and cut open vast quantities of large vegetables. Reasoning that the thrifty natives will not let the leftover vegetables go to waste, the priests thereby guaranteed that radish will replace meat on the following day's menu.

A Handy Tote for Infernal Embers

While Americans may find overgrown radishes a curious medium for pious renderings of biblical scenes, we tend to take for granted our own desire to annually hollow out vegetables, carve in some human features, and plant a candle in the cavity.

The folklore behind the Jack-o'-lantern is every bit as curious as is our general indifference to what all this gourd-gutting signifies. And what about the name itself?

The first mention of a "Jack of the Lantern" occurs in print in 1750, but only in the sense of a "Jack of all Trades," the trade in this case being a night watch-man, and the "Jack" being generic. All it means then is "Jack Who Carries a Lantern Because He's a Night Watchman." Pretty dull. And certainly nothing that would inspire one to extract all the slimy guts from a pumpkin.

But the seven hundred thousand or so Irish immigrants who came to this country during the potato famine of the 1840s were much better storytellers and enlivened this generic lamp carrier with quite a bit more personality. First of all they scrapped the night watchman bit and made him a blacksmith. And a stingy one at that. And one with a pronounced penchant for drink.

After playing a series of tricks on the devil, this Jack kicks the bucket and is denied entrance to heaven thanks to all his "colorful" traits. But his pranks on the devil also get him barred from hell. Being a social animal, Jack wants to get in with his cronies and continues to beg Old Nick for admittance. Lucifer will have none of it, and tells him to hit the road, but Jack continues with his objections, whining that the path back from Hell is too dark.

At this, the exasperated Lord of Hell picks up a coal from the eternal flames and hurls it at Jack telling him to take *that* for his light and beat it. To protect the glowing ember from the wind, Jack sticks it inside a hollowed potato he'd just happened to be munching through, and thus begins his lost wandering, eerie lantern in hand.

Thus, on Halloween, a night when the recently departed are said to walk the earth like Jack, the Irish acknowledge their ghostly presence by placing a candle in a hollowed out potato, or the closest thing they could find in America—a pumpkin.

■ **JUST DON'T BITE IT** ■

The Man with the Edible Head

Cabin fever during the period between harvest and warm weather must've been particularly severe in the days before effective birth control and state-run schooling. With so many kids underfoot, it shouldn't be surprising that a few

The very first Mr. & Mrs. Potato Head kit (1954).

In 1952, reworking this tradition for a baby-boomer toy market, Hasbro, Inc., in Pawtucket, Rhode Island, gave birth to a new toy sensation: "Mr. Potato Head." As first introduced, Mr. Potato Head suffered from a sort of multiple personality disorder. No more than a loose collection of plastic arms, eyes, noses, shoes, lips, and so forth, the toy depicted on the box showed Mr. Head with variable onion, tomato, and eggplant bodies.

Advertising displayed indifference to the potato body we now take for granted, proclaiming, "any fruit or vegetable makes a funny face man."

pumpkins, potatoes, or radishes might be sacrificed as playthings to quiet the kids. Carving vegetables into dolls or doll heads would be a natural pastime to divert children from mischief. Since in most societies, tending to kitchen chores and minding the kids fall under the same job description, it's no wonder that foodstuffs—dough, nuts, empty gourds, and dried apples—have been such common material for doll-making.

Jumpin' Mr. & Mrs. Potato Head (1966). She cleans the house and then prepares dinner; he works with a jackhammer and then goes fishing.

Mr. Potato Head's Tooty Frooty Friends (1964).

Though Mattel and Hasbro may feud over the topic, Hasbro maintains that this "Spud of a Thousand Faces" was in fact the first toy advertised on television—a possibility that may explain the remarkable success and abundant spin-off products, including Willy Burger, Franky Frank, Mr. Ketchup Head, Mr. Mustard Head, Frenchy Fry, Mr. Soda Pop Head, Oscar the Orange, Pete the Pepper, Katy Carrot, Cooky Cucumber, and Dunkie Donut Head. Equally remarkable

> **T**he tuber's proudest moment came in the heady days of the early Apollo mission, when in 1968 Hasbro produced the historical "Mr. Potato Head on the Moon" play set.

The rare Mr. Potato Head on the Moon set (1968). Check out those moon monsters!

is the toy's longevity, demonstrated by the unceasing flow of new accessory packs and potato acquaintances as well as Head's starring role in Disney's 1992 computer-animated blockbuster, *Toy Story*. But perhaps the tuber's proudest moment came in the heady days of the early Apollo mission, when in 1968 Hasbro produced the historical "Mr. Potato Head on the Moon" play set.

Mmm . . . Plastigoop!

In the 1960s, kids a bit old for Mr. Potato Head might instead be into making Creepy Crawlers. While these youngsters would be squirting "plastigoop" into metal molds, heating them on a hot plate and picking out the vulcanized rubbery bugs, reptiles, and other critters, more practical minded youth were using similar tools and techniques to feed their siblings and friends on Incredible Edibles, Creepy Crawler's digestible cousin.

Incredible Edibles were less frightening for their insectoid shape than for the fact that they were created from "Gobble DeGoop," a substance more or less indistinguishable from colored Elmer's Glue—and made no less sinister by the manufacturers evasive identification of the product as "liquid food." The budding gourmet could select from among cherry, raspberry, butterscotch, mint, cinnamon, licorice, root beer, and tutti frutti liquid foods, fill one of eight different metal molds, and pop it into a "Sooper Gooper" oven to cook up his Edibles.

Introduced by Mattel in 1966—two years after the highly successful Creepy Crawlers hit the market—Incredible Edibles was one of the more short-lived products in the Thingmaker series. One reason for its abbreviated life span was parental concern over the exact content of this mysterious "liquid food." Nonetheless, even the Incredible Edible toy spawned sequels, including the "Makery Bakery," a contraption for manufacturing little cupcake-like creatures with plastic arms and feet. These "Kooky Kakes" were fabricated by heat-treating "Kakeroop" and quickly covering up the results with "Frosteroop." These two substances were received with suspicion as great as that shown "liquid food," and the product did not remain on toy store shelves for long.

The Burgermeister

Full-Throttle All-Beef Patty Preoccupation

Some people like their hamburgers fried on a griddle. Others prefer them broiled on a grill. Still others seek out the variety that's steam-broiled. And then there's the true burger lover, like "Hamburger" Harry Sperl, who'll snatch up any kind of burger—broiled beef or molded plastic, inflatable vinyl or plush fabric, ceramic, plastic, wax, and sterling silver. Specifically, it's the inedible variety that's earned him a reputation.

Sperl's got five hundred or so of them squirreled away in his home in Daytona Beach, Florida. Opened once a year as the "International Hamburger Hall of Fame," his horde includes toys, models, and more functional burger-shaped items such as clocks, banks, cups, bowls, glasses, cookie jars, salt shakers, music boxes, pencil holders, erasers, telephones, and bean bag furniture, to name a few.

Besides hamburger-shaped collectibles, he's got plenty of others that bear an image or other connection with the sandwich, including burger-emblazoned posters, menus, T-shirts, postcards, calendars, magnets, caps, badges, towels, and hors d'oeuvre trays. Sperl, a native of Wetterburg, Germany (several hundred miles south of Hamburg, unfortunately), gleefully embraces the all-American favorite as an icon of his adopted home, and not a day goes by that the former Wetterburger doesn't eat at least one.

His collection began when, on a lark, Sperl purchased some hamburger display pieces from a toy store. Seeing these casually

exhibited on his desk at work, a coworker assumed they were part of an actual collection and offered further donations. From these humble origins in 1989, the collection has grown to include such marvels as a $3,500 hamburger-shaped waterbed, complete with sesame-seed-sprinkled bedspread.

But the most impressive bogus burger in Sperl's collection must be the one on wheels—three to be exact. The "Hamburger Trike" is a 1100cc Harley with the engine tucked between a pair of immense fiberglass buns, a melted cheese fender, and ketchup bottle shocks. Completing the effect are wisps of steam emitted by the burger and an onboard stereo sizzling with the sound of frying beef.

Inspired by the success of this undertaking, Hamburger Harry's vision for the future includes a Mini-Burgermobile for his young son Karl, a Hamburger Dragster, Hamburger Golf Cart, Hamburger Bus, and Hamburger Helicopter, as well as a double bacon cheeseburger shaped structure to house his Hamburger Collection.

Eat Your Chia Pet!

Or at least its fur. The chia seeds sprouted on those TV commercials for pottery planters are actually the edible sprouts of the *salvia columbariae*. A member of the watercress family, they're the same sprouts as those commonly sold for use in salads, sandwiches, and other hippie-pleasing foods. However, Joseph Enterprises, Inc., the maker of the Chia Pet (as well as that other holiday TV classic

> The chia seeds sprouted on those TV commercials for pottery planters are actually the edible sprouts of the *salvia columbariae*. A member of the watercress family, they're the same sprouts as those commonly sold for use in salads, sandwiches, and other hippie-pleasing foods.

selection of secretly edible products to include Chia cows, elephants, lion cubs, bunnies, frogs, hippos, kittens, pigs, puppies, bears, turtles, trees, as well as human Chia Heads (including a Chia Clown and Chia Professor). Once you've purchased all those, you can start on the T-shirts, sweatshirts, denim shirts, mugs, and watches emblazoned with the Chia Pet likeness. That's about $400 worth of chia—if you can restrict yourself to one of each.

WATCH IT GROW! **Chia Pet**®

Complete your collection with these Chia® Planters.

This package contains the Elephant.

ELEPHANT   COW   FROG   PIG   TREE

PUPPY   BUNNY   TURTLE   HIPPO   KITTEN

The menagerie of Chia Pets (and tree). Missing in action are the Chia lion cub, Chia bear, Chia clown, and Chia professor (among others).

"The Clapper") has never submitted their novelty planters to the FDA for approval and, therefore, cannot legally market them as the untapped food source they truly are. They've more than compensated for this shortcoming by broadening their

Teething Homemakers

Naturally, toddlers put toys in their mouths and, naturally, parents would rather see that toy be a piece of plastic gourmets can use a Fisher Price Pasta Maker with attachments to create more urbane delights such as angel-hair pasta à la Play-Doh. "Tea Time" and "Elegant Dining" accessories packs (complete with goblet, napkins, candles, and place cards) represent upscale preschool aspirations, while more down-to-earth dreamers can simulate adult dining with polyvinyl TV dinners offering compartmentalized servings of Salisbury steak, macaroni and cheese, and green beans. The even more grimly realistic tot, compelled to rehearse an adult life of meaningless wage slavery, can do so with Fisher Price's fast food employee play kits, some featuring the "McDonald's Crew Uniform" spatula, microphone, and name badge (erasable for make-believe lay-offs).

Fake Food for the Now Generation

Children growing up with plastic food in the '60s could transition to other forms of "play food" as they matured. In the early-'70s, hippies tiring of those drab all-natural beeswax candles began injecting some color into their projects, using vividly tinted wax for a wide rainbow of novelty candles. One of the more popular subjects was food, and many of these were also scented (often in disconcertingly unrelated flavors: vanilla pizza, strawberry hamburgers, etc.). Sundaes were particularly sought after. More sculpture than candle, despite the perfunctory wick, these were often sold alongside glasses of milk "levitating" on a hardened stream of white acrylic.

Imitation food was also marketed as a hiding place for all those illicit substances for which those decades are fondly remembered. "Hide-Your-Dough" was

A future fast-food worker gets some early training.

food than the barrel of a plastic gun. Fisher Price, a subsidiary of Mattel, realized this in the late 1960s and began capitalizing on kids' instinctual fascination with food as well as their desire to copy parents' kitchen activities with their "Fun with Food" series. At one point or another, most adults born in the mid-'60s or later have held in their hand one of their primary colored fruits, donuts, or bottles of milk.

Yet much has changed over the decades and, today, potty-trained

> The even more grimly realistic tot, compelled to rehearse an adult life of meaningless wage slavery, can do so with Fisher Price's fast food employee play kits, some featuring the "McDonald's Crew Uniform" spatula, microphone, and name badge (erasable for make-believe lay-offs).

a hollow plastic baguette outwardly marketed as safe-keeping for pin money, and "Lett-Us-Hide" was a cleverly disguised lettuce safe for green of one sort or another.

The '80s brought a food replica renaissance; this time it was diminutive samples of rubber or plastic food posing as refrigerator magnets. Further miniaturization reduced these to earrings.

Having grown up with artificial food, adult connoisseurs moving on to more sophisticated arenas—such as art collecting—found their dual interests supported by companies like Fax Foods in Vista, California. This food replica service offered a line of products called "Food Art by Francesco" that included pizzas, quesadillas, and pies turned into clocks as well as sculptural constructions of plastic fruits and vegetables or bakery items modeled after the imaginary portraits of the sixteenth-century Italian artist Giuseppe Arcimboldo.

Tastes as Good as it Looks

If you thought ornamental arrangements of fake fruit were something your Aunt Edna invented just to beautify her mobile home, seventeenth-century interior décor might throw you for a loop.

Modeled after the painterly still-life genre, formalized compositions of fruit in bowls were a fixture in better homes of the period. Handcrafting these wax replicas became the pastime of well-bred and idle ladies and remained a popular hobby up through the Victorian age.

In Japan, wax was also used to model fruit, not for ornamental use but as an offering to the gods. Exacting replicas carved in ivory were also used for this purpose. Centuries later, similar skills were turned about and used in fabrication of plastic food commonly displayed in Japanese restaurants. Used in place of advertising signs throughout the island, these food replicas showed up on U.S. shores transformed to refrigerator magnets or other novelties during the 1980s as sushi was hitting the American mainstream.

In this country, our use of such facsimiles is largely limited to plastic garnishings on salad bars, but Americans are perfectly willing to forgo that third dimension if we can get some really juicy two-dimensional representations. While the food photographed in various domestic advertisements may not be plastic, it's far from natural. And that's all thanks to the obsessive food grooming of the photographer's aesthetic conscience—the food stylist.

A bevy of food fridge magnets looking good enough to eat.

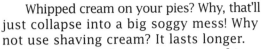

The Food with Collagen Lips

Ever wonder why your feeble attempts to follow a recipe fail to yield the sumptuous masterpiece portrayed in the cookbook?

Probably because you didn't individually trim your green beans with scissors. Or brush them with glycerin. A professional food stylist would have plenty to say about your manner of presentation.

Did you neglect to mist your roast with a solution of glucose or flesh it out with a hypodermic full of cooking oil?

> **W**hipped cream on your pies? Why, that'll just collapse into a big soggy mess! Why not use shaving cream? It lasts longer.

Did you pull out the soldering iron to touch up those grill marks on your steak?

That pool of juices running off the meat—did you just intend to let it run into the veggies? Don't you have a Q-tip to swab that ragged edge?

Whipped cream on your pies? Why, that'll just collapse into a big soggy mess! Why not use shaving cream? It lasts longer.

Oh, you'd rather use a scoop of ice cream? Don't you mean nonmelting whipped potatoes? I mean, unless you really want a soggy crust!

Don't forget the salt in the beer for a nice sudsy head.

And that soda—it'll just get diluted if you use ice. Try acrylic resin instead.

Now that it's all in shape, don't forget to polish all those fingerprints off the plate. People like food that's fresh and natural, not too fussed over by human hands.

More akin to mortuary cosmetics than anything that might normally transpire in your kitchen, these are some of the tricks in the arsenal of the food stylist. In the context of advertising (rather than cookbook photography), this work is strictly regulated by consumer protection law. All the trouble started with a 1970's landmark decision against a major soup producer, who had allowed a stylist to use glass marbles to nudge veggies up to the surface of a soup, thereby creating the illusion of a heartier stew than the thin stuff they really canned.

While adulteration of products can lead to prosecution, intense selectivity cannot. Therefore, it is not uncommon, for instance, for a half dozen crates of vegetables to be tossed in the search for that one photogenic specimen, or for makers of a breakfast cereal to hand select each individual flake or otherwise scrupulously audition each element granted a role in the shoot.

Food stylists in action: Is that ice cream or whipped potatoes?

■ BIGGER THAN GROCERIES ■

Oh, I'd Love to Drive an Oscar Mayer Wiener

It would have been interesting to be a fly on the wall when, in 1936, an apparently earnest young businessman suggested to his colleagues that their firm (a solid Midwestern venture founded by solid German immigrants around the turn of the century) should promote itself by dressing a midget in a chef's outfit and having him tool around the streets of Chicago in a 13-foot motorized sausage.

But Carl G. Mayer, the man who opened his big mouth, just happened to be the nephew of the company's founder, and it didn't take much discussion for his far-flung Wienermobile notion to get some wheels. Midgets were big at the time, and they knew just the man to play the "Little Oscar" character—Meinhardt Raabe, the actor who'd recently played the Munchkin coroner in *The Wizard of Oz*.

Raabe is no longer with us, and—like the Wicked Witch he examined—the notion of using midgets as an advertising gimmick is "most sincerely dead." But the Weinermobile's promotional career has continued for six decades despite this loss.

Vintage Oscar Mayer Weinermobiles. These were originally driven by "midgets," including Meinhardt Raabe—the Munchkin coroner in The Wizard of Oz.

This sleek, contemporary version of the Weinermobile features a sunroof and amplified sound system. It is 27 feet long and can reach speeds up to 90 mph.

Today, from among 1,000 applicants, 12 desperately eager college grads are chosen for enrollment in "Hot Dog High," where rigorous training turns them out as full-fledged "Hotdoggers," now capable of traversing the country, handing out Wienermobile whistles and coin banks.

The vehicle also has been souped up a bit since Raabe's day. In the '50s, the length expanded to 22 feet, and luxuries like a sunroof and amplified sound were thrown in. A late-1950's model even sported a space-age glass bubble cockpit along with the addition of buns covering the previously nude wiener. (Buns stayed, the bubble didn't.) In 1988, the "Wienebago" model was introduced, upholstered in relish green, featuring fridge, microwave, and sophisticated sound system to play 21 variations of that insidious corporate jingle.

> **T**oday, from among 1,000 applicants, 12 desperately eager college grads are chosen for enrollment in "Hot Dog High," where rigorous training turns them out as full-fledged "Hotdoggers," now capable of traversing the country, handing out Wienermobile whistles and coin banks.

The current model burns asphalt at about 90 mph (clocked in Cal Tech wind tunnels) and is the longest wiener yet at 27 feet. It also comes loaded with large-screen television monitors, as well as a wiener-shaped glovebox and dash. Six of these currently motor around the country bearing license plates such as "BIG BUN," "YUMMY," and "OSCAR." Older models still roam the streets of Mexico, Canada, Puerto Rico, Spain, and Japan.

Mattel has issued a number of Hot Wheels Wienermobiles including the highly coveted all-chrome Silver Series 1996 model. Radio controlled Wieners and small peddle-car versions for children can also be found by the diehard collector. In 1997, a classic 1950's model was parked outside the Henry Ford Museum in Detroit, Michigan, and converted to a snack stand selling soft drinks, chips, and probably an Oscar Mayer wiener or two.

Milton Black's Wiener Proclaimed Cultural Landmark!

Perhaps the most famous frankfurter-shaped café is the Tail o' the Pup fast food stand in West Hollywood, California. This 17-foot hot dog, slathered in mustard and tucked between enormous stucco buns, does double duty as popular local eatery and international icon of all that is

Tail O' the Pup—The Los Angeles landmark hot dog stand located at San Vincente and Beverly Boulevard.

pop. With cameos in countless commercials, videos, and films (*LA Story, Ruthless People*), the Pup is also a favorite stop for celebrities from Jay Leno to Luke Perry.

Constructed in 1945, the building was actually designed seven years earlier by Milton J. Black. In 1987, the building narrowly escaped demolition by a developer who'd purchased the site for a new hotel. Designated a cultural landmark by the city, it was moved a couple blocks away to its current location, where it now doles out the dogs seven days a week.

The Big Chicken

The "Big Chicken" in Marietta, Georgia, is indeed that—56 full feet of towering sheet-metal poultry. Now open as a Kentucky Fried Chicken franchise, the seven-story bird was built in 1963 by S.R. "Tubby" Davis to seduce motorists off the I-41 and into his chicken 'n burger joint, "Johnny Reb's Chick, Chuck and Shake." Selling the Kentucky Fried variety since 1974, the location was among the most lucrative of the Colonel's many franchises until a new highway parallel to the I-41 drew away business.

The Chicken was further threatened in 1993 when it was badly rattled by a storm and KFC balked at undertaking the extensive repairs. But the people of Marietta wanted that bird back and raised such a fuss that the corporation not only patched the structure, they also refurbished the original mechanics that once allowed the wind to animate the bird's beak and eyes. This machinery had given out decades ago and had never been repaired, thanks in part to a flaw in the original design that caused vibrations from the moving parts to shudder through the structure so violently that windows would occasionally burst out of their frames.

Such inconveniences have now been engineered away, and visitors can not only drop in for a drumstick but also linger over an exhibit of historical Big Chicken photos, press clippings, and old bits of sheet metal the bird molted during repairs.

Lost World of Chicken Boy

A more humanoid big chicken became an unlikely cult figure in a story beginning in the early-'80s with the closing of the Chicken Boy Restaurant in downtown Los Angeles. Perched atop the restaurant for more than 20 years was the restaurant's iconic namesake: a 22-foot fiberglass human male recapitated with the head of a chicken.

Chicken Boy. A pop culture masterpiece miraculously saved from the wrecking ball.

Architectural conservationists and lovers of kitsch alike rallied to save the endangered mutant, but after rescuing him from the wrecking ball, no museum or collector could be found to accommodate the displaced giant. Eventually, Chicken Boy was relegated to a warehouse rented by Future Studio, a graphics design firm.

In the "Chicken Boy Catalog for a More Perfect World," the man-bird's mythology blossomed briefly, even generating a short "mocu-drama" by Tom Dusenbery, in which an actor in precisely matched costuming portrays the troubled bird. Posing the question: "Can an accordian-playin', grain alcohol-drinkin', lovesick chicken-headed boy find love, fame, and a healthy psyche in Southern California?" the film's poignancy was largely lost on an uncaring world, and Chicken Boy continues to languish in ever more remote warehouses of Southern California.

Saluting the Banana: Size Matters

Carnivores are not the only ones exhibiting larger than life devotion to favorite foods. Fruits and vegetables also inspire their share of grandiose visions. That most evocative of fruits, the banana, has stimulated some of the grandest—roughly 43 by 16 feet in certain cases.

These dimensions scaled up proportionally from a prize-winning specimen selected at a regional agricultural fair describe the mammoth ferrous concrete behemoth that greets visitors to Coffs Harbor, Australia.

Erected in 1964, this fruity colossus was originally intended as a roadside advertisement for produce stands operated by agriculturist John Landi. He was inspired to construct what's now known simply as "The Big Banana" after seeing the colossal pineapple towering over the Dole cannery in Hawaii. Over the years, the Big Banana grew from the focal point of a handful of vendor's stalls into the centerpiece of a sprawling bananacentric tourist wonderland, featuring exhibits on banana farming, rides, gift shops, and a banana-milk bar.

More Giant Fruit

Others pay tribute to favorite fruits in a variety of monuments scattered throughout the country. Some heroically scaled replicas are raised as gestures of

You Say Monro, I Say Monroe

Bombshell in Burlap

Far less erotic than the banana and hardly as exotic as the orange, the earthy potato, nonetheless, has its share of enthusiastic devotees. Testimony exists in the form of numerous potato behemoths that dot the North American landscape from Driggs, and Pocatallo, Idaho, to New Brunswick, Canada.

glamorous past, its space-age adventures as an experimental subject on the Space Shuttle, a Mr. Potato Head retrospective, and a short documentary on the art and science of potato farming. A sign promising "Free Taters for Out-of-Staters" is good to its word, and disgruntled natives are placated by a slightly smaller

World's largest potato chip.

There is also an enormous recumbent potato languishing outside the World Potato Exhibition in Blackfoot, Idaho. This storehouse of spudly lore is rivaled only by Munich's Potato Museum in its extensive exploration of everyone's favorite tuber.

The Blackfoot collection's official prize jewel is "The World's Largest Potato Chip," authenticated by the Guinness Book of World Records at a whopping 24 by 14 inches. Ensconced in a vitrine of honor, the chip exhibited unfortunately does not come from a proportionately monstrous tater but, rather, is a reconstituted Pringles chip donated by Proctor and Gamble. The museum features other exhibits showcasing the potato's

sign offering the same "to the local who's vocal." Mutant Pringles aside, the real unacknowledged treasure of the collection is the display on potato sack couture. Featured is the ceremonial suit once belonging to Idaho's original Potato Commissioner. Tailored entirely of burlap, it would probably qualify for the ultimate in potato sack apparel, were it not outshone by the nearby image of Marilyn Monroe barely contained within a form-fitting Twin Falls potato sack. Dreamed up as a stunt for the press by one of the starlet's publicists in the early-'40s, the photograph unquestionably serves the intention of demonstrating that Monroe would indeed look great "even in a potato sack."

civic pride, while others are created with more commercial interests in mind. Most are to be found along the country's interstates where barn-sized facsimiles speak more clearly than even the largest billboard.

If you want to sell orange juice, for instance, the folks in Redfield, Arizona, figured that a juice stand in the shape of a house-sized Valencia Orange would best do the job. In Lemon Grove, California, an immense concrete lemon at a downtown intersection lets you know where you are, while visitors to Strawberry Point, Idaho, can orient themselves by the town's gargantuan berry. In Gaffney, South Carolina, peach farmers

El Cajon, CA—Once home of the world's largest orange.

go about their business beneath the shadow of a peach-shaped water tower, while in Colborne, Ontario, in Harcourt, Australia, and in Winchester, Virginia, it's giant apples that loom large on the horizon.

In Sunnyvale, California, they idolize

> If you want toast with your eggs, there's a giant loaf stuck up on a pylon over what used to be a bakery in Montgomery, Alabama. On the way there from Washington, swing by Collinsville, Illinois, if you want ketchup on your eggs. They've got a converted water tower painted to resemble a 70-foot-tall bottle of Brooks Catsup circa 1949.

no single fruit but, rather, celebrate the entire fruit rainbow with an immense water tower painted to represent a can of fruit cocktail. Originally the site of the Libby's cannery, alleged birthplace of the cocktail, the facility is no more, and the trademark can has been repainted to represent a more generic cocktail of fruit bits.

Breakfast of the Giants

To further illustrate our nation's wealth of architectural food, consider this scenario:

You wake up one morning hungry as hell and one hundred feet tall. As a giant, your choices will naturally incline toward giant breakfast foods. If you happen to have awakened in the U.S., you're in luck, as this country supplies a well-balanced array of gargantuan breakfast options.

If you want eggs, you've got quite a few to choose from. There is an enormous egg in Newberry, South Carolina, or another giant egg in Mentone, Indiana. There's also a large egg in Winlock, Washington, and, though it's no bigger than the 11-footer in Indiana, it's nearer the world's largest frying pan in Long Beach, Washington—so that's probably your most convenient bet.

If you want toast with your eggs, there's a giant loaf stuck up on a pylon over what used to be a bakery in Montgomery, Alabama. On the way there from Washington, swing by Collinsville, Illinois, if you want ketchup on your eggs. They've got a converted water tower painted to resemble a 70-foot-tall bottle of Brooks Catsup circa 1949.

You'll probably want milk too, and a giant bottle can either be had from the former Richland Dairy in Richmond, Virginia, or from the abandoned dairy up on the Charles River in Boston.

If you decided not to traipse over to Illinois for ketchup or Alabama for bread, then you might want to stay put near your frying pan in Washington and just pick up your milk from the bottle in Spokane.

If you'd rather skip the eggs altogether, you've got plenty of enormous dough-nuts scattered around the country to choose from (including a drive-through specimen housing a donut shop near

Randy's Donuts, yet another Los Angeles landmark.

Los Angeles, California). Or if oatmeal's your thing, you can try the converted water tower in Oatmeal, Texas.

Whatever you go with, you will surely want coffee. Now with coffee, your choices tend to come down to a choice of celebrity endorsement. Tacoma, Washington, offers a giant coffee pot named "Bob's Java Jive," an amazing Tiki-themed dive where legendary surf-rockers The Ventures once played as the house band. If you're not so big on the surf theme, Stanton, Iowa, offers a more sedate choice. Their towering coffee-pot-shaped water tower is dedicated to hometown girl Virginia Christine who, as "Mrs. Olsen," got thou-sands hooked on Folger's "mountain grown" finest.

Bon Appétit!

The world's largest bottle of ketchup is located in Collinsville, IL.

CHEWING on METAPHORS

"*I am for U.S. Government Inspected Art, grade A art, Regular Price art, Yellow Ripe art, Extra Fancy art, Ready-to-Eat art, Best-for-less art, Ready-to-cook art, Fully cleaned art, Spend Less art, Eat Better art, Ham art, Pork art, chicken art, tomato art, banana art, apple art, turkey art, cake art, cookie art.*"

—Claes Oldenburg, May 1961

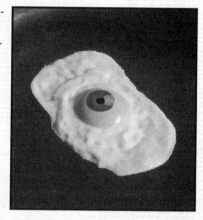

Food works in the same way as art. It draws us in with tantalizing aromas, vivid colors, and varied shapes. But aroma, color, and shape are not the most important thing about food. Its most essential task— keeping us alive— goes on invisibly as nutrients sneak into our bloodstream. Ditto for art. You don't eat it for the meaning, you eat it for the taste, but the meaning sneaks in as you digest it.

Food keeps us alive. Some would say meaning helps with that too.

Anyway, it's flattering for the vagaries of "art" and "meaning" to be associated with something as real and essential as food. It makes art look good and solid. It's no wonder then that many artists have used food metaphorically.

A very few instances examined in this chapter represent the chef's achievements as analogy for all mortal endeavors. But more often the focus is not so purely aesthetic, and most often it's less sympathetic, reminding us instead of specific or general forms of cultural dyspepsia.

In these critiques, the kitchen pops up as a metaphor for feminine enslavement or the table as the prison of etiquette. Fine food represents bourgeois decadence or materialistic gluttony. Food packaging signifies an enfeebling distancing from our primal roots or comments on our irrepressible tendency to conceptualize along certain lines.

Naturally, the most uncritical of the bunch discussed here are the advertising artists, who in trying to sell food reach into the brain's most virginal nooks and crannies and end up speaking an archetypal baby talk that in academic circles could pass as "mythic."

All of them, however, basically want the same thing: to make you hungry. Maybe they want to make you hungry for a certain brand of peas, for social change, or maybe they just want to make you hungry so you can feel the space within your own stomach.

■ YUMMY CELLULOID ■

Babette's Feast

Receiving the Academy Award for Best Foreign Film in 1987, this French film set in nineteenth-century Denmark tells the story of Babette—a wizard of *haute cuisine* displaced from her native France to a desolate village on the windswept coast of Denmark. Following up a distant connection in her search for employment, she becomes housekeeper to a grimly puritanical and domineering minister. Somewhere amidst all the austere living, Babette happens to win the lottery, and when the old patriarch kicks it she offers to donate her winnings to finance the titular feast, a sort of postmortem birthday celebration for the old spoil sport and his priggish congregation. After a bit of light comedy with provincials wriggling uncomfortably over such fine food bought with gamblers' winnings, Babette's financial and spiritual generosity are given their due with sumptuous photography of the exquisite feast. Hope (and maybe even a hint of sensuality) blossoms in that barren region, and audiences go home craving expensive food. Despite its fable-like simplicity, this film remains one of the more pleasing "food films," with its healthy balance of historical chill and soft-focus warmth.

A Chef in Love

Like Babette, Pascal Ichac, a wandering

French chef and apostle of *haute cuisine*, is the protagonist of *A Chef in Love*, a 1997 production filmed in the former Soviet state of Georgia. Unlike Babette, however, Ichac is an outright hedonist, intellectually drooling over opera, women, and food. He falls in love with a refined Georgian princess and begins a passionate affair. Together they open a Shangri-La of a restaurant, but like Babette, meet with ideological opposition. In this case it's Communist revolutionaries who take a dim view of his temple of bourgeois decadence. They confiscate the restaurant for the People and the princess for a commanding officer.

The film stumbles on for a while after that, showing Ichac's various half-hearted attempts to reclaim some joy or defy fate. It also staggers back and forth in time, indifferently leaping from pre-Revolutionary Georgia to the present day with scenes of the next generation examining letters and diary entries documenting the smoldering ruin of the former *bon vivant*.

The critical reaction to this film was cool, probably because of the way in which it includes these merciless morning-after sequences tastefully omitted from *Babette*.

Big Night

In the case of *Big Night*, the bad guy is commercialism, flash, and noise substituted for the loftier subtleties of fine cuisine. Immigrating from Italy to New Jersey in the 1950s, two brothers set up a restaurant and confront this enemy as personified in a rival eatery where substandard cuisine is bolstered by a happening house

"Louis Prima? Here? I'll make my timballo di maccheroni!"

From the Dalicatessen

Surrealist Recipies for Film

Luis Buñuel Can't Go Home

The Surrealists regarded bourgeois institutions such as the dinner party with overt disdain. Long after the movement's heyday, the filmmaker Luis Buñuel (who had collaborated cinematically with Salvador Dali on Un Chien Andalou back in 1928) gave vent to the Surrealist contempt for these middle-class gatherings in his 1962 film The Exterminating Angel.

In the film, a dinner party mysteriously refuses to end. The captive guests at first cover politely for their inexplicable inability to leave and settle in to stay overnight on the sofas and rugs. As this continues night after night, primitive instincts take over. A wandering sheep is captured, butchered, and roasted over a fire of broken furniture. Guests quench their thirst by chopping through a wall to open a water pipe. Two lovers commit suicide and the bodies are piled in a closet. Concerned outsiders are unable to enter. Soldiers ordered to breach an entrance are unable to carry out commands. In all instances, the unwritten law prevails.

Ten years later, Buñuel followed up this film with The Discreet Charm of the Bourgeoisie, balancing the first film with this story of two couples who endlessly discuss intentions of throwing a dinner party and even sit down to a meal together but are repeatedly constrained from eating.

Biting Critiques

Buñuel is one of the few filmmakers able to claim a historical connection with the original art movement, yet many Hollywood latecomers come close to the Surrealist's agenda of stripping away the veneer of rationality to reveal primitive or absurd impulses.

The charming bourgeoise engage in a little pre-dinner gunplay.

Cannibalism popping up amidst civilized ladies and gentlemen is a favorite cinematic image for the theme. In 1991, Jean-Pierre Jeunet and Marc Caro spun out a tale along those lines in their film Delicatessen, set in a decadent post apocalyptic future where base instincts coexist with a desire for fine dining.

Their story involves a former clown, a "fool" innocently volunteering his services as a handyman for a

Yummy! Charleton Heston just can't get enough of those little green squares.

crumbling tenement where the landlord makes his living by butchering humans for meat (a commodity now more valuable than gold). Thanks to their quiet complicity, the primitive tenement dwellers—referred to in the film as "cave dwellers"—enjoy an ironically sophisticated diet provided by the landlord's delicatessen.

Likewise, the film Parents (1989) jostles the ideals of society against savagery. Set in the red-meat-eating 1950s, in a quintessentially uptight suburbia, the story focuses on the source of a young boy's constant nightmares of backyard barbecues consisting of human flesh. The film is filled with implicit puns on the notions of conformity, "swallowing," and "being swallowed," as well as the "dog-eat-dog" metaphor of '50's capitalism.

The food-chain metaphor makes a class-conscious appearance in Stephen Sondheim's Sweeney Todd: The Demon Barber of Fleet Street (1979), the story of a barber turned cannibal-entrepreneur. In this case, the murderous barber who sells his victims as ingredients for meat pies becomes a sort of folk hero of the downtrodden, encouraging London's poor to literally "eat the rich," á lá Jonathan Swift's A Modest Proposal.

In Soylent Green (1973), the logical conclusion of this brutal ethic is played out in a world circa 2022, in which humans reproduce faster than their food supplies. Charlton Heston plays a cop who accidentally discovers the yucky source of soylent green, a cheap government-produced food source.

band. In the face of all this, lofty brother #1 voices the opinion, "to eat good food is to be close to God" and rants about "the rape of cuisine," while less-lofty brother #2 listens dutifully and nervously tends the register.

In this instance, the *Big Night* is a single meal (like Babette's). This meal consists of the monumentally baroque *timballo di maccheroni,* a four-course tower of baroquely layered meatballs, filled pastas, and other goodies encased in a pastry shell. The idea behind all this is to wow a traveling Italian-American celebrity (Louis Prima), and thereby create a buzz for the restaurant, but the film leaves serious doubt as to whether the gambit pays off financially.

Success or failure, the director's operatic staging of the all-important night creates a sense of fleeting triumph, though the film's most powerful scene takes place the following morning as the two brothers share a humble omelet. Shot without dialogue and in painfully real time, the episode strikingly conveys the less glamorous yet more fundamental role of the cook as one who provides sustenance and solace rather than edification.

> ***Big Night's*** **most powerful scene takes place the following morning as the two brothers share a humble omelet. Shot without dialogue and in painfully real time, the episode strikingly conveys the less glamorous yet more fundamental role of the cook as one who provides sustenance and solace rather than edification.**

■ COMFORTS OF THE TABLE ■

> *"The joys of the table belong equally to all ages, conditions, countries and times; they mix with all other pleasures and remain the last to console us for the others' loss."*

—Anthelme Brillat-Savarin, early nineteenth-century French gastronome

Nourishing a Flagging Relationship

The term "comfort food" became popular in the 1990s. It's an expression of nostalgia usually applied to foods like macaroni and cheese by those whose tastes have moved on to *maccheroni con parmigiana,* i.e., a more heartfelt way of describing "guilty pleasures."

The concept's at the very core of the 1991 film *Fried Green Tomatoes,* based on a novel written by Fannie Flagg. An obviously homesick Alabama transplant to Hollywood, Flagg's been involved in film and television since the age of 19, and

her nostalgia is emphasized in the novel by its flashback structure, which has nursing home resident Idgie Threadgoode relating Depression-era anecdotes from her small Alabama diner. The listener, in this case a woman in the midst of marriage difficulties, and the old woman's sense of perspective and the whiff of tradition from the diner's no-nonsense food, presumably help ground the younger woman in her time of instability.

Tears in the Batter

Another "food film" filled with yearning, but more acute passion, also began as a novel penned by a woman involved with the film industry. Laura Esquivel's novel *Like Water for Chocolate*, set in turn-of-the-century Mexico, became the number-one best-seller in Mexico in 1990 and was made into a film in 1993, setting a record in American box offices as the top-grossing foreign film.

This time, it's frustrated erotic desire that gets things bubbling in the kitchen. It begins with protagonist Tita's true love proposing to her and her traditionalist mother prohibiting the marriage on the grounds that, as the youngest, Tita's obliged to remain at home as the mother's caretaker.

The film has the flavor of magical realism and is spiced with uncanny omens of Tita's romantic tragedy and culinary consolation. Her birth, for instance, takes place on a delivery bed improvised from a kitchen table piled high with tear-provoking onions, which produce preternatural floods of tears drying into piles of salt.

As a means of staying close to her true love, Tita accepts the mother's suggestion that the older sister instead marry the young man, and then the lucky girl is assigned the duty of creating

> *Like Water for Chocolate* has the flavor of magical realism and is spiced with uncanny omens of Tita's romantic tragedy and culinary consolation. Her birth, for instance, takes place on a delivery bed improvised from a kitchen table piled high with tear-provoking onions, which produce preternatural floods of tears drying into piles of salt.

the couple's wedding cake. Her tears fall into the batter with supernatural results as wedding guests consuming the cake likewise fall into outbursts of unbridled weeping.

Like Water for Chocolate may have given one of the more literal treatments to this theme of emotions spilling over into the cooking pot, but it's certainly not alone in tackling the subject.

Family Formalities

Also communicating nonverbally through cooking is the semi-retired Taiwanese Chef Chu, who shows his love and support for three daughters in the film *Eat, Drink, Man, Woman*. In this film, as in the 1997 film *Soul Food*, a traditional Sunday dinner is depicted as an all-important ritual binding a family that

Men, women, and children eat and drink.

Damnit Jim, I'm a Doctor, Not a Chef!

Let the Force Do the Dishes

When we love something very much, we "eat it up." We want to incorporate it orally. This can apply to fleshy parts of the body for a lover or to sacramental bread for someone deeply devoted to their faith. But what's a science fiction fan to do? There's not much taste to be had from cardboard lobby cards, and plastic action figures are hard on the esophagus. Luckily, a number of sci-fi oriented cookbooks have been published within the last few years to remedy this problem.

The year 1998 saw the publication of Robin Davis' Star Wars Cookbook: Wookiee Cookies and Other Galactic Recipes, wherein aspiring masters of Jedi culinary arts can learn to make C-3PO Pancakes, Jedi Juice Bars, Obi-Wan Kebabs, Sandtrooper Sandies, Ewok Eats, Boba Fett-uccine, Tusken Raider Taters, Twin Sun Toast, and Yoda Soda. The most endearing feature of the book, however, would have to be the illustrations consisting of miniature dioramas of Star Wars action figures conducting their adventures amidst the foods, i.e., a small plastic Jabba the Hutt glowering over a pit of slimy lime Jabba Jell-O Jiggle.

While that's all fine for the more playful Star Wars fan, devotees of Star Trek have had longer to develop a more earnest allegiance to their love object. Beginning with a short-lived television show in the 1960s, the series went on to spin off several theatrical films as well as a Next Generation family of shows broadcast from 1987 and into the twenty first century.

With more emphasis on "authenticity" than fun, and punning recipe titles, The Star Trek Cookbook appeared in 1999, authored by Majel Barrett-Rodenberry—editor and wife of series creator, Gene Rodenberry—Ethan Phillips, and William J. Birnes.

Written in the personae "Starfleet Chef Neelix," the book's recipes are extrapolated from three decades of television shows and movies, as well as a number of novelizations, fan concordances, and encyclopedias. The collection not only includes recipes for realistic (yet more-or-less palatable) re-creations of Klingon's Rokeg Blood Pie, Blood Wine, worm-like Gagh, and Ferengi Slug Liver, but also accommodates terrestrial preferences with teatime recipes such as those enjoyed by the good Captain Picard (watercress sandwiches, Madeleines, Earl Grey tea, and so forth). Even actor Leonard Nimoy contributes a bit of Yiddish-vulcan nostalgia with Kasha Varnishkas a la Vulcan.

Even before all those spin-offs, the original series inspired its own cookbook. Published in 1978, The Official Star Trek Cooking Manual by Mary Ann Piccard featured recipes for Captain Kirk's favorite apple pie, as well as for Plomeek, "a thick orange Vulcan soup" concocted, in this case, from pureed pumpkin and served cold.

The ever-popular Plomeek is back again in the most recent 1999-2000 publication The Star Trek Cookbook: Food from the 23rd Century and Beyond by Theresa Robberson. Tapping into this apparently inexhaustible market, Robberson comes up with 130 recipes for final frontier food, including Bularian Canapés, Cardassian Taspar, and Heart of Targ.

needs support in troubled times.

Director Ang Lee of *Eat, Drink, Man, Woman*, however, shows some ambivalence toward this kind of communication done with the mouth full. Short on words but long on culinary skill, Chu is depicted as somewhat misguided in giving his daughters what they need most. The stultifying effects of tradition are clearly portrayed as the daughters react with frustration to the old-fashioned formality of these meals (no matter how much Ang Lee's camera delights in these exquisite feasts).

■ THROWING PIES ■

From the Ground Up

Though director Mack Sennett (of Keystone Kop fame) deserves every bit of recognition he's received for popularizing the pie fight as a slapstick essential, it's unlikely the gag originated with him. Sennett, like all directors in the early days, drew their talent from the theater (and from burlesque and vaudeville in the case of comedy). And as any thespian who knows his history can tell you, the idea of throwing pies or other food on stage is a tradition as old as theater itself.

Oddly enough, it was probably during a drama rather than a comedy that the gag was first employed, and it was most likely a member of the audience rather than a playwright or actor who first employed it.

The original Elizabethan theater drew a mixed crowd, and the more disreputable element, the "groundlings," sat not in the shaded comfortable seats, but on the ground immediately in front of the stage in the direct sun. The discomfort of the hot sun and rough seats made these the cheapest seats in the house, yet they also afforded the best vantage point for hurling rotten fruit or vegetables at actors who failed to please the groundlings, either by performing poorly or having the misfortune of being scripted into tedious scenes.

It's not hard to imagine how an actor suffering the indignity of a full-frontal barrage of slimy food might indeed become the high point of a mediocre play. A few decades later, when the ancient Romans' equestrian circuses were reincarnated in Europe, food naturally became a part of the act when many theatrical actors—who had joined the traveling troupes as clowns—borrowed on their stage experience by utilizing the crowd-pleasing effects of projectile food.

As mainstream theater evolved into an indoor activity of more refined sensibilities, food-hurling audience interaction may have been discouraged, but in the melodramas of America's wild west and the British music hall shows, such rowdy involvement was often part of the evening's entertainment. Both these forms contributed to vaudeville and, therefore, to early Hollywood's bag of comedic tricks.

Mack Sennett

"A pie in the face, provided the recipient does not anticipate it, has no equal in slapstick comedy. It can reduce dignity to nothing in seconds."

— Mack Sennett

Before directing his first pie-in-the-face scene, Sennett used rotten vegetables hurled by the audience at a lousy musical

Oliver enjoys a cup of joe in-between pie fights while Stanley, well, Stanley's just being Stanley.

combo in *The Ragtime Band* in 1913. He must've liked the effect, because later that same year he had Mabel Normand—who had appeared in *The Ragtime Band*—fling the first cinematic pie into Roscoe "Fatty" Arbuckle's mug in *A Noise from the Deep.*

Substituting soft pies for stinking and heavy vegetables was certainly a welcome switch for the actors, and the effect turned out to be even more spectacular

(with a little tweaking of the recipe). Sennett's pie-makers made extra-sloppy throws using gloppy wheat-paste topped with whipped cream. For blondes and light-colored clothing, dark berries were added to the mix for better contrast. Six to eight feet was said to be optimal throwing distance, though Arbuckle could nail a target ten feet away. Aim was sometimes assisted by stringing the pies on fishing line, and surreal double flips and other fancy throws were often obtained by puppeteering the pies from above.

Laurel and Hardy

Laurel and Hardy were no amateurs when it came to tossing pies. In fact, they are responsible for what most film lovers regard as the ultimate cinematic pie fight.

The 1927 short *Battle of the Century*—lost for many years and now partially restored—has Hardy in need of money and taking out an insurance policy on Laurel. To see to it that Laurel will incur the necessary injuries, Hardy plants a banana peel in his path. Laurel never makes it to the peel, but one of the many who do slip and fall is a pie vendor who has arrived dangerously armed with a wagon full of pies. Spotting Hardy as the perpetrator, he quickly dispatches a pie that misses Ollie and hits an innocent passerby instead—the classic cinematic means of enlarging a pie fight.

As more and more pedestrians are thus engaged in the melee, the exchange quickly escalates from pie fight to pie war, and the camera pulls back to reveal

"You're gonna pay for that pie! It's ruined!"

an astounding view: an entire city block of pie-hurling madness. To realize this groundbreaking scene, director Hal Roach budgeted in the entire daily output of the Los Angeles Pie Company, the biggest supplier in town—amounting to a pastry apocalypse of over three thousand pies!

The Three Stooges: Film to TV

The Three Stooges carried this pie-throwing nonsense on from the '30s into the '60s, using pie gags in about 10 of their films, including *The Pest Man Wins* (1951) and *Pies and Guys* (1958). But by far their finest pie film is *In the Sweet Pie and Pie* (1941), with a total of 33 on-target (mostly facial) pies, including one groundbreaking accidental auto-pieing by Curly. The Stooges also helped bring the pie gag into the television era. Indeed, one of their early co-stars from *Three Little Pigskins* (1934) was Lucille Ball. Besides creating her notorious mess as a new chocolate factory employee, Lucy also took a pie while dressed as a clown in one episode of "I Love Lucy," found herself covered in pie makings and other kitchen mess during her cinematic venture with Desi Arnaz in *The Long Long Trailer* (1954), and was smeared with yet one more pie in an episode of her 1960's "The Lucy Show."

Soupy Sales

But when it comes to television, the real Prince of Pies has got to be Milton

> **B**ut when it comes to television, the real Prince of Pies has got to be Milton Hines (though you'd know him as "Soupy Sales"). He's thrown at least nineteen thousand by now, and that's including some pretty high-profile profiles like Frank Sinatra and Sammy Davis Jr. (Would you pie a man with Sinatra's connections?).

Hines (though you'd know him as "Soupy Sales"). He's thrown at least nineteen thousand by now, and that's including some pretty high-profile profiles like Frank Sinatra and Sammy Davis Jr. (Would *you* pie a man with Sinatra's connections?).

Soupy began his career as a script-writer and DJ, eventually launching a kiddy show of his own, *The Soupy Sales Show*, first broadcast in Los Angeles in the early '60s and then aired nationally by 1966. At the height of the "spy music" craze, Soupy also released a chart-topping recording entitled "Spy with a Pie."

Soupy's success was fueled along by a contemporary nostalgia for the slapstick era. In 1961, a documentary about Sennett and his ilk, *Days of Thrills and Laughter,* was released, giving audiences a simultaneous peek into the past as well as the future of film. By the middle of the decade, "old-time" pie fights and undercranked camera (speeded-up motion) were firmly re-established in the language of film comedy.

■ ADULTS PLAY WITH FOOD TOO ■

Wild Strawberries

Tickling two of the ticket buying public's most basic appetites, sex combined with food also satisfies a third appetite for novelty. As such, this synergistic pairing has served a number of films as a particularly delicious selling point.

Among these, the film *9 1/2 Weeks* (1986) was one to generate perhaps more controversy than ticket sales, but it's nonetheless widely remembered for its erotic use of food. The plot, as it is, revolves around a mysterious Wall Street exec entering into a sexual relationship of sado-masochistic play with an art dealer. But forget about the characters! What's important here is the sex, and in particular which foods are involved: strawberries, honey, champagne, and just about anything else that can be pulled off the shelves of the art dealer's refrigerator. Specifically aimed at the art house market, the film expands upon the sense of cosmopolitan kink first lubricated by that butter Marlon Brando ordered Maria Schneider to apply in *Last Tango in Paris* (1972).

The '70s not only saw Brando and Schneider tangoing in Paris but also witnessed a food-slathered Ann Margaret wriggling in the film *Tommy* (1975). Though the effect is sexual, the context is satiric. Margaret portrays the guilt-stricken mother of Tommy, who, after attempting to drown her regrets with champagne downed in front of the television, is literally carried away in a flood of advertisements for chocolate, baked beans, and other messy substances spewed from the TV in the course of her drunken hallucination.

A more recent example of food, sex, and celluloid would be in the "Spaghetti Eastern" *Tampopo* (1986). This story of a struggling cook's attempts to rejuvenate a noodle house with the help of an old west-style "mysterious stranger" type

features a side-plot with a gangster and his lover whose hedonistic repertoire emphasizes food. Particularly memorable is their sexual play with a raw egg, the yolk of which is gently coaxed over the woman's breasts, across her naked body, and from mouth to mouth without breaking.

It's Not Dirty—It's Literature!

While there is plenty of bedroom bawdiness in the 1963 cinematic adaptation of Henry Fielding's *Tom Jones*, one of the most erotically charged episodes takes place at a table where Albert Finney as Jones and Joyce Redman as his mistress give new meaning to the phrase "oral sex." Anticipating a rendezvous after dinner, they pass the meal memorably, exchanging smoldering glances, tossing back wine, slurping up pears, and sucking the meat off chicken legs in an overtly naughty way.

A few years later, director Ken Russel would take on more earnest literary material with his adaptation of D.H. Lawrence's *Women in Love*, in which Alan Bates as Rupert Birkin makes an unforgettable erotic spectacle out of merely peeling a fig. Lawrence himself was occasionally preoccupied with fruits (the kind on trees and perhaps otherwise), at least as far as they suggested themes of fertility and eroticism. He even wrote an entire series of poems called *Fruits* while living in rural Sicily in the early-'20s.

"Forbidden Fruits" happens to be one of the classes of aphrodisiacs given literary treatment in Isabel Allende's 1998 publication *Aphrodite: A Memoir of the Senses*. More often associated with tales of political oppression spun out within a context of magical realism, the Chilean Allende brings an earthy appreciation to the topic, interspersing literary musings with personal recipes for aphrodesiacal dishes of all descriptions. Her own autobiographical recollections are woven together with passages by Anais Nin, W.B.Yeats, and Pablo Neruda, as well as more than one hundred recipes for dishes such as Filet Mignon Belle Epoque, Alicante Cream Soup, and Widower's Figs.

> **T**earing at poultry with greasy fingers, gnawing, smacking, and tossing bones over his shoulder, Charles Laughton won an Oscar for Best Actor as the monarch in *The Private Life Of Henry VIII* in 1933, a film best remembered by many for Henry's imperious indifference to twentieth-century table manners.

Films to Diet For

Indulging the appetites is, however, not always as sexy as it is in Allende's memoirs, Lawrence's prose, or Tom Jones' rakish adventures. Sometimes it's downright disgusting.

Among filmmakers, we find this more jaundiced view of the topic first in 1925 with Eric von Stroheim's *Greed*. Epic, in all senses of the word, this film, cut down from Stroheim's original 10-hour running length to a mere 7 hours, tells the tale of the MacTeagues and their moral dissolution after winning the lottery. One of the most graphic illustrations of this is the frenzied gorging that takes place at the MacTeauges' wedding banquet.

Tearing at poultry with greasy fingers, gnawing, smacking, and tossing bones

over his shoulder, Charles Laughton won an Oscar for Best Actor as the monarch in *The Private Life Of Henry VIII* in 1933,

a film best remembered by many for Henry's imperious indifference to twentieth-century table manners.

Advertised as the film with "something to offend everyone," *The Loved One* (1965) no doubt offended problem eaters everywhere with its nightmarish depiction of undertaker "Mr. Joyboy's" immensely overweight mother and her nocturnal assault on the refrigerator. 1973's *Blow Out* graphically depicted the excesses of four bored middle age "success stories" who hole up in a luxurious Italian villa with the intent of eating themselves to death. Ten years later, these excesses were outdone when *Monty Python's The Meaning of Life* left heavy eaters with a phobia of after-dinner mints thanks to a scene in which a grotesquely stuffed restaurant patron literally explodes after hesitantly downing this final addition to his gargantuan meal.

Gluttony: Cinematic Sin and Sideshow Attraction

In 1990, epicurean excess of another kind was the object of satiric treatment in *The Freshman*. In a curiously comic recasting, Marlon Brando does his Don Corleone thing as the boss of a highly

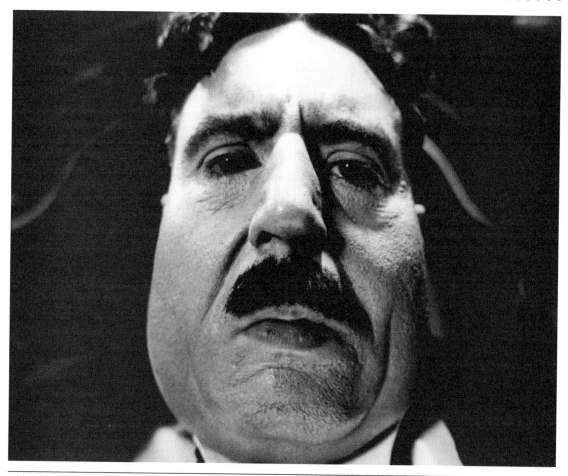

The infamous Mr. Cresote from Monty Python's The Meaning of Life. *"May I have my after-dinner mint, now, please?"*

suspicious importing business in need of a stooge to make deliveries. First-year film school student Matthew Broderick is the man for the job, and the business turns out to be one trafficking in endangered animals imported for consumption by novelty starved gourmets.

In 1995, the film *Seven* rode out the early '90s serial killer fad, depicting the nasty adventures of a murderous moralist who themes each of his killings according to one of the Seven Deadly Sins. Our first taste of this rather unappetizing world comes with Gluttony's leftovers, i.e., a forensic exploration of the decomposing flab of a glutton force-fed to death.

Shock effects produced by the grossly omnivorous can easily draw a crowd, whether on film or on stage. One of the most memorable performers in the punk-rock-flavored "new vaudeville" of the '90s was the gastronomically invincible "Enigma" of the Jim Rose Circus. This magnificently tattooed beast not only displayed amazing ability in downing all manner of living insects but was most notorious for his "anatomical smoothie," a vile concoction of yogurt, blue sports drink, bong water, and ginseng ("for health reasons"). Loathsome enough the first time down, this brew would be swallowed and then recycled via stomach pump in order to be swallowed again.

Enigma has since been replaced in the Jim Rose Circus by the equally fascinating Amago. While his primary aim is the "pursuit of a radical full body transformation"—including a wide variety of piercings and tattoos, as well as tongue splitting, implants, and teeth filing—Amago has also been known to swallow worms, insects, and other assorted creepy crawlies by the handful. And Amago has his own version of Enigma's "anatomical smoothie" act. During the performance of "The

> **W**hile his primary aim is the "pursuit of a radical full body transformation"—including a wide variety of piercings and tattoos, as well as tongue splitting, implants, and teeth filing—Amago has also been known to swallow worms, insects, and other assorted creepy crawlies by the handful.

Gavage," Amago places a large tube in his nose and runs it into his stomach. A pump is attached and yellow juice, followed by a blue sports drink, is pumped into his stomach. The result? Out comes a green mixture, of course!

of molten lead, boiling oil, and red hot iron were reported on as early as 1920 by Harry Houdini in his book *Miracle Mongers and Their Methods.*

The Cook, the Thief, His Wife, Her Lover, Culture, History, Art, and so Forth

Lurid shock effects and a neo-classical cool, gluttony, and minimalism, combine disconcertingly in British director Peter Greenaway's 1989 film *The Cook, the Thief, His Wife and Her Lover.* The production is staged almost entirely in a palatial temple of haute cuisine (over which the Cook presides and where the Thief and his Wife are to be found every night dining with the thief's scurrilous band of lackeys). The restaurant is also the point of rendezvous between the Wife and the Lover.

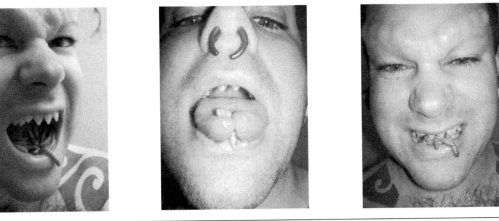

Three views of Amago eating assorted creepy crawlies. Dig the filed teeth, forked tongue, implants above the brow, tattoos . . .

But live performances such as these predate MTV by more than a few decades, and the techniques involved in swallowing living snakes, umbrellas, spoonfuls

With characteristic detachment, Greenaway's film details the moneyed boorishness of the Thief, the desperate passions of the Wife, and the inevitable

LUST...MURDER...DESSERT.
BON APPETIT!

THE COOK, THE THIEF, HIS WIFE & HER LOVER

fate of the Lover, a man of genuine intellect and sensitivity, crushed and consumed (literally) by the Thief and his Wife.

Though set in the present, the film's visual style, staging, and set design is heavy with history. The end result is to suggest parallels between the Thief's patronage of this majestic restaurant and the flowering of Renaissance art under the patronage of the criminal Medicis, the opulence of St. Peters funded by the machinations of a corrupt papacy, or other historical analogies involving low morals and high culture.

Interestingly, the restaurant in which all this plays out is called *Le Hollandaise*, and this association with the Dutch and the typically Dutch genre of still-life painting is reinforced by Greenaway's visual compositions explicitly mimicking the Dutch Masters.

Having begun his artistic career as a painter, Greenaway's visual references signify more than a game of "name that

painting." So what is it that still-life painting says about our culture? Or about gluttony, for that matter.

■ THE STILL LIFE SYNDROME ■

Moral Art

Today, the idea of painting a bowl of fruit seems astoundingly unoriginal; yet in the 1500s, after centuries of artistic effort strictly devoted to religious and myth-ological themes, the notion of a painter earnestly dedicating himself to rendering scenes of food and everyday household items must've seemed rather novel. But society was bending rules in plenty of ways at the time, and this particular development, like many others, had to do with the birth of the merchant class.

Originating in Spain, the Dutch quickly picked up on and expanded this genre as a means of celebrating the newfound luxuries being carted home to Europe by Dutch traders. While, on the one hand, Holland's Protestant work ethic kept the merchant class feverishly busy hoarding stuff, Protestant asceticism also spoiled much of the fun of their newfound wealth.

Oddly enough, this ambivalence was expressed by painting pictures of food and household luxuries. While still-life

Italian Table-Mannerists

He Painted Human Vegetables

Few artists of the sixteenth century, when called upon to paint the portrait of the Holy Roman Emperor, would choose to replace the imperial nose with a pear. Giuseppe Arcimboldo, however, was not afraid to commit such an outrage against the royal proboscis and, in fact, replaced every noble feature with an analogous shape from the vegetable kingdom.

Arcimboldo's "mosaics"—strange composite portraits composed of themed clusters of objects—had already made a name for the Italian mannerist as he worked under Emperor Maximilien II as a court painter and copyist, and the artist continued to crank them out under the reign of Maximilien's son, Emperor Rudolph.

Some of these mosaic portraits include a cook made out of food, a librarian made out of books, and a vegetable gardner, which when viewed right-side-up appears to be a still life consisting of vegetables in a metal pail but when inverted appears to be a gardener, his face composed of fruits and vegetables and wearing that pail as a hat.

Best known among these paintings are Arcimboldo's seasonal cycle in which summer is portrayed with a face assembled from fruits of the season, spring personified with features composed strictly of flowers, and winter's visage created from dead leaves and barren branches. In portraying the Emperor in the person of autumn, the artist's intent was, in fact, to represent a flattering association between the ruler and the most abundant time of the year, depicting the royal personage resplendent in the season's bounty of overripe pears, figs, grapes, and pomegranates.

The conceit is one that might not have flown in the court of another emperor, but Rudolph II was not your ordinary monarch. Arcimboldo's patron was, in fact, known for his cultivation of highly unusual interests, in particular for a preoccupation with alchemical pursuits and the occult, and for reputedly exhibiting signs of mental derangement, including the habit of keeping the fingers of a dead man on his person at all times. Rudolph's court in Prague also employed the English mathematician, astrologer, and necromancer John Dee and his assistant Edward Kelly, who regularly held discourses with angels for the benefit of the emperor. Arcimboldo's eccentric artwork fit right into an atmosphere that was "Bohemian" in all senses of the word.

Arcimboldo contributed not only painting to this lively environment but also art-directed the emperor's coronation, royal weddings, tournaments, processions, and other theatrical productions. When not designing set pieces or costumes for these extravaganzas, or engaged in his painterly activities, Arcimboldo further indulged his love for analogy in attempts to transpose music into visual form, transferring the "Pythagorean harmonic proportions of musical tons and half-tons" into colors.

After the halcyon days of Rudolph's patronage, Arcimboldo's outlandish art was dismissed as a tasteless novelty until it was "rediscovered" by the Surrealists. Today, in Arcimboldo's adopted home of Prague, the great Czech animator Jan Svankmajer continues this Surrealist infatuation with the Italian artist, using clearly Arcimbold-esque imagery and borrowing explicitly from the artist's idea of anthropomorphic assemblages in his film Dimensions of Dialogue.

painting takes obvious pleasure in luxurious surfaces and rich textures, it also historically undercut these materialistic delights by assigning to many of the objects symbolic meanings that expressed the more otherworldly values of the Church.

Wealthy burghers could, therefore, proudly decorate their homes with these handsome masterworks, knowing that the paintings testified not only to their wealth but also to their humility, since each item in the composition was painted by the artist as a symbol of vanity, a *vanitas*.

The lusciously rendered exotic lemon, for instance, represented superficial beauty hiding a sour reality. Grapes, on the other hand, might (by suggesting wine) affirm a gloomy preoccupation with the shedding of Christ's blood. The luxury of tobacco could indicate the smoke-like and insubstantial nature of material wealth. The fleeting beauty of blooming flowers could signify the transience of life, and an overturned glass might represent mortality or the toppling of the mighty.

This was the perfect moral way to have your art and eat it too!

> The lusciously rendered exotic lemon, for instance, represented superficial beauty hiding a sour reality. Grapes, on the other hand, might (by suggesting wine) affirm a gloomy preoccupation with the shedding of Christ's blood. The luxury of tobacco could indicate the smoke-like and insubstantial nature of material wealth. The fleeting beauty of blooming flowers could signify the transience of life, and an overturned glass might represent mortality or the toppling of the mighty.

■ THE BAD MANNERS OF THE AVANT-GARDE ■

Food Shenanigans

Now, since the artistic avant-garde has historically served as a goad to the bourgeois conscience, it's only natural that the neurotic conflicts embodied in still lives should be picked up three centuries later and smeared all over the respectable countenance of the middle class. Fruits, meat, and other vain symbols of the "good life" were, therefore, quintessential props in 1960's Fluxus actions and Pop happenings.

Because there are so many taboos

In 1997, art historian Jack Sheffler built this 10-foot-high, 113-square-foot pyramid at the University of Pittsburgh-Bradford out of Hostess Sno Balls and Cupcakes.

associated with what we eat and how we eat it, it's only natural that many artists have chosen to provoke spectators by the "misuse" of food. As such, during the last several decades, hundreds of variations on the theme of transgressive play with food have trickled from galleries into underground clubs, where "performance art" often takes on a much looser meaning.

Karen Finley's 1985 solo piece, *I'm an Ass Man*, generated the widely circulated myth that Finley stuck a yam where the sun don't shine. In reality, the incident involved the dramatization of a grandson who smears yams across his grandmother's buttocks; Finley was using the yams as a symbol of sexual abuse and the oppression of women.

level, is still being appealed by the government.

Her 1985 solo piece, *I'm an Ass Man*, generated the widely circulated myth that Finley stuck a yam where the sun don't shine. In reality, the incident involved the dramatization of a grandson who smears yams across his grandmother's buttocks; Finley was using the yams as a symbol of sexual abuse and the oppression of women. *I'm an Ass Man* also featured Finley's use of kidney beans to represent menstruation

Karen Finley and the Myth of Yams

Widely acclaimed as one of the most compelling performance artists of her time, Karen Finley is unfortunately known to most Americans for the controversy she generated as a result of her 1989 solo piece *We Keep Our Victims Ready*. During the piece, Finley covered herself in chocolate as a commentary on the circumstances surrounding Tawana Brawley, the young black woman who, after being found alive in a garbage bag with feces on her body, charged she had been abducted and raped. This led conservative columnists Evans and Novak to vilify Finley (they dubbed her "the chocolate-smeared woman") and her Bessie Award-winning performance in the national media. Ultimately, Finley became one of the "NEA Four," four artists whose NEA grants were denied because of the content of their art. Finley successfully sued the NEA, and her 1990 grant was finally awarded, although the reversal of the decency language provision at the NEA, which the artists won at the lower court

Karen Finley takes on Martha Stewart.

during a scene in which a young woman is nearly raped on a subway, as well as melted ice cream sandwiches to symbolize a young girl having to perform oral sex on a neighbor.

Food also played a role in Finley's play *The Theory of Total Blame*, in which Finley, as an alcoholic matriarch of a dysfunctional household, berates her son for his inability to have a relationship, and in an angry, drunken rage places meatloaf up to her crotch before smearing it all over her son's face.

In 1996, Finley attacked the house-broken mind with a send-up of the frivolous world of Martha Stewart called *Living it Up: Humorous Adventures in Hyperdomesticity*. Published by Doubleday after Crown dropped the book out of fear over objections by Stewart, Finley followed the happy homemaker's formula of a month-by-month trifling with themed projects. October, for instance, is the month to invite guests for marshmallow pancakes in the form of life-size ghosts, and June brings Father's Day commemorations with Lyle and Erik Menendez makeovers for the bedroom.

Judy Chicago Throws a Party

Just as controversial as Finley is Judy Chicago, whose *Dinner Party* installation has drawn criticism not only from the right but also from the left.

Created in 1979, and still without a permanent home due to both enormous scale and enormous controversy, the work consists of an immense triangular table upon which are laid 39 place settings allegorically uniting 39 female figures from Western history and mythology. Right-wingers aren't too happy about the hand-crafted plates with motifs suggesting female genitalia, prompting one conservative congressman in 1990 to introduce a bill threatening to cut funding to any university offering to permanently house

this piece of "clearly pornographic weird sexual art."

The settings also feature individually hand-embroidered table linens, executed in a style of needlework indicative of each symbolic guest. Chicago's complacent use of these stereotypical feminine and "frivolous" forms of expression (china-painting, needlecraft, and throwing dinner parties) is the cause of much grumbling on the left no matter how loudly the artist claims allegiance to the feminist cause.

Anorexia, Lipstick, and Lard

A visual artist using food to convey critical messages about domesticity, eating disorders, and the cult of beauty is Janine Antoni. As the daughter of a plastic surgeon, these were perhaps inevitable concerns for Antoni, who has made use of food both in performance and sculptural installation. In her 1992 piece, *Gnaw*, Antoni produced two 600-pound blocks, one of chocolate and one of lard, from which she took bites, which were chewed and spit into piles. From the mouthfuls of chewed lard, she fabricated 300 lipsticks, and from the chocolate, she molded candy hearts.

The relationship of eroticism and consumerist culture is also alluded to in Jean Dunning's installations of photographs

Three images from Jeanne Dunning's Icing.

and video of nude female models slathered in cake icing, whipped cream, and instant pudding. Superficially sweet and sexy, Dunning's art, like Antoni's lardy lipstick, also conveys a latent sense of disgust or menace. This is evident, for instance, in Dunning's claustrophobic video images of a model's head—including her eyes and ears—being gradually covered with cake icing.

Does My Meat Offend You?

When it comes to pushing buttons, meat's the food for the job. Especially when raw and bloody, it makes a fine symbol of institutionalized violence. Not surprisingly, it was during the buildup of hostilities in Vietnam that one of the first and most notorious performances using meat was staged.

Characterized by its creator, Carol Schneemann, as "a celebration of the flesh as well as an assault on repressive culture," *Meat Joy* was a 1964 performance in which Schneemann and other partially naked collaborators writhed about ecstatically amid bloody piles of raw chicken, sausages, and fish.

That same year, in New York's Washington Meat Market, in a refrigerated locker measuring approximately 14 by

Characterized by its creator, Carol Schneemann, as "a celebration of the flesh as well as an assault on repressive culture," Meat Joy was a 1964 performance in which Schneemann and other partially naked collaborators writhed about ecstatically amid bloody piles of raw chicken, sausages, and fish.

90 feet, hundreds of curious art scenesters made their way through a maze of hanging meat and bloodied lingerie fabric in a *Meat Show* organized by Robert Delford Brown. Eight uniformed police officers were also present at the festivities, dispatched by nervous city officials expecting obscenities or confrontations.

By 1972, Suzanne Lacy and others were squirming through blood and smashing raw eggs in *Ablutions*, and a few years later, in 1979, Lacy shot a video called *Learn Where Meat Comes From*, featuring her efforts to demonstrate a butcher's technique on a joint of a cow. In 1975, Paul McCarthy shot the video *Sailor's Meat*, in which he fornicates with a pile of raw hamburger while sporting black lingerie, blonde wig, and hot dog protruding from his anus. In 1979, he recreated a similar scene for *Contemporary Cure-All.*

In 1991, Canadian artist Jana Sterback was still at it with her controversial "meat

dress" created from $260 worth of raw salted steak stitched into a tunic and displayed on a hanger in the National Gallery next to a photo of a model wearing it. After six weeks of conspicuous aging, the meat was replaced by another 50 pounds of fresh steak. At least two hundred righteously huffy politicians, miffed citizens, and affronted food-aid agencies disgruntled by the "waste" protested the display by mailing leftovers to the museum.

Hearkening back to the Dutch still-life tradition, Sterback had titled the work *Vanitas: Flesh Dress for an Albino Anorectic.*

Blood Rituals: Cutting-Edge Historicism

Most famous, long-lived, and controversial among those artists working in the carnal medium would have to be the Viennese Actionist Hermann Nitsch, who, since 1965, continues to direct productions of his *Orgies Mysteries Theater*, incorporating huge quantities of raw meat, blood, and even animal sacrifice. Staged in a castle in rural Austria, these week-long festivals are the next best thing to stepping back a millennia or so to attend the rites of the ancient Mystery religions.

While there is a frenzied aspect to these performances, there is also a closely choreographed focus—a formal structured ceremony participated in vicariously and sometimes actively by the attending audience/congregation. The slaughter of dozens of pigs and cattle, and the bathing of performers in their blood, is balanced with stately choral presentations and periods of meditative quiet in surrounding orchards.

While the intention to uproot spectators from their normal frame of reference is obvious, the use of crosses, processions, the castle setting, the musical accompaniment of string ensembles and brass tavern bands, all suggest Nitsch's desire to root his theater in more recent European tradition (as well as its bloodier predecessors).

Arising around the same time, and diverging in a more-or-less opposite direction from the somewhat solemn and historical character of Nitsch's theatrical reconstructions, was the work of the Pop artists. Food, in particular the still life, functioned for them as a springboard of a different kind.

■ **POP GOES THE STILL LIFE** ■

Warhol's Groceries

While Nitsch may have been trying to connect man more directly with the primal realities of his food (meat in this case), Pop Art was celebrating precisely what separated the two—the packaging.

Andy Warhol's Campbell's Soup cans are perhaps the most famous icon of the Pop movement, but Warhol also silk-screened Del Monte Peach cans, Coca-Cola Bottles, Pepsi Cola bottle caps, Heinz Tomato Ketchup, and made sculptures of Brillo Boxes with labels he'd produced himself.

Even Warhol's *Banana* cover for the debut album by the Velvet Underground and Nico focused attention on the

THE VELVET
UNDERGROUND

◄ PEEL SLOWLY AND SEE

Andy Warhol

economic critique. Later, Warhol himself would simply say, "I was looking for something that was the essence of nothing, and the soup can was it."

Much like his stupendously boring films, his silk-screen work simply showed without telling. His subject matter, like that of the still-life artist, was simply the household object, and his technique was simply the silk-screen he'd been using as a commercial artist before embarking into the galleries.

In a similar vein, Edward Ruscha's painting *Actual Size* depicts a can of Spam with two-foot tall letters spelling out the product name. Like Warhol, Ruscha's trademark use of typography simply exploited technical skills he'd used during his career in advertising.

The Futurist Cookbook and Oldenburg's Store

Though Pop Art often passed itself off as utterly neutral toward its subject, it did have an implicit agenda, which was to define itself as unique from the heroic "spirituality" of its Abstract Expressionist's predecessors. It did this in part by choosing prepackaged food and other "ordinary" subject matter and by using mechanical means of art-making, such as collage and silk-screen.

By embracing what was "vulgar" and new, it recalls the mood of the earlier Dada and Futurist movements. Both of those earlier movements also occasionally used food as a subject.

These movements also sought to move beyond traditional gallery-accepted forms of art-making. Pop artist Claes Oldenburg set up an environment called "The Store" in 1961 from which he sold painted plaster models of various foods, and the Futurist poet Filippo Tommaso Marinetti advocated a future form of cooking as a Futurist form of art in 1932.

Marinetti even published the *Futurist Cookbook*, in which he envisioned dining

"natural packaging" of the fruit's peel. (The original release of the album sported a yellow Colorform sticker showing the banana alongside the small inscription "Peel Slowly And See." Underneath was the exposed fruit rendered in a suggestive pink.)

Early reactions to all this package-friendly populism ranged from simplistic outrage at "consumerist" gestures to disheveled Marxist's notions about intended

In his Futurist Cookbook, *poet Fillippo Tommaso Marinetti wrote that advancing technologies would raise dining to a purely aesthetic experience.*

Licorice Pizza

Cibo Matto

Cibo Matto is Italian for "food madness." It's also the name of a post-punk New York band writing songs like "Sugar Water," "Birthday Cake," "Know Your Chicken," "Artichoke," "White Pepper Ice Cream," "Beef Jerky," "Le Pain Perdu" (French Toast), and even covering Sammy Davis Jr.'s "The Candy Man."

Drawing their name from a smarmy Italian sex comedy, Seso Matto (Sex Madness), their obsession is clearly metaphoric. The not even

pleasantly plump members consist of Yuka Honda, Miho Hatori, Timo Ellis, and Duma Love, and they were recently joined on tour by Sean Lennon playing bass (thanks in part to his relationship with Yuka Honda).

In their few years together since 1994, they've released a number of singles and promos and four LPs: Cibo Matto (1995), Viva! La Woman (1996), Super Relax (1997), and Stereotype (1999).

The sound is an urban mix of trip-hop, acid jazz trumpets, punk, Afro-Cuban beats, and even a little swing and spaghetti Western soundtrack tossed into the stew. Along with the guitars, drums, loops, and scratching, you'll also hear a little unexpected oboe and hurdy-gurdy. Presiding over it all is the bilingual rapping, screaming, and sighing of lead vocalist Miho Hatori.

There are plenty of bands people have been willing to compare them to, among them Shonen Knife, the farcical '80s bunny-punk Japanese

import. But while Cibo Matto may have its playful aspects, it's not all farce and gimmick, and some of their songs are downright painful, like the ballad "Artichoke," in which emptiness and luxury combine ruefully in the lyrics—"My heart is like an artichoke . . . I eat the petals . . . myself . . . one by one."

But Cibo Matto is hardly the first band to sing about food. As the following list demonstrates, food and music have gone together like red beans and rice for years and years:

30,000 Lbs. of Bananas—Harry Chapin
A Chicken Ain't Nothin' but a Bird
   —Cab Calloway
Alice's Restaurant—Arlo Guthrie
Alligator Meat—Johnny Otis
All That Meat & No Potatoes—Fats Waller
All You Can Eat—Candye Kane
Animal Crackers—Shirley Temple
Artichoke—Hemlock/Cibo Matto
Attack Of The Killer Tomatoes—Lewis Lee
Banana Chips—Shonen Knife
Bananas & Cream—Kinky Friedman
Bananas—Louis Jordan
Bangers and Mash—Peter Sellers and
   Sophia Loren
Barbeque USA—Mojo Nixon
Beans & Cornbread—Louis Jordan
Black Coffee—Peggy Lee
Bread & Butter—The Newbeats
Breakfast in America—Supertramp
Butcher Pete—Roy Brown & His Mighty
   Mighty Men
C Is For Cookie—Cookie Monster
Cajun Cookin'—Queen Ida
Call any Vegetable—Frank Zappa
Candy by the Pound—Elton John
Cheese & Onions—The Rutles
Cheeseburger in Paradise—Jimmy Buffett

Chew, Chew, Chew, Chew—Chick Web
Chicken—The Cramps
Chicken Fried Snake—Ron Levy
Chili Sauce—Louis Prima
Chittlin' Ball—King Porter
Chocolate Cake—Crowded House
Chocolate—Lisa Hall
Coconut Woman—Harry Belafonte
Coconut—Harry Nilsson
Coffee Cantata—JS Bach
Cooking Breakfast for the One I Love
    —Fanny Brice
Cotton Candyland—Elvis Presley
Crawdad Song—Harry Belafonte
Crawfish—Elvis Presley
Curry—Taj Mahal
Cut Off The Fat—Charles Brown
Dinner Bell—They Might Be Giants
Dixie Chicken—Little Feat
Do Fries Go With That Shake?
    —George Clinton
Dumplin Dumplin—Margie Day
Eat at Home—Paul & Linda McCartney
Eat It—"Weird"Al Yankovic
Eat the Menu—Sugarcubes
Eat the Music—Kate Bush
Eat to the Beat—Blondie
Eat Your Greens—Lloyd Cole
Egg Cream—Lou Reed
Everyone Eats at My House—Cab Calloway
Fast Food—Richard Thompson
Fatman—G Love And Special Sauce
Feed Me—Little Shop Of Horrors
Feeding a Hungry Heart—KT Oslin
Fish Heads—Barnes & Barnes
Food Chain of Fools—Reverand Billy Wirtz
Food Glorious Food—Oliver!
Food—The Turtles
French Fried Potatoes and Ketchup
    —Amos Milburn
Frim Fram Sauce—Nat King Cole

Frog Legs—Lloyd Price
Fruits & Vegetables—Shonen Knife
Gettin' Hungry—Beach Boys
Gimme a Pound O Ground Round
    —Ivory Joe Hunter
Girl Scout Cookies—NRBQ
Git with the Grits—Wynonie Harris
Goober Peas—Kingston Trio
Good Biscuits—Memphis Minnie
Gravy—Dee Dee Sharp
Green Eggs & Ham—Moxy Fruvous/Dr.Suess
Green Onions—Booker T & The Mg's
Gris Gris Gumbo Ya Ya—Dr. John
Guacamole—Texas Tornados
Hamburger Hell—Todd Rundgren
Hamburger Midnight—Little Feat
Happy Meal]—The Cardigans
He's a Jelly Roll Baker—Lonnie Johnson
Hog Maw and Cabbage Slaw—Todd Rhodes
Hot Chocolate—Shonen Knife
Hot Dog and a Shake—David Lee Roth
Hot Pastrami—Joey Dee & The Starlighters
Hot Potatoes—The Kinks
Hot Sauce—Thomas Dolby
Hot Tamale Baby—Clifton Chenier
Hungry Man Blues—Nathan & The Zydeco
    Cha-Chas
Hungry—Paul Revere & The Raiders
I Ate The Wrong Part—Gus Jenkins
I Hate To Eat Alone—10cc
I Like Bananas Because They Have No Bones
    —Hoosier Hot Shots
I Like Food—Descendents
I Need Lunch—The Dead Boys
I'm Hungry—Sugarcubes
Ice Cream Man—The Tornadoes
Ice Cream—Sarah Mclachlan
It Was a Real Nice Clambake—Carousel
Ito Eats—Elvis Presley
Jambalaya—Hank Williams
Java Jive—The Inkspots

Jellied Eels—Joe Brown
Jelly Roll—Richard Berry
Junkfood Junkie—Larry Groce
Kidney Stew—Eddie Vinson
Kraft Dinner—Annihilator
Life In The Foodchain—Tonio K
Life Is a Minestrone—10cc
Lollipop—The Chordettes
Malted Milk—Robert Johnson
Mashed Potato Time—Dee Dee Sharp
Maximum Consumption—The Kinks
Mayonnaise—The Smashing Pumpkins
Memphis Soul Stew—King Curtis
Milkcow Blues—Elvis Presley
Monkey Hips and Rice—The Five Royales
Mother Popcorn—James Brown
Nighthawks at the Diner—Tom Waits
Okra—Olu Dara
One Meatball—Anne Rabson
Orange Juice Blues—Bob Dylan & The Band
Pancake Man—Catfish Hodge
Peaches—Presidents Of The United States
Peanut Butter—The Marathons
Peelin' Taters—Junior Brown
Pink Sugar and Purple Salt—Sammy Turner
Pizza Pie—Norman Fox & The Rob Roys
Plant a Radish—The Fantasticks
Popcorn—Hot Butter
Popcorn Sack—Spike Jones & The City Slickers
Pork Chops & Mustard Greens
    —Ernie Andrews
Pound Cake—Count Basie
Quiche Lorraine—B-52s
RC Cola & a Moon Pie—NRBQ
Red Beans and Rice—Booker T & The Mgs.
Red Beans—Marcia Ball
Riffin' At The Barbeque—Nat King Cole
Roast Possum—Carter Brothers
Rubber Biscuit—The Chips/The Blues Brothers
Rump Steak Serenade—Fats Waller

Salad Days—Procol Harem
Saturday Night Fish Fry—Louis Jordan
Savoy Truffle—The Beatles
Scenes from an Italian Restaurant—Billy Joel
Seafood Mama (Hold Tight)—Andrews Sisters
She Cooks Me Cabbage—Jack Dupree
Shish Kebab—Ted Heath
Sing for Your Supper—Mamas & Papas
Slow Cooked Pigmeat—Memphis Sheiks
Small Fruit Song—Al Stewart
Smokey Joe's Cafe—The Robins
Snack Attack—Godley & Creme
Solid Potato Salad—Ella Mae Morse
Soup for One—Chic
Soup Is Good Food—Dead Kennedys
Soup of the Day—Chris Rea
Spam—Monty Python
Squirrel Sandwich—Henry Qualls
Stringbean—Ray Charles
Struttin' with Some Barbeque
    —Louis Armstrong
Sturgeon—Primus
Sugar Dumpling—Desmond Dekker & The Aces
Sugar, Sugar—The Archies
Supper Time—Irving Berlin
Sushi Bar—Shonen Knife
Taco Wagon—Dick Dale & His Del-Tones
Tavern on the Green—Chic
The Candy Man—Sammy Davis Jr.
The Coffee Song—Frank Sinatra
The Peanut Vendor—Desi Arnaz
Too Much Pork for Just One Fork
    —Southern Culture on the Skids
Tupelo Honey—Van Morrison
TV Dinners—ZZ Top
Vegetables—The Beach Boys
Wild Honey—Beach Boys
Worst Pies in London—Angela Lansbury
Yes, We Have No Bananas—Billy Jones
You're My Meat—Joe Jackson

as part of a multisensory aesthetic experience. One scenario presents the Futurist diner using one hand to pluck foods from unusually sculpted and visually appealing dishes, while the other is busy stimulating the fingertips on sandpaper, velvet, and silk. With hands thus occupied, the subject would also listen to a combination of roaring airplane engines and a Bach concerto, while simultaneously having the nape of his neck sprayed by a waiter equipped with an atomizer of perfumed water.

Advancing technologies, Marinetti believed, would raise dining to a purely aesthetic experience, with actual nutrition being accomplished through the intake of synthetic vitamins and chemicals (or possibly even through radio waves). Heavy pasta dishes, he claimed, were responsible for his countrymen's sluggish advances into the future. While much of his cookbook is clearly an exercise in hyperbolic poetry and polemic, Marinetti did actually produce a few recipes, which he and companions served to potential converts on a brief and bizarre lecture tour in 1932.

Eating Big, Thinking Small

Futurism was perhaps a bit too contemptuous of public tastes to make it in the long run; it died quietly and quickly, undiluted by a legacy of impostors. Without such troublesome manifestos, Pop Art,

> **O**ne scenario presents the Futurist diner using one hand to pluck foods from unusually sculpted and visually appealing dishes, while the other is busy stimulating the fingertips on sandpaper, velvet, and silk. With hands thus occupied, the subject would also listen to a combination of roaring airplane engines and a Bach concerto, while simultaneously having the nape of his neck sprayed by a waiter equipped with an atomizer of perfumed water.

however, continued to produce crowd-pleasing works, some of these again focusing on food as a subject.

Claes Oldenburg's interest in making props for happenings evolved from the hand-made objects sold in a store to larger and more public works, including a large bean-bag-like *Floor-Burger* in 1962. He went on to fabricate the large and furry *Good Humor Bar* a year later, then a *Floor Cake*, a *BLT*, *Two Cheeseburgers with Everything*, a *Roast*, *French Fries*, a *Baked Potato*, *Pie*, an *Ice Cream Cone*, an *Apple Core*, and Swedish *Knäckebröd* crackers. Through the mid-'60s and into the '90s, his work evolved from the 5–by–7–foot *Floor Burger* to state-commissioned monuments of public art, such as the Minneapolis Sculpture Garden's 51–foot *Spoonbridge and Cherry*, representing a spoon holding a 1,200–pound maraschino cherry.

Claes Oldenburg's Spoonbridge and Cherry *(Minneapolis, MN).*

Critics who formerly found a mock heroic irony in the monumental scale of Oldenburg's inflated objects and a further critical "deflation" in their bean-bag laxity, may have been somewhat put off by what appears to be an increasing capitulation to economic and popular demand. But Oldenburg, in his own statements, never stressed this ironic aspect. Instead, he values the way the scale of his work can stir a sense of childlike wonder and sensual appreciation of certain qualities of the objects. In a sense, then, it was really more about using large cartoonish images to bypass critical reasoning and reach a more basic level.

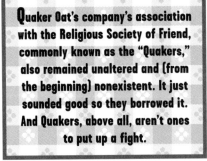

Quaker Oat's company's association with the Religious Society of Friend, commonly known as the "Quakers," also remained unaltered and (from the beginning) nonexistent. It just sounded good so they borrowed it. And Quakers, above all, aren't ones to put up a fight.

All of which is merely a very complicated way of talking about something pursued by those interested in selling us food. These are the people who really know "pop" and really know packaging—the advertising agencies.

■ YOUR IMAGINARY FRIENDS ■

Mythic Heroes from Madison Avenue

If you survey the shelves of your neighborhood grocery, you'll obviously find thousands of attempts to personify products. It's a basic law of advertising that products need "personality," and that this personality better be one the consumer would like to invite into his home—or at least walk to the checkout counter.

For the adult, the attempts are geared to making the product seem as if it might be an essential prop in belonging to a community (athletic and health-minded, well-traveled cosmopolitan, earth-friendly, family-value family, etc.). The product personifies the abstraction of a collective personality through subtleties of the label's copy, layout, and even typeface. At least to the more sophisticated adult.

But in the case of products aimed at children (or "inner children," for that matter) it all gets more concrete. For that, your best bet's identifying your product with a cartoon (or at least cartoonish) personality, i.e., a trademarked character.

Quaker's Wild Oats

One of the oldest of these still in use is the Quaker representing Quaker Oats. Appearing first in 1877 as a figure holding a banner inscribed with the inscription "Pure," his form has evolved slowly over decades, while his purpose of conveying wholesomeness remained unaltered. The company's association with the Religious Society of Friend, commonly known as the "Quakers," also remained unaltered and (from the beginning) nonexistent. It just sounded good so they borrowed it. And Quakers, above all, aren't ones to put up a fight.

But the stern figure of the Quaker seemed in some cases a little too solemn and static. By 1920, the company had solved this problem with more animated and fanciful members of this faith miniaturized into "Quaker Quakies." This primitive kiddy cereal was advertised with images of traditionally clad, yet

When is a Quaker not a Quaker?

strangely athletic and elfin, Quakers leaping out from the box and scurrying toward a bowl filled with the product.

The legend explained, "Everywhere about us live Good Spirits, Elves, and Pixies. The first Quakers in America had befriended the Indians, who then shared

with them the secrets of corn. The Quakers were told that the corn contained the Three Good Spirits of Beautiful Youth: the Spirit of Strength, the Spirit of Courage, and the Spirit of Truth."

While adult consumers could content themselves with the moral exemplifications of Strength, Courage, and Truth, young children were caught up in the half-belief that magical fairy figures hid just below the surface of the bowl in the next spoonful, or deep within the box.

Breakfast Cereals Get Lives

Interestingly, the "Quakies" are associated with animistic earth spirits of the Native Americans as well as the elves and pixies of pagan-Europe. Quaker Oats Quakies were now "magical" via elfin association, like the gifts produced in Santa's workshop, a modernized version of the even older folk tale "The Shoemaker and the Elves," in which a cobbler's production lag is solved by magically produced shoes. And the mythic motif employed by Quakies goes back further still to the enchanted weapons crafted underground by the dwarves of Germanic legends or the rings created by Celtic fairy folk. With Quakies, advertisers were beginning to speak the insidious language of archetypes—and it sure sold cereal.

It worked well enough, in fact, that it gave birth to imitations. Around the same time Quakies was being sold, "Dwarfies Wheat Food" appeared on shelves, produced by the Dwarfies Corporation Council located in Bluffs, Iowa. Dwarfies, like Quakies, were depicted as literally inhabiting the box along with the cereal.

By 1923, General Mills had begun marketing via weekly radio shows, and by 1929 they'd switched their adult format broadcasting to a show documenting the adventures of a cartoon character popular with children. Trademark characters no longer merely *posed* with samples of the product—they'd made the leap from static image to dynamic narrative. Now they had their own commercials and programming.

They got lives.

The Snap-Crackle Population

While other fairy folk came and went as cereal shills, Kellogg's hired on Snap as the first member of the trio of elfin

reps for Rice Krispies cereal. Oddly, it wasn't until 1941 that Crackle and Pop were enlisted to assist him, and not until 1949 that they were redrawn as more human and less grotesquely gnonem-like creatures.

By the mid-'60s, the Krispies Elves were joined by another diminutive cereal maker and promoter, Lucky the Lepre-chaun—associated with the "magically delicious" Lucky Charms. Post had its own more short-lived, short-statured

representatives in Postem Elfins and Raisin Bran Fairies.

Keebler borrowed the magic of elfin endorsement and created a long-running campaign for their "uncommonly good" cookies baked in a "magic oven" within a hollow tree occupied by lead elf Ernie and his anonymous subordinates.

The notion of elves helping with bak-ing or other duties of hearth and home is also archetypal. From Italy to Scandi-navia, invisible or tiny entities often associated with the kitchen have appeared in folk tales to assist with domestic duties.

In 1960, Poppin' Fresh, the Pillsbury Doughboy became America's most promi-nent player in this role.

Poke His Stomach! Buy His Peas!

The Doughy One was created by the Leo Burnett ad agency of Chicago to assist homemakers with baking and, in particular, to personably demonstrate the use of Pillsbury's new-fangled tubes of refrigerated dough that had to be smacked on a hard edge in order to open. Over the years, the characters transformed from humble servant to celebrity. In the '70s, in fact, Fresh became so popular

A couple of happy-go-lucky pieces of dough, vintage and contemporary.

Pass the Quisp, Please

Space Cadet's Breakfast

Thanks to folks like Dr. Sylvester Graham and Harvey Kellogg, science metaphors became attached to breakfast food. Science metaphor is second cousin to science fiction, so it should come as no surprise that within a few decades of their appearance, breakfast cereals were being described as "rocket fuel" for little spacemen about to soar off into their day of adventure.

As early as the 1920s and '30s, association with sci-fi radio shows, newspaper strips, and movie serials were helping get those boxes of grain onto consumers' tables. In the 1930s, Kellogg's had Buck Rogers hawking boxes of Pep "The Vital Food" and "The Peppy Cereal." In the '40s, Buck pushed Post Corn Crackos and Toasties.

But in the '50s, things really blasted off. Television space hero Tom Corbett (the original "Space Cadet") was great at selling cereals to kids because he went to school like them, albeit a much cooler "space academy." Regardless, Corbett knew a good breakfast cereal when he endorsed one (or many). His favorites were Kellogg's Corn Flakes, Raisin Bran, and Pep—The Solar Cereal.

At some point in the late 1950s, General Mills, eager to cash in on the growing enthusiasm for the dawning Space Age, realized that instead of paying expensive endorsement fees to celebrity spacemen, they'd do better just inventing their own space explorers and fashioning advertising and indeed products around these.

"Jets," later marketed as "Sugar Jets," was their answer—originally a "sugar-toasted" version of Kix cereal, those boring little spheres of grain evolved into "space age shapes." With each mouthful chewed, children crushed entire planetary systems, stars, comets, and armadas of sugary jets. Boxes advised growing astronauts to charge up on the cereal more than once a day: "For breakfast and snacks all smart kids know it's SUGAR JETS for JET UP AND GO!"

Adventures of Space Pilot Major Jet and sidekicks Johnny Jet, Mr. Moonbird, Gogol the Alien, and the Sugar Jet Kids were chronicled on the backs of the boxes. Occasionally, you might also find coupons for some useful space gadget, decoder glasses, or glow-in-the-dark astronomical stickers. The space frenzy even spilled over into General Mills' other more neutrally themed cereals like Kix, which offered a "Space-O-Gage" control panel for navigating the far reaches of your bedroom.

As Space Operas died out, and the cinematic form of science fiction entered suspended animation during the '60s and early-'70s, "inner space" became a more popular field of exploration, and in 1965, Quaker Oats wisely introduced a more psychedelic spaceman, the eternally cross-eyed and "quazy" Quisp, a diminutive propeller-headed alien from some planet far beyond our galaxy of acceptable adult behavior. His frenetic antics in animated commercials pushed the product's popularity, eventually making it a "cult classic" (as cereals go).

Borrowing purposefully from the adventures of old space opera cereal-shills like Buck Rogers, Star Wars hit the screen in 1977, and science fiction was reborn.

By 1984, Kellogg's gave C-3PO, the gold protocol and etiquette droid from the film, his own cereal, and General Mills followed suit the same year, providing E.T. the Extra-Terrestrial with a chocolate and peanut butter cereal to sell. Shortly after its 1977 release, Star Wars promotional giveaways also appeared at Pizza Hut and Taco Bell, and it was around this time that the idea of fast-food chains licensing characters from films gave birth to a vast new market of toys.

that Pillsbury marketed not only a flexible vinyl doll of the character, but dolls representing other members of his doughy household, including dough dog, dough cat, and Uncle Rollie (yes, also made of dough). A house-shaped carrying case and Doughboy car completed the set.

> **A**nother advertising old-timer with mythological associations, the Jolly Green Giant, first appeared in 1925 as an illustration more or less copied from a book of fairy tales. Leo Burnett again was the company chosen to take over and transform the original rendering, which depicted a rather stubby giant in scruffy bearskin cradling an oversized pea in his arms like an infant. Not only was the 1925 character poorly dressed, a bit effeminate, and not very giant—he wasn't even green!

(his identifying "ho, ho, ho") just in time for his first appearance in a TV commercial in 1959. The effects were quite memorable—impressive to adults and terrifying to many children. The next decade saw the introduction of a sidekick, Sprout, scaled down, childlike, and much less likely to figure prominently in children's nightmares.

Interestingly, the voice talent behind Fresh's dialogue and trademark giggle was Paul Frees, the same actor responsible not only for the cold-war comedic stylings of Boris Badenov on *The Rocky and Bullwinkle Show*, but the brain behind *Paul Frees and the Poster People* (a one-album novelty featuring Frees singing The Beatles' "Hey, Jude" in the persona of Peter Lorre and The Archie's "Sugar, Sugar" as Sidney Greenstreet).

Another advertising old-timer with mythological associations, the Jolly Green Giant, first appeared in 1925 as an illustration more or less copied from a book of fairy tales. Leo Burnett again was the company chosen to take over and transform the original rendering, which depicted a rather stubby giant in scruffy bearskin cradling an oversized pea in his arms like an infant. Not only was the 1925 character poorly dressed, a bit effeminate, and not very giant—he wasn't even green! In 1935, the agency gave the giant a smart leafy suit and a big boost in size by losing the out-of-scale pea and rendering the giant as a 50-foot behemoth towering over an agricultural landscape.

In an attempt to make this rather intimidating character a bit more benevolent, he was given some catchphrase jollity

The Trixter's Trix

Besides offsetting the frightening scale of the giant, the Sprout character served to offset the monolithic "goodness" of the giant's personality. By the '60s, advertisers were beginning to pick up on the fact that a little mischief was good for the soul (and for sales).

Sprout's minor misadventures were, however, not to be compared with the more flamboyant escapades of the many other characters of the period intent on stealing a product that was inevitably not theirs to have. Thus the Trix Rabbit ingeniously yet fruitlessly schemed to acquire Trix cereal despite the oft-spoken law that "Trix is for kids." Sonny the Cuckoo Bird, despite his mad genius, never tasted Cocoa Puffs, and Charlie the Tuna's pathetic attempts to gain acceptance by Starkist Tuna were forever snubbed.

The fact that these characters keep trying to obtain these products despite inescapable and bitter failure and humiliation helps establish these foods (a bowl of puffed corn or what-have-you) as a sort of Holy Grail. It implicitly pats that consumer on the back for his ability to "attain" this reward for himself. The failures also serve to prolong the dramatic dynamic sustaining the campaign. Their devious, crafty, yet flawed characters are what generate interest. Could their longevity and fascination be rooted in an even longer-lived myth?

An obvious mythological connection could be drawn between the Trix Rabbit, for instance, and the name of his cereal. "Trix" is eerily similar to "Trickster," the popular Native American character showing up in folk tales as a rabbit. Carl Jung, Joseph Campbell, and legions of folklorists have agreed upon "Trickster" as a conventional label for this greedy, crafty, comic, and imperfect character turning up in myths, legends, and stories the world over.

Does this represent, then, a scheme to tap into the collective unconscious to make cereal even *more* "magically delicious"?

The Trickmeister, in all his plush glory.

Kentucky F. Chicken

KFC's advertising takes the real and the personal and explodes it into a global abstraction. Though its corporate empire stretches from Kentucky to Abu Dabi, KFC advertising insists on an illusory bond between its product and a single homey and historic individual, Harlan Sanders, who in the mid-1930s began serving humble dinners at a roadside diner and garage he operated in Corbin, Kentucky.

While the Colonel's mortal remains have lay buried in Louisville's Cave Hill cemetery since 1980, KFC, a subsidiary of PepsiCo, Inc., sees to it that his ghost lives on as an advertising construct, encouraging the consumer to enter into an imaginary scenario of Southern hospitality upon visiting the restaurant. Year after year, the deceased Colonel putters about in an otherworldly kitchen coming up with new recipes for Chicken

Twisters, Spicy Buffalo Crispy Strips, and other dishes, while continuing to hand mix the "11 herbs and spices" according to his secret personal recipe.

Guarded like an occult secret, these mystic herbs and spices come closer than anything else to retaining a wisp of the corporeal Harlan Sanders. They are, in effect, an expression of his individuality. Not developed through a battery of market focus groups or consultation with teams of food scientists, they represent a single subjective personality, something Harlan himself mixed up and took a liking to. And "the

> **And "the Colonel's own" remains as much as possible his own, locked away in a Louisville, Kentucky, bank vault—according to spokesperson Jean Litterst—and known by "less than a handful of people." Strict KFC protocol maintains this secret by ordering spices from separate vendors and premixing components at two separate and remote sites with the aid of an IBM processing system.**

The Colonel has been buried in Louisville's Cave Hill cemetery since 1980.

Colonel's own" remains as much as possible his own, locked away in a Louisville, Kentucky, bank vault—according to spokesperson Jean Litterst—and known by "less

than a handful of people." Strict KFC protocol maintains this secret by ordering spices from separate vendors and premixing components at two separate and remote sites with the aid of an IBM processing system.

The Goddess and Mr. Peanut

Aunt Jemima and her syrup, Mrs. Olsen and her coffee, Mama Celeste and her pizzas, the Land o' Lakes "Indian Maid" and sticks of butter suggestively tucked against her breasts . . . are these to be regarded as expressions of the Great Mother archetype? Wouldn't this then represent the ultimate ploy in "suckling in" the consumer via depth psychology?

Entertaining as it is to stretch the mental taffy, it should be remembered that there are plenty of other sociologically determined reasons that maternal females might have been associated with these foods and their representation on the market.

The development of long-lasting trademark characters rarely fits this paranoiac vision of academic alchemy. Long living and "successful" trademark characters may, of course, be nothing more than lousy characters living parasitically off a self-sustaining business venture. They may be engineered in consultation with psychologists and consumer focus groups, or they can just be created by some kid with a pencil—as was the case with the ever-dapper "Mr. Peanut," whose unchallenged reign dates back to 1916 when Planters hosted a contest in schools in Suffolk, Virginia, offering $5 for the best design for their new trademark.

While these characters are essentially two-dimensional "cartoons," understood by the conscious mind as symbolic, the case of Betty Crocker, America's favorite figurehead of food, is interesting in the way she is presented as at once iconic and "real," despite the fact that no such historical individual ever existed.

■ BREEDING BETTY CROCKERS ■

Genetic Betty

Eager to update the image of Betty Crocker in honor of her 75th birthday, General Mills sponsored a contest in 1996 to find 75 contestants representing Betty's "spirit." From this group, a composite image would be created to represent Betty into the twenty first century.

The several thousand contestants who entered needed to show four essential qualities. They had to enjoy cooking and baking, be committed to family and friends, be involved in their community, and be resourceful and creative in handling everyday tasks.

Beyond these basic requirements, other more obscure attributes were weighed by the company in the selection of the 75. Winners received donations to a charity of their choice, a copy of the latest cookbook, a Betty Crocker Red Spoon Diamond Pin, and, most importantly, the chance to be photographed, digitally scanned, and morphed into the new Avatar of Homemaking.

While the technology of computer compositing may not quite jibe with Betty's previously homey feel, even stranger are the weird eugenic overtones of this attempt to synthesize a perfect being using virtual "genetic code" of mysteriously selected parties. Yet these attempts to play god

The first Betty Crocker portrait (1936).

characterize Betty's history since her artificial inception.

Betty was created in 1921 by the Washburn Crosby Company, manufacturer of Gold Medal flour and other baking goods. As part of a promotional campaign, consumers who correctly assembled a jigsaw puzzle depicting a milling scene received a pincushion in the shape of a Gold Medal flour sack for their trouble. Along with the thousands of completed entries, the company had to deal with accompanying letters posing questions and offering comments on baking.

A Hyper-Personal Response

To project a more personable image, they wanted to individualize response letters with a signature, but for reasons that remain unclear, no single individual on staff seemed to possess exactly what it took. Thus began the weird process of human synthesis.

A last name was borrowed from a recently retired member of the board of directors, William Crocker, while the first name, Betty, was selected

> A last name was borrowed from a recently retired member of the board of directors, William Crocker, while the first name, Betty, was selected for "its warm, approachable feel."

for "its warm, approachable feel." The signature came from an anonymous employee chosen via a company-wide search for the style of handwriting that

personal endorsements began to be applied to packaging in the form of a trademarked red spoon logo. According to a 1945 survey, only Eleanor Roosevelt beat out Betty as "best known woman in America." By the 1950s, the American public had walking, breathing proof of Betty's reality as she appeared regularly

Betty in 1955. Notice the touch of grey.

A thoroughly modern woman (1965).

would add the right "personal" touch.

Homemakers during the 1920s became further acquainted with their imaginary peer Betty though opinions, tips, and recipes found in syndicated columns throughout the country's papers. Beginning in the mid-'20s and continuing for nearly a decade, yet another Betty Crocker appeared—this time on radio in the *Betty Crocker's Cooking School of the Air.* By the late-'40s, the familiar homemaker's

on television as a guest on the *Burns and Allen Show.*

The Many Masks of Betty

But even those un-American families who weren't tuning in to Burns and Allen had been seeing Betty's portrait in advertisements since 1936 and on products since the '50s. Though it's been recomposed eight times over the years, there appeared to be Four Unbreakable Laws of Betty:

1) Betty's hair is always brown (though in 1955 it clearly shows gray, and in 1980 it took a walk on the red side).

2) Betty always wears a red dress, jacket, or sweater.

3) Betty always has white at her neck, either collar, necklace, or scarf.

4) Betty has always been Caucasian.

features, Betty did not fail to disappoint.

Not only had her skin tone lost a bit of its gleaming whiteness, but her eyes for the first time had gone brown, and what's more, the shape had been nudged just a bit toward almond.

There is also a greatly relaxed feeling to her portrait, particularly when compared to her 1986 embodiment. Betty '96 is smiling, showing her teeth even, something only Betty '86 had attempted and,

Yet another change for 1968.

Betty during the Watergate years.

The fourth "law" had become the cause of some grief to General Mills, thanks to shifting demographics, and in the early '90s, Betty's highly Caucasian visage was quietly escorted off the packaging.

Then, in March of 1996, when the results of General Mills genetic experimentation were unveiled and the more racially mixed group of expectant mothers crowded around to see if the new incarnation did indeed share their

then, only with tight-lipped prudishness.

Betty '96 is also dressed in a casual red sweater and collarless white shirt, while '86 wears what looks like a wardrobe for an English fox hunt.

While Betty '86 appears to be regally seated, posed in the traditional half-turn preferred by Renaissance artists, '96 appears to be on her feet, standing with head and shoulders flatly facing the camera. The effect is much more that of a snapshot. The new Betty clearly does not have time to waste sitting for portraits. The new Betty has to work for a living and is obviously better equipped to communicate with working-class consumers than her forebearers.

But there is one further inescapable change that has nothing to do with Betty's genetic contributors. In what appears to be an attempt to accentuate her new shorter stature, Betty '96 is framed very

could help you serve up food for 8 after a 12-hour work day, she doesn't quite look like someone you'd trust to help you celebrate life's special moments with food.

Which is to say, she might not be the type to confidently construct that perfect four-story *timballo di maccheroni* as in the *Big Night*. But remembering the closing scenes of that film, what really seemed important was not the visionary cookery of the night before, but the sturdy

Freshened up for the early '80s.

Regal Betty '86.

low in the composition, by far the lowest of the previous eight portraits—drastically low—low enough to elicit critique in an introductory photography class. The truth is, the poor girl looks beaten down!

Though the new Betty clearly looks like someone who

> **T**he new Betty clearly does not have time to waste sitting for portraits. The new Betty has to work for a living and is obviously better equipped to communicate with working-class consumers than her forebearers.

sustaining omelet the morning after. Betty '96 would be good at those.

She could probably play mom to homesick types, but by the look of her, the comfort she'd offer would be backed by life experience. She's bound to have jumped a few hoops because she's not from

1996—the 75th anniversary portrait. Genetically superior? What would Betty *think?*

the privileged class, so novelists Fannie Flagg and Laura Esquivel might be happy with her. It's no stretch to see her as an independent single mom, and she's got community activist genes from her virtual donors, so maybe those angry women artists wouldn't be too mean to her.

She'd probably find some common sense way out of Luis Buñuel's inescapable dinner party, and the Futurists might have approved of her high-tech eugenic retooling. The fact that she'd been machined down to a demographically neutralized blank would've been a good joke for Warhol and his pals in the Pop art movement.

But what about Betty herself? What would *Betty* think? 🍴

FOOD
SEX
DEATH
...and Then?

Many good things begin with food. It's quite possible that many of our lives began during some passionate squirming amidst the leftovers of an intimate dinner for two.

A meal as an overture to sex is one of the oldest tricks in the book, an overpowering one-two conspiracy by your most powerful drives. Though the hunger and sex drive do tend to get their way, not everyone's thrilled about those old animal impulses running the show. But you can't really beat them down without submitting yourself to an even nastier taskmaster: Death.

So one polite answer has always been to just build a nice, legitimate-looking structure over and around it all and hope people will have the decency to focus on that instead. Over all that sweating and grunting of sex, for instance, we construct a rather

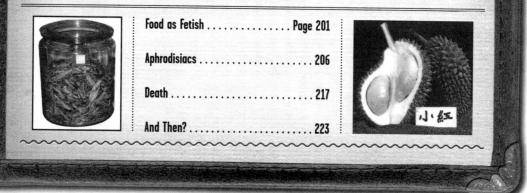

小紅

Things get a little hot and heavy at this 18th century French dinner.

stiff Victorian structure like the wedding cake.

But look at that cake again! What *were* those Victorians thinking when they added all those classical pagan columns between each tier? That just brings it all back to the Roman orgy your parents were having on the dining room table!

In one form or another, crude realities of sex and death show up again and again in our food traditions. This chapter simply examines how rational societies ice the cake of instinct and let it go at that.

But cultures don't just use food to deal with the type of impulses that pummel our bodily selves. We've also used food to look into those other worlds we only intuit. This tends to take the form of food rituals, sneaking by today as "games." These games allow us insight beyond the rational as well as beyond the animal realities. Or at least allow us to have a good laugh.

■ FOOD AS FETISH ■

Oral Sex Toy Fixation

"He who sees a satiated child sink back from a mother's breast and fall asleep with reddened cheeks and blissful smile will have to admit that this picture remains as typical of the expression of sexual gratification in later life."

This is Freud's take on the erotic meaning of breast-feeding at the "oral phase" of psychosexual development. And it commonly stirs up both vaguely pederastic anxieties and academic argument. Nowadays, people tend to want to smack Freud around and drag him into reality. Come along, old man! That connection between the mouth and erotic stimulation is not so obscure as all that!

Even before the days when President Clinton made oral sex national headlines,

Edible Undies, Kandie Kondoms, Tastee Tattoos, Edible Bra . . . good to the last, er, nibble.

Everyone loves an all-natural—and lickable— massage creme.

and employed Freud's iconic cigar in a most Freudian manner, Americans were wholeheartedly embracing this activity as evidenced by a 1998 survey of college students revealing that 62 percent of the men and 67 percent of the women had engaged in oral sex in the past month (and these were students identifying themselves as virgins!).

This oral diversion has come a long way since the "genital kiss" was first discretely mentioned in marriage manuals of the 1920s. And, like any good hobby, it's generated a market for all sorts of peripherals, mostly edible. Today, any man or woman can entice finicky or inexperienced sex

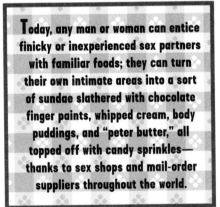

Today, any man or woman can entice finicky or inexperienced sex partners with familiar foods; they can turn their own intimate areas into a sort of sundae slathered with chocolate finger paints, whipped cream, body puddings, and "peter butter," all topped off with candy sprinkles— thanks to sex shops and mail-order suppliers throughout the world.

partners with familiar foods; they can turn their own intimate areas into a sort of sundae slathered with chocolate finger paints, whipped cream, body puddings, and "peter butter," all topped off with candy sprinkles—thanks to sex shops and mail-order suppliers throughout the world. If you're burning those calories in bed anyway, you're free to indulge in a few, too, right?

Practical jokers can enjoy the X-rated fortune cookies and the high-risk novelty of Licketty Dicks Edible Condoms (the manufacturer *really* doesn't want you to sue them, warning that they are not to be mistakened for real protection against pregnancy or STDs). Fantasy lovers can not only chew up condoms but also nibble their way through role-play costuming like pasties, bow ties, and lickable tattoo transfers.

Or perhaps you are a solitary type? Not sure about going all the way? Maybe just a whiff of sex with a Peaches and Cream Sweet-n-Tasty Pussy simulated in rubbery "Flavorful peach gelle'" or the International Hot Cock 12" Double Dong with a subtle aroma of French vanilla?

Then you got your spices and flavorings: Cinnamon-Hot Nipple Drops, Lick A Pussy Gel, Cotton Candy-Flavored Kandy Ass Erotic Oil, and the "Ultimate Blow Job" in a tube which is a mint gel marketed as a "centuries-old technique used in brothels around the world."

If all these tire out that tongue of yours, you can always rely on Sex Rocks, an effervescent candy that can ad its own sizzling and popping action to your lovemaking.

Sound like just one more way to sell Pop Rocks candy, mint toothpaste, cinnamon oil, chocolate, whipped cream, pudding, and cake sprinkles?

Well even the good doctor from Vienna wouldn't be so taken aback by any of this. The consumers purchasing these products, he would surmise, are merely fixated at the oral stage of development, thanks to overindulgence by the mother during breast-feeding; they carry this need for overindulgence into all spheres, betraying their oral fixation in obsession with oral sex as well as related tendencies to indulge in food and drink, smoking, and shopping—the metaphoric consumption of consumer goods. Ja?

Well, sure! Even post-Freudians agree that various human desires to consume are related and compensatory. The meaning is particularly transparent when packaging identifies the product with sex, and the act of purchase itself becomes a form of foreplay.

But, hell, any daytime talk-show host can tell you that—and more! It's a favorite topic on the talk-show hot seat. Alcoholics, shopaholics, and sexaholics playing musical chairs on Oprah, talking about times that they lived on sex alone and other times they sank into more interesting forms of degrading overindulgence. Everyone, even Freud, understands the rough mechanism at work here. Everyone knows sex sells, particularly by its absence.

Watch out for limp noodles.

Iced Beefcake

Speaking of absence, what if rather than an actual human, you might prefer something just whipped up in the kitchen? Of course, you can always pick up one of those suckers or chocolates molded in the shape of naughty parts of either sex. And, for a more substantial meal, there's novelty pasta twisted into miniature breasts and penises.

But say you want something a little more personal and intimate. Not an off-the-shelf surrogate but, let's say, an erotic cake baked just for you? Well, you could probably find something among the eight hundred possible design suggestions offered by Sweet-n-Nasty in Boston.

Eat me!

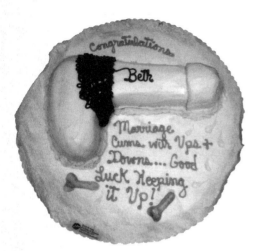

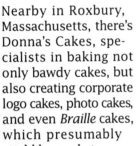

lovemaking and artfully crafted sweets remains with us in courting rituals today.

A less traditional take on the subject is represented by Toefood Chocolate of Berkeley, California. Specializing in "edible foot products" for 15 years, Toefood has walked a dangerously fine line, selling Foot Suckers and full-scale chocolate replicas of human feet both as fetish objects and as innocent novelties. The distractingly punning ingenuousness of products like Mistle Toe, Valentoes, or A Foot of Feet (25 small milk or white chocolate podiatric candies packed into a tube disguised as a ruler) helps those blithely unaware of the sexual connotations to remain so. Toefood advertising quotes a host of wholesome examples of yuck-it-up salesmen giving their candies away

Nearby in Roxbury, Massachusetts, there's Donna's Cakes, specialists in baking not only bawdy cakes, but also creating corporate logo cakes, photo cakes, and even *Braille* cakes, which presumably could be made to say something provocative.

> **S**pecializing in "edible foot products" for 15 years, Toefood has walked a dangerously fine line, selling Foot Suckers and full-scale chocolate replicas of human feet both as fetish objects and as innocent novelties.

But the award for realism must go to Cyráko Erotic Cake International, whose bakeries in Switzerland, Holland, and Germany offer grimly accurate anatomical models of male or female torsos and crotches, crafted from Bavarian cream-, Amaretto-, or Grand Marnier-flavored cake and skinned over with lifelike marzipan epidermis (colored to the race of your choice). Best of all, Cyráko cakes come luxuriously attired in their own sexy undies, provided as a wearable keepsake—once you get all that icing out of the crotch.

Lingerie-clad baked goods may be a fairly recent novelty, but Europeans have a long tradition of handcrafting naughty marzipan novelties. During medieval banquets, figurative decorations of sugar, pastry, or almond paste—known as "subtleties"—often represented erotic themes, and this early association between

For the chocoholic and foot fetishist in all of us.

to "get a foot in the door" and matronly party planners purchasing Mazel Toe candies for family bar mitzvahs. The Foot Health Foundation of America has even sent them along with press kits without any foot-in-mouth sense of *faux pas.*

When Neatness Doesn't Count

Novelties such as these are for mere dabblers, however. Those who really get into food, really *get into it*. For them, the pie fight, the comedian sitting in a cake—all those messy cinematic sight gags from a more innocent era—are not really quite so innocent. The fetish goes by many names: sploshing, wetlook, wam, and gunging. What it all comes down to is women (it's mostly a male heterosexual obsession) covered in mess—pies, rice pudding, chocolate, colored corn syrup, or nonfood items like paint and mud.

While the American mainstream was getting an inkling of this fetish with Herb Alpert's 1965 Coolwhip-clad cover model for the album *Whipped Cream and Other Delights*, and then the "discovery" of mud-wrestling around 1976, the Europeans

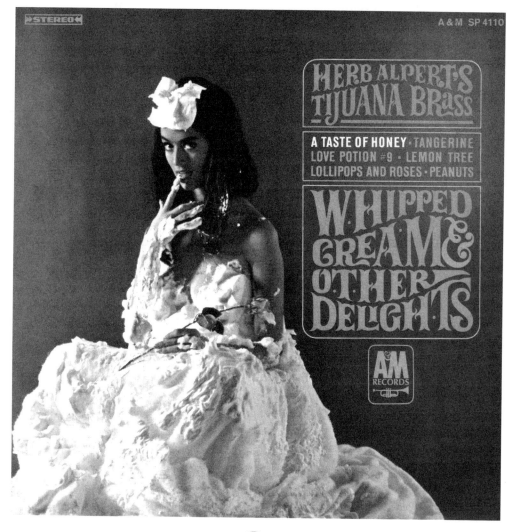

had been getting themselves into erotically sticky situations decades before with the mud and food wrestling debacles featured on the German cabaret scene back in the 1930s.

Americans didn't get to luxuriate in all this untidiness until the pioneering English-language magazine *Splosh!* appeared in the UK in 1981 and copies began making their way across the Atlantic. The slick periodical has inspired many to come out of the closet with like-minded publications including *WAM Newsletter* from Chattanooga, Tennessee, *Messy Fun* from Austin, Texas, and the German *Nasse Klamotten,* as well as many more web sites and newsgroups devoted to the subject.

The fetish comes in a variety of flavors including "wam" (acronym for "wet and messy" and the most universally accepted term for this interest), "wetlook" (those turned on by wet bodies, wet hair, and clingy, shiny clothing—either fashion-conscious latex or regular old street clothes drenched with liquid), "aqua" (underwater photography), and "gunge" (that's British for "slime," referring to any uncategorizable mucky stuff).

Besides professionally produced materials, members of this underground community swap fantasy fiction, homemade videos, and "cliptapes" of messy scenes dubbed from mainstream movies or television. Wamtec.com, an online special interest site, not only organizes participatory get-togethers for insiders (auditions and video shoots) but also coordinates field trips to events like the Water and Mud Olympics held in Florida's "mermaid capital" Weeki Wachee. Even more ambitious was the group's 1998 outing to New Year's festivities in Thailand, where it's traditional for celebrating strangers to dowse each other as they pass in the streets.

Other even more curious food or eating-related fetishes represented on the Internet include vorephilia or "vore," a fascination with human beings getting themselves swallowed by large, usually mythical beasts. Those occupying this especially kinky corner of sci-fi fandom also often enjoy stories and images of cannibalistic themes. On the other side of things are those who fantasize about being swallowed themselves (usually by a big-bosomed sexy giantess). Dominance-submission themed fantasies of forced feeding, forced weight gain, and artificial simulation of such via balloons swallowed and inflated in the stomach also can be ferreted out from certain dank cubbyholes on the web.

■ A P H R O D I S I A C S ■

It's All in the Shape . . . and the Pocketbook

Fantasies are fine and good, but some people expect food to do a little more than just fire up the imagination; they expect it to help them realize those fantasies by acting as an aphrodisiac. The belief that certain foods can be used to bend the will of a potential partner toward sexual compliance is nearly universal, and there's also some fairly widespread agreement as to what kinds of foods best do the trick.

A common starting point is visual analogy—does the

> **T**he belief that certain foods can be used to bend the will of a potential partner toward sexual compliance is nearly universal, and there's also some fairly widespread agreement as to what kinds of foods best do the trick.

food *look* like the right tool for the job? From the male perspective, the tool in question is pretty much the shape of a banana, right? And, indeed, in Central Africa, that fruit is regarded as such a potent aphrodisiac that even the blossoms of the tree are treated with caution in the belief that they can induce pregnancy. Carrots and asparagus fit the criterion also and were regarded by the ancient Greeks as potent in stirring desire.

Peppers, too, are sometimes regarded as an aphrodisiac, and their suggestive shape is recognized in the designation of certain species such as the "peter pepper" in Texas or similarly named peppers referred to in Swahili, Korean, and other languages with a sense of fun. Their presumed effectiveness may also relate to the physiological effects they produce when eaten—increased blood flow and swelling in the tongue and mouth, which nicely mimics sexual arousal.

For just such reasons, chilies were shunned by our Puritan forefathers. Eager Cajun men, on the other hand, used to sprinkle ground pepper on dance floors in hopes that at least the inhalation of what's stirred into the air would get the ladies all hot and bothered.

One of the best known aphrodisiacs, Ginseng, derives its name from the Chinese expression meaning "man's root," presumably because the root of the plant bears resemblance to the legs and other extensions of the male anatomy.

The shape of the *unagi* eel plays no small part in the Japanese belief in its aphrodisiac powers, and the resemblance is reiterated by the eel's traditional side dish, a pickled plum of equally phallic proportions. Regarded by the Chinese and Arabs as an aphrodisiac, the sea slug dramatizes its penile personality in

life by swelling indecently when touched.

A visual kinship with parts of the female anatomy no doubt has had something to do with the status of oysters in the pantheon of Western aphrodisiacs. The oyster in classical myth is in fact the godmother of all such substances, ever since it bore Aphrodite from the sea, giving birth not only to the goddess of love but her namesake "aphrodisiacs." More earthy legends relate how Casanova would begin his day's amorous exploits with 50 oysters, ideally shared in a morning bath with the woman of the hour. (Aside from their visual or tactile associations, the reputation of oysters possibly could be related to their high zinc content, an element required in the production of testosterone).

> One of the best known aphrodisiacs, Ginseng, derives its name from the Chinese expression meaning "man's root," presumably because the root of the plant bears resemblance to the legs and other extensions of the male anatomy.

Almond Joy

Ultimately, of course, the best aphrodisiac is in the mind.

As empirical science discredits the perceived pharmacological effect, this becomes increasingly obvious. For this reason, much of what passes today for sexual mood enhancers are high-price items—effective not because of an inherent effect, but effective because they're expensive.

That is to say, oysters, artichokes, asparagus, chocolate, champagne, and caviar are seductive because they symbolize wealth equated with rank equated with power equated with sexual potency. In the world of aphrodisiacs, you get what you pay for.

Some historical aphrodisiacs have acquired their value because of the difficulty in acquiring them—truffles, saffron, and other spices either made expensive by importation or harvesting costs.

Fennel, cardamom, cloves, caraway, cinnamon, mint, rosemary, salvia, and thyme have all been classed as aphrodisiacs. Ginger is almost universally regarded as such. Caviar has only been regarded as an aphrodisiac since the turn of the century when it was first imported to Western Europe. And importation costs make some people horny.

One recent craze in aphrodisiacs—powdered emu shell—is an import of an import, an Australian substance first imported to China, and then imported to the West. All that shipping and handling drives up the price, thereby driving up the libido of those eager to believe.

This association of the exotic, sensual, and sexual recurs throughout the history of the West. When the tomato was brought from the New World to be cultivated in Europe, it was literally regarded as the forbidden fruit of Eden. Presumed poisonous, the "love apple," as it was called, was grown merely as a colorful ornamental.

While the penis may be the delivery system, the real source of male potency is recognized by many cultures as residing in the testes. Thanks to the shape and seed-bearing function of this part of the body, an ancient Roman hanging out with impolite company here in contemporary America would have no trouble picking up on the slang use of the word

The Nut Museum's Elizabeth Tashjian, "the Nut Lady," shows off her coco-de-mer.

"nuts." They called them that too, classing the walnut, for instance, in the genus *juglans* ("Jupiter's Glans"). Naturally, this meant the nut for the Romans was also an aphrodisiac symbol of fertility, and as such the perfect thing to sling at newlywed couples, just as Americans might throw rice or birdseed. Hazelnuts were recommended by Roman doctors to restore masculine vigor, and are still considered to have this invigorating quality in traditionalist regions of Italy and France.

Near Eastern fertility cults may have some role in getting the Greeks and Romans worked up about the nut. Throughout that region, the almond tree is regarded as sacred and associated with sexual potency, and Almonds are still used in Italian folk medicine to enliven the libido. The amorous Queen of Sheba is said to have found pistachios so useful in this respect that she nearly drained Syria of the resource.

In Arabic countries, pine nuts do the trick, and in Northern India the coconut's the thing. Our word "avocado" comes from a Spanish explorer's take on the Aztec's word for the fruit (*ahuacatl*), which happens also to have been the Indian's word for "testicle." Though not a nut, it performs the duties of one, being regarded as an aphrodisiac in certain Mexican cultures.

An interesting exception to the masculine quality of the aphrodisiac nut is the coco-de-mer, native to the Seychelles Islands in the Indian Ocean. Rather than evoking the image of male genitalia, this baby's all girl. Also called the "double coconut," the two lobes of this immense specimen come together in an explicitly labial fashion, distinguishing the coco-de-mer not only by its indecent appearance but also as the largest seed in the plant kingdom, weighing in at around 30 to 40 pounds.

More Things to Do with the Penis

But why should it all stop at metaphors of peppers and bananas? If you want real effects, why not ingest the real thing? In fact, many cultures have.

Bull and lion penises ("pizzles") are served in soups and made into wines in Asia and most notably Singapore. Though protected by conservationists, the Indian tiger penis is particularly sought after, and one organ is said to fetch thousands on the black market. Naturally, all of the bits and pieces of the reproductive system listed above are believed to be potent aphrodisiacs.

Snake penises, for instance, currently command a high price in Thailand and are sold on black market street stands catering to an upper-class clientele of health enthusiasts who stop for the snack as a break from their morning jog.

An assortment of dried animal private parts as displayed in your friendly local herbalist's shop.

The Romans were very thorough in this respect, chowing down on a wide variety of genitalia in hopes of increasing their virility. Deer, rooster, and monkey all gave up their penises and testes, while pigs and cows sacrificed their wombs to wealthy patricians hoping to increase fertility. History also records the use of crocodile semen as an aphrodisiac in ancient Rome (though no mention is made as to the method in which it was obtained).

Have Some Balls

The testicles of bulls were regarded as especially efficacious and the Romans would not only eat these but also brewed aphrodisiac drinks using the blood drained from these little nuggets. Deer testicles were likewise employed. In Moslem countries and throughout Asia, animal testicles also figure into a variety of folk remedies.

Bull testicles or *criadillas* are enjoyed by the Argentinean gaucho and other Spanish-speaking people hoping to ingest a bit of machismo. In the same spirit, their cowboy counterparts in the American West gobble "Rocky Mountain Oysters." Breaded or deep fried, these testicular treats were also enjoyed in the San Franciso of the "gay nineties" at certain restaurants like the Mason Dorree and the Poodle Dog, where upstairs bedrooms were reserved for those looking to enjoy the effects of their glandular repast.

These "oysters" were often harvested from sheep as well as cattle, depending on what flock or herd in the area had been recently gelded. In Persia and Sweden, it is sheep that would often give up their manhood for man's gastronomic enjoyment. In ancient Rome, it was testicles of turkeys and lamprey eels that tended to get extracted, though more than anything the citizen of Rome preferred

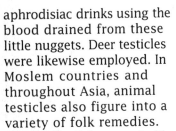

eating the gonads out of sea urchins.

Found in temperate tidepools in all temperate waters, these prickly little aquatic porcupines turn over their gonads to the Japanese, Samoans, Chileans, Peruvians, and many Mediterraneans. The French puree and slightly brown the stuff, sprinkle it with parmesan, and call it *oursin*.

Similarly, the Chinese extract the ovaries from jellyfish; these can be eaten either deep-fried or dried. The Japanese serve *uni*, the eggs of sea urchins, as well as the testicles of *fugo* (the poisonous puffer fish). The latter is considered an especially virility-inducing treat, thanks in part to the dangers presented by the fish. The eggs of the lady urchin can be called roe (hard roe), whereas the soft membraned semen or milt of the gentlemen urchin is known as soft roe or white roe.

To add to the confusion, eggs of the urchin (but more commonly crustaceans such as lobster) are sometimes called coral. Caviar is roe of any fish that's been salted (though that of the Caspian Sea-dwelling beluga sturgeon is preferred).

> **T**he testicles of bulls were regarded as especially efficacious and the Romans would not only eat these but also brewed aphrodisiac drinks using the blood drained from these little nuggets . . . Bull testicles or *criadillas* are enjoyed by the Argentinean gaucho and other Spanish-speaking people hoping to ingest a bit of machismo.

Eggs: Grown Up and Grown Old

Asian Americans call it "the treat with feet" or "the egg with legs." In the Philippines, they're called *baalut* and in Vietnam *hot vit lon*.

Fertilized eggs that happen to turn up in a grocer's carton are regarded by

most Americans as unseemly and even a mildly horrifying mistake, but in many parts of Asia they're a delicacy. A fertilized duck or chicken egg is eaten by tapping a hole in the top and sucking out the white. The one- or two-week old embryo can either be hardly distinguishable as such or might display distinctly recognizable bones and even black feathers. In either case, it's spooned out and eaten with great relish.

Perhaps a hair's breath more alluring on the Western scale is the "thousand (or hundred) year old eggs" eaten in China. While an egg genuinely aged a full century would be most highly regarded among the Chinese, most of these are actually only one or two years old and are prepared by first soaking briefly in brine and then plastering the shell with a paste of mud and/or ash, lime, or salt.

The cheesy flavor and texture of the interior are, by Western standards, an acquired taste.

Pureed Uterus à la BBC

Other female odds and ends are enjoyed throughout the world. The French, British, and Argentines prepare dishes from the udders of cow, and the ancient Romans used both the pig's mammaries and uterus. Pig uterus shows up in Mexican *carnitas*. And many mothers giving birth in tribal cultures will consume the umbilical cord, placenta, and afterbirth of their newborn—none of which served in the least to deflect public outcry when the host of England's Channel Four's television cooking show "TV Dinners" decided to follow suit in a 1998 broadcast. The culinary use of the afterbirth was conceived as a particularly meaningful dish to be shared on-air by both mother and father. The placenta was served to studio guests on focaccio bread after being fried with shallots, flambeed, and pureed.

After censure by the Broadcasting Standards Commission, host and placenta-eater Fearnley-Whittingstall responded defiantly: "If I wasn't getting a number of complaints I would consider I wasn't

doing my job. It was one of the stories I most enjoyed doing. There's a lot of complacency in the way we approach our diet and food production, which is

The Taste of Heaven . . .

Mystery of the Durian

to be found on the ground. Durian trees are rather finicky about when they give up their fruit, and fruit plucked before it's ready to drop tends to be inferior. For this reason, durians are always allowed to fall naturally, and this—thanks to some mystery of nature—occurs almost exclusively at night.

Devotees often seek out the company of one another for clandestine durian-eating parties. What goes on behind closed doors is a matter of intense speculation, as some ascribe to the fruit not only exquisite taste

Strange Devotions

Southeast Asia is home to the mysterious durian, a melon-like figure of controversy. Tough and covered with yellow-green spikes on the outside yet soft as pudding inside, the enigmatic durian is known throughout Thailand, Singapore, and Malaysia as "the King of Fruits." Its mushy pulp can be spooned directly out of the rind but is also sold frozen, served over sticky rice, or as a fermented side dish. Asian markets that might not sell the fruit fresh will often offer cookies, crackers, cakes, custard, ice cream, candy, and extract all with the flavor of durian.

Durian is one of the world's most expensive fruits, going for around $4 per pound (about $10 a fruit). But price is not an issue to its fanatical devotees, some of whom spend several thousand dollars yearly to feed their relentless craving.

The Durian Underground

Some durian addicts resort to crime to obtain a precious mouthful of the stuff, and armed guards are regularly posted on Malaysian durian plantations during nocturnal hours when the fruits are most likely

A street vendor in an exotic land sells the mysterious Durian fruit.

but also aphrodisiac qualities. The locals have a saying: "When the durians come down from the trees, the sarongs come off."

But it's all love on the run for this outlaw fruit.

Singapore bans the durian from public buildings, and from transport on subways, buses, airplanes, ferries, and taxis. Malaysian rental car companies inflict stiff penalties on drivers who give the fruit a ride, and hotel owners and airports post notices in hotel rooms prohibiting its presence.

Why?

The fruit doesn't smell good. In fact, it stinks. Even supporters admit to this, saying that the durian "has the smell of hell and the taste of heaven." But this is not a matter of subjective bias or hypersensitivity. Cutting open the fruit is equivalent to detonating a gas bomb.

No Durians Allowed

Immediately as the surface is pierced, the durian explodes with an incomparably nauseating stench. People become clammy and desperate. Fights break out. Those too close are incapacitated.

A former British governor of Singapore

"Honey, I'm home! And I've got a special surprise for you!"

once compared the King of Fruits to "carrion in custard." And it's not just colonialist outsiders offended by the smell. Disgust is widespread if not unanimous. Finding uncharitable expressions to describe the scent is something of a national pastime for Malaysians. Sweaty socks, backed up sewers, natural gas, rotting cheese, rotting fish, rotting flesh—all have been suggested, yet no single description seems to sum up the charms of this loathsome yet seductive fruit.

why I'm quite happy to be seen eating squirrels and, indeed, placenta. People need to be shocked to make them think about the issues in eating food."

And You Expect Me to Kiss You?

Unpalatable as these tidbits may sound, at least there's an intuitive link between the substance and the desired effect. Then there's those items considered aphrodisiacs that are simply unappetizing and seemingly unrelated to the cause. Among the Romans, for instance, this would include bone marrow, hippo snouts, hyena eyes, and liquamen, a sauce made from decomposing fish entrails.

Then there's those items that seem unrelated and, for the lack of a better word, *uninspiring*. Celery, beans, peas, leaks, and radishes, not to mention prunes (which the Elizabethan brothels supplied as a sexual pick-me-up), have all, at one time or another, been regarded in the West as aphrodisiacs.

Some of these rather ordinary vegetables, such as beans, which were outlawed by many religious orders, were classed supposedly because of their notorious gastrointestinal effects, which brought attention to parts of the body best ignored.

Modern squeamishness about odors would likewise seem to rule out the use of garlic and onions in this respect, yet both of these have held a significant place in

Hmmm . . . must be a lot of lovin' goin' down in Gilroy.

the European's cabinet of love potions. Onions for the ancient Greeks were the most popular aphrodisiac and were also highly praised by the Romans. The Egyptians, Greeks, Romans, Chinese, and Japanese likewise prized garlic. Go figure.

In France, newlyweds exhausted by the adventures of their wedding night are traditionally encouraged to restore their vigor with a morning-after bowl of onion soup. Celibate priests in ancient Egypt were forbidden onions because of the overpowering effect they were believed to have. And in "The Perfumed Garden," a sort of sixteenth-century Arabic take on the *Kama Sutra*, the author, Sheik al-Nefzawi, relates that "The member of Abou el Heiloukh has remained erect for thirty days without a break because he did eat onions."

Melts in Your Mouth, Now How 'Bout Some Hands?

Chances are you've never wrapped up a valentine's gift of onions, peppers, nuts, garlic, or celery. But chocolate, an ancient pre-Columbian aphrodisiac from the New World, still retains its value today as a symbolic if not physiological love charm. Originally consumed as a warm drink, the Aztecs regarded the cacao bean as sacred to fertility goddess Xochiquetzal and made offerings of the substance in rites marking births, deaths, weddings, and the coming of age. At the time of the cacao harvest, the drink fueled orgiastic rites in honor of the goddess of the fields, and according to legend, Montezuma primed himself with 50 cups of the stuff before servicing those 600 wives of his.

Despite all these carnal associations, when Cortez returned to Europe with the beans, it found an unlikely niche in Spanish monasteries, where it served to sustain monks during fasts from solid food.

As its use spread through Europe during the years of religious reformation, Protestants came to view the drink as symbolic of Catholic excess and hedonism. In the seventeenth century, chocolate was prohibited from French monasteries, while in the French Court, chocolate became a symbol of seduction. By the reign of Louis XIV, chocolates were offered to the ladies surrounding the Sun King as a symbolic yet explicit invitation to sexual rendezvous.

Henry Stubbs, royal physician of the English court, formally proclaimed chocolate "provocative to lust," in the seventeenth century.

Phenylethylamine Luxury Assortment

From the late 1800s on, chocolatiers began to capitalize on this notion of chocolate as an aphrodisiac. In 1868, the UK-based company Cadbury began marketing the first chocolates packaged in a box decorated in the sentimental Victorian style exchanged at Valentine's Day today, and in 1922 the Italian firm Perugina introduced the chocolate kiss (*bacio*) for Valentines Day. The wife of the company's cofounder (who was having an affair with the son of her husband's partner) is said to have developed the candy from her custom of twisting papers containing invitations to rendezvous around chocolates sent to her lover inspecting chocolates down the line.

Ever since, chocolatiers and empiricists have eagerly attempted to vindicate this mystique through science. While much has been made of the fact that chocolate contains the stimulant caffeine as well as the endorphin phenylethylamine (associated with euphoria), this hardly represents a mainline to the libido. Moreover, the amounts of these substances you'd find in your average chocolate bar are pretty paltry—there's a dozen times more caffeine in a cup of coffee and one hundred times more phenylethylamine in a serving of sausage or of cheese. All told, science offers less support for chocolate's effect as a physiological aphrodisiac than for Ogden Nash's assertion that "candy is dandy, but liquor is quicker."

Necco-Philia

Sugar, corn syrup, gelatin, and flavoring. It's not exactly the height of confectionery art, but the words speak volumes: "Be Mine," "Be Good," "Be True," "My Man," "Kiss Me," and "Sweet Talk."

considerations: Slogans have to be of the sort that won't fly over the heads of first graders or raise eyebrows at the PTA, but the bottom line is letter count. No matter how clever or crowd-pleasing, they've got to be clever and crowd pleasing in two lines of no more than five letters each (or the equivalent allowing for spaces.)

There are 100 Necco messages in all, and only about 20 of those have been updated since the candies first appeared, with superlatives like "Groovy" and "Hot Stuff," biting the dust some time ago.

Anyone who's ever spent a Valentine's Day in the United States has probably chanced upon a bit of sugary pastel-colored love thanks to Sweethearts Conversation Hearts. It wouldn't be hard as there's around 8 billion of them out on the market in the 6 weeks leading up to the big day. Necco candies cranks them out all year long in plants in Wisconsin, Louisiana, and in the company's Cambridge, Massachusetts, headquarters, where company Vice President Walter "King of Hearts" Marshall puts the words in Cupid's mouth.

His lexicon of love is circumscribed by a few

> There are 100 Necco messages in all, and only about 20 of those have been updated since the candies first appeared, with superlatives like "Groovy" and "Hot Stuff," biting the dust some time ago. Also, slogans hot during the sexual revolution like "Try Me" and "Dig Me" have now been swapped for the more remote "Email Me" and "Page Me," at the suggestion of Marshall's nine grandchildren.

Also, slogans hot during the sexual revolution like "Try Me" and "Dig Me" have now been swapped for the more remote "Email Me" and "Page Me," at the suggestion of Marshall's nine grandchildren. Other recent arrivals include "Be My Icon," "Web Site," "You Rule," "You Go Girl," "Cool Dude," and "Yeah Right." Sometimes demoted phrases may even be reinstated like "Only You," which was resurrected in 1998.

The evolution of the Conversation Hearts can be traced back to Necco's "Cockles," a crisp shell-shaped candy hiding bits of colored paper printed with romantic sentiments.

Necco enters the world of cyberspace: "Email Me," "Page Me," "Be My Icon."

Cockles were first marketed by Necco back in the late 1860s, and the company moved one step closer when Daniel Chase, brother of Necco founder Oliver Chase, invented the Lozenge Printing Machine in 1866. Finally, by 1902, the first batch of "Conversation Candies" rolled off the line and became an instant success at conveying valentine's wishes in the sweetest way possible.

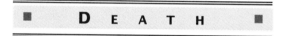

D E A T H

The Final Fling

What's the difference between an Irish wedding and an Irish wake?

One less drunk at the wake.

That's the way the Irish pin it down. And though they're more notorious for emptying bottles than clearing plates at these affairs, the Irish wake is probably the species of funeral feast most familiar to Americans. Since the 1600s, the church has fought against the overindulgence a wake traditionally entails, and finally, within the last century, some Irish are having the body laid out not in the home but in commercial funeral homes, and are laying out money not so much on innumerable bottles of whiskey as the fees demanded by more upscale caterers.

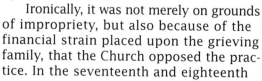

Ironically, it was not merely on grounds of impropriety, but also because of the financial strain placed upon the grieving family, that the Church opposed the practice. In the seventeenth and eighteenth centuries, various laws were even passed to prevent freeloaders from overwhelming the grieving family. But popular sentiment has always demanded the biggest blowout possible, and then some. The feeling of communal responsibility is well summed up in the old Irish rhyme:

"Deal on, deal on, my merry men all,
Deal on your cakes and your wine.
For whatever is dealt at her funeral today
Shall be dealt to-morrow at mine"

The traditional way of announcing the death was via paid professional mourners (keeners), whose ancient stylized mode of wailing suggests a link to earlier

Mediterranean, Near Eastern, or Indo-European cultures. Paid from whatever was on the table of the funeral feast, the intensity of keening was always said to be directly related to the quantity of food and, more importantly, drink provided.

Broadcasting the news as widely as possible, superstition dictated that the death even be announced to the aggrieved family's cattle and at the bees' hives, which would sometimes be wrapped in black crepe for the occasion. Thanks to an ancient connection between bees and the spirits of the dead, the "telling of the bees" was particularly important not only in Ireland, but in parts of England. Like the keeners, the bees would also be "paid" their tribute in food. Bee-sized portions of each item from the funeral feast would be smeared onto a saucer set out by the hives. What services the bees rendered probably has to do with the Celtic Goddess Brigid and her other-worldly orchard home to bees, as well as to similar mythological associations contributed by the Romans.

Funeral Club Potluck

The ancient Romans, at least the wealthy citizens, were under similar obligations to go out with a bang. Along with paying mourners, there were additional expenses involved in staging elaborate torchlight funeral processions, including hiring musicians, clowns, actors to wear wax masks of deceased family ancestors, artisans to create various memorial props carried in the parade, and orators to eulogize the dead.

To meet those expenses, the Romans resorted to potluck dinners. These dinner gatherings served as meetings for the Roman "funeral clubs" (*collegia funeraticia*). Members not only served (when the need arose) as mourners for their fellow diners but also paid dues at these dinners that went into a kitty to pay off all those musicians, jugglers, and so forth when their time came.

These societies had their predecessor in similar Greek groups dedicated to collective devotional meals (*eranos*) shared by special societies. Many historians also relate these pagan gatherings to the early Christian *agape* or love feasts.

This Christian practice served both as a social means of building fellowship as well as a mode of distributing food donated as an act of charity (*agape*). The connection to Roman gatherings in honor of the dead also calls to mind Christ's final meal, at which he instructed his followers to gather for wine and bread in his remembrance. The love feast, however, was generally distinct from sacramental bread and wine, preceding the ritual as a sort of social hour before the main event.

But within a couple of centuries, the Church was experiencing the same problem as Irish villagers had with freeloaders overrunning wakes. In 363, the Council of Laodicea forbade participants more eager for free food than fellowship from showing up at these handouts with doggy bags. By the sixth century, the practice had disappeared altogether.

A proper Roman Funeral lasted nine days, with the mourners, both intimate and professional (along with all of the participants in the elaborate funeral production), sharing a funeral meal at the gravesite or pyre. In cases of burial, there would be one final feast at the graveyard. Some cemeteries even came equipped with their own banquet halls. In both cases, food was also offered to the deceased, and sacrifices ranging from valuable spices to birds, dogs, and other small animals might also be burned on the funeral pyre.

Wealthy Egyptians likewise staged elaborate funeral processions with hired mourners and made feasts and food offerings at the gravesite. The Babylonians considered a proper funeral feast so important that they devoted a special

> **A proper Roman Funeral lasted nine days, with the mourners, both intimate and professional (along with all of the participants in the elaborate funeral production), sharing a funeral meal at the gravesite or pyre. In cases of burial, there would be one final feast at the graveyard. Some cemeteries even came equipped with their own banquet halls.**

Things begin to get out of hand at this Roman funeral feast.

demon by the name of Edimmu solely to the task of bedeviling those who failed to show deceased kin the proper respect.

You Can Die After We've Eaten Your Funeral Feast

The scale of the spread at these feasts is a pretty accurate measure in many cultures of just how high up the totem the dead guy stood. But it's in certain regions of Indonesia, in southern Sulawesi among the Torajan people, that the importance of that final festivity is so great that the moribund individual is not even *allowed* to die until all preparations are complete.

This is not to say that the body in question must maintain respiration and circulation and all that; it may fall down and start to smell funny, but no one among the Torajan will call it "dead" till the family has suitably stockpiled for the big event, which is generally postponed until September.

Underneath a festive funeral tower containing the not-quite-dead honoree, the villagers then gather for chanting, dancing, cockfighting, kickboxing, and fights between bulls—all interspersed with frequent slaughter and consumption of a generous number of water buffalo and pigs. (In former times, as many as one hundred buffalo would be eaten; now the number is somewhat less.) It is only after at least a week of holiday gluttony that the individual is finally regarded as "dead," and the coffin may be tucked away in a cliffside graveyard.

Elaborate funeral meals, often at the burial or cremation site, are common on every continent. Particularly if you look at it as an attempt to comfort the dead with a bit of familiar sustenance, then

> **U**nderneath a festive funeral tower containing the not-quite-dead honoree, the villagers then gather for chanting, dancing, cockfighting, kickboxing, and fights between bulls—all interspersed with frequent slaughter and consumption of a generous number of water buffalo and pigs.

it's clear it has some common basis in universal associations made during infancy between food and the security provided by the mother. Eating is a near universal way of drawing close socially— essentially a domestic event, eating together symbolically brings friends and lovers into a more intimate familial bond. So, naturally, by sympathetic magic, a graveside meal has been used to affirm the enduring bond with the deceased just about everywhere.

The practice appears to be very old, indicated by the remains of charred bones of food animals nearby those of human graves at Neanderthal burial sites at La-Chappelle-aux-Saints. Archeologists excavating these sites also believe these to be the remains of *numerous* meals, eaten as a series of commemorative feasts in the presence of the grave. Recurrent symbolic affirmation of ties with the world beyond—that pretty much gives you rudiments of religion. No surprise then, that annual observances in honor of the dead are part of most contemporary religions.

Eat the Cookie or Your Grandma Goes to Hell

One of the most familiar examples of this sort of observance is the Catholic's All Souls' Day. On the British Isles, the commemorative funeral feast here became more of a funeral snack with little "soul cakes" standing in for an entire meal. These small, square, cake-like cookies not only fed the dead metaphorically but resembled them (at least in their original gingerbread-man-like form).

Since the Catholic Church wasn't really keen on the idea of straight-out ancestor worship, the idea of food offerings

in purgatory." The Belgians, too, consume a special type of cookie, encouraging children to glut themselves in the belief that "the more cakes one eats the more souls will be saved from purgatory." But if you're really looking for otherworld-pleasing confections, Mexico's the place to check out.

Take a Bite out of Your Skull

Pre-Columbian Mexicans didn't need any Catholic priests to teach them how to honor departed souls with a holiday of their own. They were already celebrating one, and not a single day, but a month-long observance dedicated to the Aztec Queen of the Dead, Mictecacihautl, and the war god Huitzilopochtli. The holiday focused particularly on the recently departed and dead children.

The Spanish priests pushed the Indians to synch up the celebration with the November 1st All Soul's Day, and succeeded in obscuring the roles of Mictecacihautl and Huitzilopochtli in the proceedings and condensing the month-long celebration down to a mere four days, but they kept the emphasis on departed children with October 30 and 31 dedicated to the souls of children (*angelitos*) and November 1 and 2 to the souls of adults.

On those days, particularly in the Mexican state of Oaxaca, families celebrate with grave-side picnics and night-long candlelight vigils and parties in cemeteries. Graves are cleaned, repainted, and decked with flowers, and wandering musicians are hired to serenade the dead with musical favorites. Elaborate altars, *ofrendas*, are constructed in homes and offerings are left upon them.

on behalf of the dead was reworked into a means of bargaining the souls out of the halfway house of purgatory. Not only were kids encouraged to eat these on behalf of the departed souls, but to encourage more baking and eating of soul cakes (and, hence, more saving of souls) the tradition of "souling" evolved (the origin of Halloween trick-or-treating). Souling involved kids wandering from house to house begging for soul cakes and other treats, promising a prayer for each tidbit received, and singing souling ballads as they strolled along, such as: "Soul! soul! for a soul-cake! I pray, good missus a soul-cake. An apple or pear, a plum or a cherry, Any good thing to make us merry, One for Peter, two for Paul, Three for Him who made us all."

The Czechs likewise remember the dead by eating special cakes on All Soul's Eve along with traditional glasses of cold milk to "cool the souls

Graves are cleaned, repainted, and decked with flowers, and wandering musicians are hired to serenade the dead with musical favorites. Elaborate altars, ofrendas, are constructed in homes and offerings are left upon them. Children receive toys, candies, gifts of food, and skulls made of sugar inscribed with their name, as well as skulls, hearses, and funeral wreathes of chocolate and marzipan.

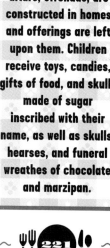

Some awfully tasty-looking pan de los muertos.

Children receive toys, candies, gifts of food, and skulls made of sugar inscribed with their name, as well as skulls, hearses, and funeral wreathes of chocolate and marzipan.

Departed adults are remembered with sweets, traditional foods, and the sweet egg-rich *pan de los muertos* "bread of the dead," sometimes sprinkled with decorative bits of dough shaped like bones and skulls. Usually baked as a simple round loaf, but sometimes formed in the shape of a human being or animal (particularly a rabbit), the loaf can also contain a tiny skeleton figurine bringing luck to whomever receives the portion in which it's contained. Elaborate tamales and moles are often prepared for the dead, sometimes made from huge green Mexican pumpkins especially grown for the occasion.

Sticky Pink Buns for a Ghost

Throughout Asia, the dead get pampered with food on special days too. When the Chinese go, they get bowls full of cooked meats, rice, and offerings of wine arranged around their photo in a family altar. Every 7 days after, supplies are restocked for as long as 11 weeks.

In April, Chinese observe Ching Ming, Remembrance of Ancestors Day, or "The Festival of Supreme Light," by honoring the dead with offerings of rice and sake and graveside picnics. The day was originally dedicated to the remembrance of a patriotic hero, Jie Zitui, famous for this faithfulness to an unjustly ousted ruler of the Shaanxi Province in 600 B.C.E. Zitui's devotion knew no bounds, and when his ruler was on the brink of starvation, Zitui is said to have saved his life by offering a tasty cut of meat off his own leg. After Zitui died in a house fire, the pious began decorating his grave in the manner now typical of the holiday. In remembrance of the hero's mode of death, no stoves are lighted on that day and only uncooked food is eaten—though the cannibalistic incident does not influence the day's menu. Cooked and dyed eggs are important during Ching Ming as a symbol of rebirth.

Second in importance only to New Year's on the Japanese calendar is the festival of Obon, the Buddhist All Souls' Day. Originally from India, Obon, comes from *Urabon-e*, which means "intense pain or suffering," a description of the state in which one of the Buddha's disciples is said to have envisioned the spirit of his departed mom. To save her from hell, he was instructed to offer certain prayers and prepare dishes of food, and this practice is now observed throughout Japan on behalf of all departed relatives. During the three days of this festival, the gates of hell are said to fly open, and

the occupants are free to wander. As always, the dead are hungry, and plenty of food is prepared and left out for them.

Taoists on the tiny island of Chueng Chau outlying Hong Kong make food offerings to appease the spirits of those killed by typhoons and pirates during a week-long springtime festival called "Festival of the Bun Hills," highlighted by the construction of three colossal bamboo towers, thickly covered with pink sweet buns blessed by the priests of the island's temple and distributed to the participants at the festival's close. A meat fast, performances of classical Chinese operas, and costumed processions with stilt-walkers and floats also mark the occasion.

■ **A N D   T H E N ?** ■

The Final Frontier

So now we know the foods that put baby-making ideas in people's heads, the cakes we bake when they marry, and the feasts we prepare when they die.

And then? What kind of food could possibly follow death?

Well, we've already talked plenty about this. Those bowls of rice loved ones sit around your picture, the candies they leave on your grave, the toasts they lift toward you then gulp down before you get a taste. They're all meals of make-believe. By the time you die, they figure you've learned a thing or two about pretending. They don't expect you to really eat it! Even little kids know how to get together for an imaginary tea party of twigs, pebbles, and rainwater. They hold it to their mouth, they move their jaw, and smack their lips, but they don't actually eat a thing. It's all a game, and that's how food seems to be in the invisible world—something to play with.

You, the angels, the sprites, they're all presumably well fed, but you can still come and go from this side to the next and play games with food. Moving from present to past and future and back again, there's plenty to see and much to do with those idle invisible hands. Since humans always have food lying around, it's a good medium with which to playfully communicate. Stir up the tea leaves lingering in a cup to give a pertinent warning of something you saw in the future; give some needy soul a boost by imprinting their tortilla with a divine countenance, make someone's day by

giving them a lucky break on a wishbone.

You'll see. There are so many fun games to play with food. Why eat it?

Bobbing for Destiny

The original object of bobbing for apples, for instance, was more than a mere mouthful of fruit or the chance to enjoy another participant's damp and sputtering indignity. The game actually

Children used to bob for apples in order to determine who would become their future mates.

originated as an attempt—increasingly playful over the centuries—to foretell the future.

Of the many versions of the game to come down to us through the Celts, a primary goal was the determination of a partner for life, with the first to catch an apple firmly between the teeth being the first to marry. Other

> **T**he original object of bobbing for apples, for instance, was more than a mere mouthful of fruit or the chance to enjoy another participant's damp and sputtering indignity. The game actually originated as an attempt—increasingly playful over the centuries—to foretell the future.

versions involve paring the apples caught—whoever removed the longest strip of peel would lead the longest life. When these strips were thrown over the left shoulder, those looking for further clues to the future could inspect the shape of the peel upon landing to determine what letter of the alphabet the paring most resembled, thereby determining the initial of the future mate.

A custom lingering in some Slavic countries and once practiced in Germany also uses an apple, one sliced to the core and then inspected, in hopes that the uncovered pattern of seeds and stem will reveal various omens for the coming year.

Poultry and Prognostication

Similarly, pulling apart a wishbone to see who would get the longer end was originally more than a game to see who could find a better point of leverage. Earlier in our country's history, this bone-splintering pastime was understood as a good way to determine the harshness of the coming winter.

But our custom is actually a mercifully abbreviated version of a practice dating back to a time before the Roman Empire, when the ancient Etruscans used hens as supernatural oracles. Their process involved drawing a circle on the ground and sectioning this like a pie, designating each section as representative of a particular letter, symbol, or concept. A handful of grain was scattered over the circle and a hen was placed in the center and allowed to peck the grain. The hen's choice of particular grains designated a sequence of letters or symbols, in which

> **P**ulling apart a wishbone to see who would get the longer end was originally more than a game to see who could find a better point of leverage. Earlier in our country's history, this bone-splintering pastime was understood as a good way to determine the harshness of the coming winter.

would be found the answer to one's question. For its trouble, the hen was sacrificed, and its collarbone was extracted and hung out to dry. Finally it was broken as final confirmation or denial of the prophecy pecked out in grain.

More widespread than the use of hens to foretell the future was haruspicy—another Etruscan mode of divination utilizing food animals, in this case the divination of the future through the clues found in the internal organs of the animal slaughtered sacrificially. Practiced up into the sixth century, the use of haruspicy was even authorized by the Christian Bishop Innocent of Rome in 408 when the city was threatened by the Goths.

Though meaning might be read from the coloration, markings, or configuration of any given organ, the liver was of particular importance, and bronze instructional models illustrating significant variations have been found in Etruscan, Hittite, and Babylonian archeological sites. Haruspices, the high priests schooled in this art, were not only sought out for private counsel, but were also highly regarded by the Roman Senate and consulted on all affairs of importance. A sacred feast consisting of the meal of the animal was shared between priest and petitioner once the chicken innards had made their secrets known.

Your Future Is a Big Yolk

Related to the art of haruspicy is oomancy—that is, divination with eggs. What you find in cracking open an egg like whatever you find in cutting open an animal was rather significant to ancient prognosticators. Just as mutant births were almost universally viewed as signs of important developments—and not always gloomy ones—opening an egg with double yolk, in many European folk traditions, is interpreted as a sign of a coming marriage, by suggesting the

union of two as one. Similarly, if an egg cracks while boiling, it's sometimes likened to the opening of a door and foretells the arrival of visitors.

A more esoteric form of fortune-telling with eggs involves the inspection of forms assumed by the raw egg as it's dropped in water. Dropping your food in water could reveal much besides your own clumsiness. In Egypt, for instance, you can have your fortune read by those who specialize in interpreting the shape of oil globules drifting on the surface of

your soup. Others specialize in reading shapes assumed by soggy wheat cakes dropped in water (aeluromancy), while some favor barley cakes (alphitomancy). This particular art of mixing food and water for the purpose of fortune-telling is known as hydromancy and is most commonly exemplified by the reading of tea leaves (tasseography).

Tall, Dark, and Darjeeling

More popular in countries where tea is steeped loose rather than in bags or

"You will soon find a cure for those two tremendous humps on your back."

balls, tea leaf reading actually involves the discernment of patterns produced after swirling a more or less emptied cup enough to leave a few leaf fragments stuck to the sides. Proximity to the handle (the subject's "home") indicates greater importance or nearness of a predicted event. Time is indicated by the height of the leaves, with those closer to the bottom representing the more distant future, those closer to the rim imminent. Within these parameters, the reader searches for configurations resembling possibly significant letters or numbers or clearly delineated geometric shapes indicating various nuances of good fortune (i.e., they "wing it"). Coffee grounds likewise are sometimes swirled and read, primarily in eastern European or Islamic countries where coffee is served with grounds in the cup—"Turkish" style.

Cookie's Fortune

"In the cookie, the wise man finds much wisdom and the cook finds much gold."

While most of us haven't ever picked through chicken entrails or meditated upon soggy cakes or coffee grounds in search of our futures, almost everyone at one time or another has read some vaguely uplifting or aphoristic message on a slip of paper folded into a crispy almond-flavored cookie.

The origins of the fortune cookie are as vague as its predictions. However, one thing is certain—the custom is more indicative of Chinatown than China. Some sources say it was a Chinatown baker and noodle maker in Los Angeles, a charitable Cantonese immigrant named David Jung, who devised the cookies around 1916 to both feed and convey inspirational thoughts to homeless people living near his bakery.

More likely is the San Francisco version, setting the date at 1907 and crediting the invention to one Makota Hagiwara, a caretaker of the city's Japanese Tea Garden. At the time, Hagiwara was experiencing some difficulties with the mayor to whom he originally sent the cookies with messages of goodwill in a campaign of reconciliation. In 1915, his invention is said to have made its public debut at the Panama Exhibition and was picked up by San Francisco Chinese restaurateurs eager to cash in on the newfound Western infatuation with the exotic East. By 1960, the Lotus Fortune Cookie Company in San Francisco had created a machine that obviated the manual insertion of slips of paper, and the cookies assumed their modern form. Some sources purport that during

Food of the Gods

Edible Simulacra

Perhaps arranged by the same omnipresent hand that plasters wet tea-leaves to the sides of teacups, the following foods have struck a variety of people as testimony to divine intervention in human fate—evidence that a less observant type might have simply eaten for lunch.

Tortilla
Religion: Roman Catholic
Manifestation: Image of Jesus Christ
Discoverer: María Rubio
Where: Lake Arthur, New Mexico
Year: 1977
Comments: Caused husband to stop drinking and helped with difficulties in pregnancy. The Rubios built a shrine for the Holy Tortilla of New Mexico to accommodate a constant stream of pilgrims.

Indian Fry Bread
Religion: Roman Catholic
Manifestation: Letters "KJCB" interpreted as "King Jesus is Coming Back"
Discoverer: Ramona Barreras
Where: Phoenix, Arizona
Year: 1977
Comments: Made cover story in Weekly World News.

Sticky Bun
Religion: Roman Catholic
Manifestation: Image of Mother Teresa
Discoverer: Ryan Finney, employee of coffeehouse, where the bun is enshrined
Where: Nashville, Tennessee, Java Bongo Coffeehouse
Year: 1996
Comments: Varnished bun drew large crowds and media attention as well as a personal letter from Mother Teresa requesting that her name not be used in promotion, causing the bun to simply be known as "NunBun™"

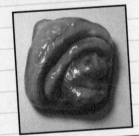

Mother Teresa or Walter Matthau? You be the judge!

Eggplant
Religion: Islam
Manifestation: Sliced open to reveal seeds spelling "ya-allah" ("Allah exists")
Discoverer: Salim and Ruksan a Patel
Where: Bolton, England
Year: 1996
Comments: Eggplant miracle reportedly foreseen in dream by Ruksan a Patel.

Tomato
Religion: Islam
Manifestation: Internal veins spell (in Arabic) "There is only one god," and "Mohammed is the messenger."
Discoverer: Shaista Javed, 14-year-old schoolgirl
Where: Huddersfield, England
Year: 1997
Comments: Local shopkeeper reported surge in tomato market as a result of miracle.

Watermelon
Religion: Islam
Manifestation: Name of Allah visible on rind
Discoverer: Anonymous farmer
Where: Taiba-Ndiassana, Senegal
Year: 1996
Comments: Sheik Absoul Moneim Zein reported additional phrase legible next to the hand of Allah: "Hamdoulillah," meaning "Praise be to God." (Found just before Ramadan).

Potato
Religion: Mammonism
Manifestation: Shaped like Mickey Mouse
Discoverer: Michelle Lachance with sons Jeremy and Andy
Where: Lincoln, Nebraska
Year: 1991
Comments: Potato purchased by Walt Disney Co. Whereabouts unknown.

Get the latest scores . . . before they happen.

the early 1900s, Chinese railroad workers in California's Sierra Nevada region enlivened the drudgery of their labors by exchanging similar cookies, but this claim is pretty shaky. Supporters of the theory identify these cookies with "moon cakes," traditionally eaten exclusively during the Chinese mid-autumn festival rather than year round. And though moon cakes are still common at this festival as celebrated in the U.S. and at home in China, no messages can be found tucked into their interior. But this was not always the case.

Throughout the thirteenth and fourteenth centuries, China suffered under Mongol occupation. Revolutionary

sentiments needed to be coordinated into an actual battle plan without alerting occupying forces. Knowing that the Mongols bore a distinct dislike for a local sweet created with lotus nut paste, Chinese patriot Chu Yuan Chang is said to have devised the moon cake from this ingredient and hidden details of the plans for revolution on slips of paper inside. The plan succeeded, giving birth to both the Ming Dynasty and an ongoing love for the sweet round cookie.

It's a great story and may have inspired David Jung in Los Angeles or Makota Hagiwara in San Francisco, but it would not have been familiar to the largely

American population that was gobbling up the cookies from the beginning. Becoming increasingly popular during the 1930s (the same era that saw Mann's "Chinese" Theater built in Los Angeles), the fortunes were couched in decidedly Confucian language intended to impress and mystify Westerners. Over the decades, more familiar and homogenized language has been adopted.

Recently, the fortune cookie has not only gained popularity in Europe but has shown up in China advertised as a novelty for Chinese eager to get a taste of the West. In Hong Kong, the cookies have been adopted as a way of getting anti-drug messages out, and American businesses or anyone with enough money to hedge his bets can today write his own fortune. Thanks to companies like Fancy Fortune Cookies in Indianapolis, Indiana, those eager to take control of such matters can not only pen their own predictions but substitute exotic flavors like orange, key lime pie, coffee, and mint for the traditional almond pastry.

Chomping Down on Good Fortune

In many Catholic countries, including Belgium, France, Spain, and Latin American countries colonized by Spain, Epiphany, or "Three Kings Day," is a day for baking cakes for a special fortune-telling game. Falling 12 days after Christmas, this day is traditionally regarded as the one on which the Magi arrived in Bethlehem bearing gifts for the Christ Child. These Epiphany cakes bear a special gift too—a hidden treasure (usually a bean or a coin)—that brings luck or predicts the fortune of whoever finds it in his slice.

In France, the recipient is treated as one of the "kings," which might either mean he is "treated like royalty" or that he is obliged, like the biblical kings, to make a gift to some worthy child. In the former French territory of Louisiana, bakers in New Orleans produce the famous "King Cake," throughout the entire "Epiphany season" (meaning from Epiphany to Lent), and in keeping with the town's party spirit, bakers are generally much

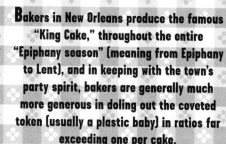

Bakers in New Orleans produce the famous "King Cake," throughout the entire "Epiphany season" (meaning from Epiphany to Lent), and in keeping with the town's party spirit, bakers are generally much more generous in doling out the coveted token (usually a plastic baby) in ratios far exceeding one per cake.

Paul's Pastry Shop in Picayune, MS ships King Cakes around the world.

Haydel's King Cake includes a mardi gras *guide, a king cake history scroll, two packs of famous* Cafe Du Monde *coffee, carnival beads and doubloons, and a handcrafted* mardi gras *collectible figure. Such a deal!*

more generous in doling out the coveted token (usually a plastic baby) in ratios far exceeding one per cake.

In Mexico, it's a tiny figurine of the baby Jesus carrying with it the obligation to give a party on February 2nd. In Greece, the cake is called Vasilopeta or "Basil's cake," and it's sliced on New Year's Day. In Scotland, the same cake game is played on Halloween and it's a ring, thimble, button, coin, horseshoe, swastika, and wishbone for different nuances of good fortune.

Most curious of all is the existence of a similar custom far away in Tibet. During Losar, the Tibetan New Year, feasts include a holiday soup with dumplings containing symbolic fortunes for the coming year, such as a pebble for longevity, hot peppers for moodiness, salt for fame, and so forth.

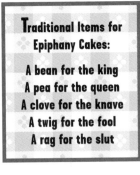

Traditional Items for Epiphany Cakes:

A bean for the king
A pea for the queen
A clove for the knave
A twig for the fool
A rag for the slut

Easy-Bake Wicca

With foods not at all uncommon in fortune-telling customs or as aphrodisiacs, and with cooks historically related to herbalists and herbalism to witchcraft, should it come as any surprise that common items from the shelves of kitchens should often be used in attempts to cast spells?

"Kitchen Witchery" is much more than a metaphor for a particularly skilled way of whipping up a date loaf. Many New Agers regard it as a traditional form of pagan practice related to the ancient idea of the hearth as the magical source of all life. The Church attempted to crush the craft by associating it with repulsive "eye of newt and toe of frog" materials, but exotic or repulsive items were not necessarily regarded as essential to these pursuits. The combination of everyday ingredients, along with knowledge of nutrition, folk medicine, and psychology blends into a shade of magic that even skeptics can appreciate.

Many modern Wiccans, in their attempts to reintegrate the sacred into everyday routines, make use of a variety of materials, such as those specified by author Lexa Rosean in her book *75 Simple Spells, Charms and Enchantments that You Can Make from Supermarket Ingredients.* Employing a chocolate cake layered with creme and rolled like a jelly roll so that slices

reveal a prominent spiral pattern, Rosean describes a spell used to reduce the number of hours your child spends glued to the television in this surprising passage:

"The spiral is an ancient Neolithic symbol that existed long before television. Anyone can be hypnotized looking into a spiral. It is a powerful image to use to send subliminal messages. You can use spiral-shaped pasta, but I find the cake roll easier to work with. . . . Simply take a chocolate cake roll and carve 'No TV' in the white filling. Move the cake roll in a circular clockwise motion before your child's eyes, tempting and implanting a subliminal message. . . . Move closer and closer until you are close enough for the child to bite into the mouth-watering treat. Once the child eats the cake roll, the message will be delivered to the child's subconscious."

Can you get any more Neolithic than that? 🍴

Auld Lang Dine

Lucky Foods for the Coming Year

Rosh Hashanah (Jewish New Year)

Apple dipped in honey = for sweetness

Challah, baked in a circle = for continuity of peaceful year

Sesame seeds = for plenitude

Dried fruits = for sweetness

Olives = for beauty and tranquillity

Carrots = representing divine decree

Pomegranates = for the mitzvahs

Japanese New Year

Fish eggs = for fertility

Root vegetables = for stability

Black beans = for health

Kombu (seaweed) = for happiness

Mashed sweet potatoes = for safekeeping

Chinese New Year

Fatt choy (dried seaweed) = for becoming prosperous

Ho see, preserved oysters = for a "fortunate occasion"

Jiaozi dumplings = means "to sleep together and have sons"

Leafy mustard green = for longevity

Fish, leaks = for surplus

Mandarin oranges = for gold

Hong zao, red dates = for early prosperity

Chestnuts = for profit

Melon seeds = for many offspring

Mushrooms = means "wishes fulfilled from East to West"

The publisher would like to thank the following individuals and organizations for contributing images to this book. While every effort has been made to contact manufacturers, companies, associations, and individuals, the sources of certain photographs and illustrations were impossible to track down. Any uncredited image brought to our attention by its owner will be gladly credited in future editions. Thank you, one and all!

California Fig Advisory Board: 9

Bat Conservation International, Inc. (Photo by Merlin D. Tuttle): 11

Library of Congress: 13, 16, 27, 31, 69, 78, Cover

The Nostalgia Collection: 18, 37, 39, 42, 47, 68, 82, 87, 88, 97, 100, 102, 115, 118, 121, 127, 154, 159, 160, 161, 163, 166, 167, 171, 173 (top), 176, 180, 181, 182, 187, 188 (left), 191 (left), 201, 202, 203 (left), 205, 230

Vivian Alexander: 21

International Pancake Day (Photo by John Avery): 26

Mike Carrig: 35

Silver World Publishing: 41

Wyoming Buffalo Company: 43

Panache: 44

Rob Hale: 46

Frescargot Farms, Inc.: 48

Frog Legs Unlimited: 49, Cover

Fur and Refuge Division: 52

J.T. Steiny: 54 (top), 86, 98, 107, 133

Zachary Huang: 54 (bottom), 55

Hotlix: 56, 57

Lamb Etc.—Scottish & Irish Imports: 58

Pork Master: 61 (top)

Bobak's Sausage Company: 65

Nathans Famous, Inc.: 70, Cover

White Castle System, Inc.: 72, 73

Hamburg Chamber of Commerce: 74

Hamburger Hall of Fame: 75

Athens Chamber of Commerce: 76

Historical Society of Battle Creek: 79, 80, 81

Vlasic Foods International: 84, 85, Cover

Hormel Foods Corporation (SPAM is a registered trademark of Hormel Foods, LLC): 89, 90, 91, 92, 93, Cover

Interstate Brands Corp: 94, 95, 96

Remarkable Things: 105

Chattanooga Bakery, Inc.: 106, Cover

Burlingame Museum of Pez Memorabilia: 110, 111, 114

Philadelphia Chewing Gum: 112, 134

Amurol Confections Co.: 113

Life Lines, Inc.: 117

Good Humor-Breyers Ice Cream (Photo by Popsicle® Ice Pop): 122, 123

Peake of Catering: 125

The Mini-Cake Museum: 132

Howard Karno Books, Inc.: 136, 137, 222

Gotham Bar and Grill: 138

Jeff Potocsnak: 142, 143

The International Hamburger Hall of Fame: 144

Joseph Enterprises, Inc. (Chia Pet is a registered trademark of Joseph Enterprises, Inc.): 145

Burke/Triolo Productions/LA: 148

Oscar Mayer Foods (OSCAR MAYER and WIENERMOBILE are registered trademarks of Kraft Foods, Inc.): 149, 150, Cover

Future Studio (Photo by Andy Caulfield): 152, Cover

Idaho Potato Expo: 153

The Catsup Bottle Preservation Group and International Fan Club (Photo by Michael Gassmann): 155 (right)

Erik Sprague (aka Amago with the Jim Rose Circus): 172, Cover

University of Pittsburgh at Bradford: 175

Jeanne Dunning: 178

CreatAbiliToys!: 187 (top), 188 (right), 190, 191 (right), 192 (right)

Cave Hill Cemetery Company, Inc.: 192 (left)

General Mills: 193, 194, 195, 196, 197

Sweet-N-Nasty: 203 (right), 204 (top)

Toefood Chocolate: 204 (bottom)

The Nut Museum: 208

Gilroy Visitors Bureau: 214

Necco: 216, 217 (top)

Bongo Java: 229

Paul's Pastry Shop: 231

Haydel's Bakery: 232

Amurol Confections Co.
2800 North Route 47
Yorkville, IL 60560
630-553-4800 • Fax 630-553-4801

Athens Chamber Of Commerce
1206 S. Palestine
Athens, TX 75751
903-675-5181 • Fax 903-675-5183
athenscc@aol.com

Bat Conservation International, Inc.
P.O.Box 162603
Austin, TX 78716-2603
512-327-9721 • Fax 512-327-9724
www.batcon.org

Bobak's Sausage Company
5275 South Archer Ave
Chicago, IL 60632
773-735-5334 • Fax 773-735-8605
bobak@bobak.com
www.bobak.com

Bongo Java
2007 Belmont Blvd.
Nashville, TN 37212
616-385-JAVA
BongoJava@aol.com

Burke/Triolo Productions
8755 Washington Blvd.
Culver City, CA 90232
www.burketriolo.com

Burlingame Museum of Pez Memorabilia
214 California Dr.
Burlingame, CA 94010-4113
650-347-2301 • Fax 650-347-3840
www.burlingamepezmuseum.com

California Fig Advisory Board
3425 N. First St. Suite 109
Fresno, CA 93726
559-224-3447 • Fax 559-224-3449
info@californiafigs.com
www.californiafigs.com

The Catsup Bottle Preservation Group and
International Fan Club
Judy DeMoisy
P.O. Box 1108
Collinsville, IL 62234
618-345-5598 • Fax 618-345-5699

Cave Hill Cemetery Company, Inc.
701 Baxter Avenue
Louisville, KY 40204
502-451-5630 • Fax 502-451-5655

Chattanooga Bakery, Inc.
900 Manufacturers Road
Chattanooga, TN 37405
463-267-3351 • Fax 423-266-2169
www.moonpie.com

CreatAbiliToys!
Museum Of Advertising Icons
1550 Madruga Ave., Fifth Floor
Coral Gables, FL 33146
305-663-7374 • Fax 305-669-0092

Erik Sprague (aka Amago with the Jim
Rose Circus)
spidergod5@aol.com
http://members.aol.com/spidergod5/index.html

Frescargot Farms, Inc.
1610 14th Street
Sanger, CA 93657
559-875-2053 • Fax 559-875-1176
frescargot@aol.com
www.etropolis.com/snails/

Frog Legs Unlimited
2689 N Kirk Rd.
West Palm Beach, FL 33406
561-968-1193

Fur and Refuge Division
Louisiana Department of Wildlife and Fisheries
2415 Darnall Rd.
New Iberia, LA 70560
318-373-0032 • Fax 318-373-0181
kinler_n@wlf.state.la.us • www.wlf.state.la.us
www.chef-parola.com

Future Studio
P.O. Box 292000
Los Angeles, 90029
323-660-0620 • Fax 323-660-2571

General Mills
1 General Mills Blvd.
Minneapolis, MN 55426
612-764-2311 • Fax 612-764-3232

Gilroy Visitors Bureau
7780 Monterey St.
Gilroy, CA 95020
408-842-6436 • Fax 408-842-6438
info@gilroyvisitor.org

Good Humor-Breyers Ice Cream
c/o McDowell & Piasecki
225 West Washington St.
Suite 1625
Chicago, IL 60606
312-201-9101 • Fax 312-201-9161

Gotham Bar and Grill
12 East 12th Street
New York, NY 10003
212-620-4020

Hamburg Chamber of Commerce
8 South Buffalo Street
Hamburg, NY 14075
716-649-7917 • Fax 716-649-6362

Hamburger Hall of Fame
126 North Main Street
P.O. Box 173
Seymour, WI 54165
414-833-9522

Haydel's Bakery
4037 Jefferson Highway
New Orleans, LA 70121
1-800-442-1342
www.haydelbakery.com

Historical Society of Battle Creek
Riverwalk Center, Suite 5
34 West Jackson Street
Battle Creek, MI 49017
616-965-2613 • Fax 616-966-2495
bchist@net-link.net
www.sojournertruth.org

Hormel Foods Corporation
1 Hormel Place
Austin, MN 55912-3680
507-437-5611 • Fax 507-437-5489

Hotlix
P.O. Box 447
Grover Beach, CA 93483
1-800-EAT-WORM • Fax 805-473-9074
www.hotlix.com

Howard Karno Books, Inc.
P.O. Box 2100
Valley Center, CA 92082
760-749-2304 • Fax 760-749-4390

Idaho Potato Expo
130 NW Main
PO Box 366
Blackfoot, ID 83221
208-785-2517
potatoexpo@ida.net • www.potatoexpo.com

The International Hamburger Hall of Fame
Owner: "Hamburger Harry" Sperl
1000 North Beach Street
Daytona Beach, FL 32117
904-254-8753 • Fax 904-255-2460
harry@burgerweb.com • www.burgerweb.com

International Pancake Day
P.O. Box 665
Liberal, KS 67905
316-626-0170 • Fax 316-626-0540
www.pancakeday.com

Interstate Brands Corporation
12 E. Armour Blvd.
Kansas City, MO 64111-1284
816-502-4000 • Fax 816-502-4216

Jeff Potocsnak
104 Braintree Court
Cary, NC 27513
Kingbolo.Com
919-468-3730
kingbolo@pipeline.com

Joseph Enterprises, Inc.
Ed Garvilla
425 California Street, Suite 1300
San Francisco, CA 94104
www.chia.com
415-397-6992 • Fax 415-397-0103

Lamb Etc.—Scottish & Irish Imports
1413 SE Mill St.
Roseburg, OR 97470
541-673-7463
www.tcfb.com/lambetc

Life Lines, Inc.
Jim Nelson
PO Box 650
Homer, AK 99603
907-235-6524
biblegum@xyz.net

Nathans Famous, Inc.
1400 Old Country Road #400
Westbury, NY 11590-5131
516-338-8500 • Fax 516-338-7220

Necco
134 Cambridge Street
Cambridge, MA 02141
617-498-0500 • Fax 617-498-0526

Nut Museum
303 Ferry Road
Old Lyme, CT 06391
860-434-7636

Oscar Mayer Foods
A division of Kraft Foods, Inc.
910 Mayer Avenue
Madison, WI 53704
608-241-3311

Panache
Russ Riseman
The Woods Resort
Route 1 Box 2210
Killington, VT 05751
802-422-8622 • RRiseman@aol.com

Paul's Pastry Shop
3247 Highway 43 North
Picayune, MS 39466
1-800-669-5180 • Fax 601-798-8945

Peake of Catering
4501 Main Street
Vancouver, B.C. V5V 3R4
Canada
604-872-8431 • www.peakeofcatering.com

Philadelphia Chewing Gum
Eagle & Lawrence Rds
Havertown, PA 19083
610-449-1700 • Fax 610-449-0563
swellgum@compuserve.com

Pork Master
www.Porkrind.com • Porkmaster@porkrind.com
Fax 630-578-0803

Remarkable Things
Larry Thomas
Long Beach, CA

Rob Hale
halerob@idryo.com • www.idryo.com\sushi

Silver World Publishing
P.O. Box 100
Lake City, CO 81235-100
970-944-2515 • Fax 970-944-7009

Sweet-N-Nasty
90 Massachusetts Ave.
Boston, MA 02115-1803
617-266-7171 • Fax 617-262-7171
www.sweet-n-nasty.com

Toefood Chocolate
2500 Milvia St.
Suite 216
Berkeley, CA 94704
888-TOEFOOD • Fax 510-849-3810
www.Toefood.com

University of Pittsburgh at Bradford
300 Campus Drive
Bradford, PA 16701
814-362-7590 • Fax 814-362-7684

Vivian Alexander
6165 Picard Lane
Maurice, LA 70555
337-898-0803 • Fax 337-898-0748
info@vivianalexander.com
www.vivianalexander.com

Vlasic Foods International
6 Executive Campus
Vlasic Plaza
Cherry Hill, NJ 08002-4122
856-969-7100 • Fax 856-969-7418

White Castle System, Inc.
555 W. Goodale Street
Columbus, OH 43215
614-559-2577 • Fax 614-228-8841
www.whatyoucrave.com

Wyoming Buffalo Company
1280 Sheridan Ave.
Cody, WY 82414
1-800-453-0636 • Fax 307-587-2318
wyobuffalo@wyoming.com
www.wyobuffalo.com

Zachary Huang
Department Of Entomology
Michigan State University
East Lansing, MI 48824
517-353-8136 • Fax 517-353-4354
www.cyberbee.net/bugeat

Books Available From Santa Monica Press

The Book of Good Habits
Simple and Creative Ways to Enrich Your Life
BY DIRK MATHISON
224 pages $9.95

Café Nation
Coffee Folklore, Magick, and Divination
BY SANDRA MIZUMOTO POSEY
224 pages $9.95

Collecting Sins
A Novel
BY STEVEN SOBEL
288 pages $13

Health Care Handbook
A Consumer's Guide to the American Health Care System
BY MARK CROMER
256 pages $12.95

Helpful Household Hints
The Ultimate Guide to Housekeeping
BY JUNE KING
224 pages $12.95

How To Find Your Family Roots and Write Your Family History
BY WILLIAM LATHAM AND CINDY HIGGINS
288 pages $14.95

How To Win Lotteries, Sweepstakes, and Contests in the 21st Century
BY STEVE "AMERICA'S SWEEPSTAKES KING" LEDOUX
224 pages $14.95

Letter Writing Made Easy!
Featuring Sample Letters for Hundreds of Common Occasions
BY MARGARET MCCARTHY
224 pages $12.95

Letter Writing Made Easy! Volume 2
Featuring More Sample Letters for Hundreds of Common Occasions
BY MARGARET MCCARTHY
224 pages $12.95

Nancy Shavick's Tarot Universe
BY NANCY SHAVICK
336 pages $15.95

Offbeat Food
Adventures in an Omnivorous World
BY ALAN RIDENOUR
240 pages $19.95

Offbeat Golf
A Swingin' Guide To a Worldwide Obsession
BY BOB LOEFFELBEIN
240 pages $17.95

Offbeat Marijuana
The Life and Times of the World's Grooviest Plant
BY SAUL RUBIN
240 pages $19.95

Offbeat Museums
The Collections and Curators of America's Most Unusual Museums
BY SAUL RUBIN
240 pages $19.95

Past Imperfect
How Tracing Your Family Medical History Can Save Your Life
BY CAROL DAUS
240 pages $12.95

Quack!
Tales of Medical Fraud from the Museum of Questionable Medical Devices
BY BOB MCCOY
240 pages $19.95

Silent Echoes
Discovering Early Hollywood Through the Films of Buster Keaton
BY JOHN BENGTSON
240 pages $24.95

What's Buggin You?
Michael Bohdan's Guide to Home Pest Control
BY MICHAEL BOHDAN
256 pages $12.95

Order Form
1-800-784-9553

	Amount
The Book of Good Habits ($9.95)	_____
Café Nation ($9.95)	_____
Collecting Sins ($13)	_____
Health Care Handbook ($12.95)	_____
Helpful Household Hints ($12.95)	_____
How to Find Your Family Roots and Write Your Family History ($14.95)	_____
How to Win Lotteries, Sweepstakes . . . ($14.95)	_____
Letter Writing Made Easy! ($12.95)	_____
Letter Writing Made Easy! Volume 2 ($12.95)	_____
Nancy Shavick's Tarot Universe ($15.95)	_____
Offbeat Food ($19.95)	_____
Offbeat Golf ($17.95)	_____
Offbeat Marijuana ($19.95)	_____
Offbeat Museums ($19.95)	_____
Past Imperfect ($12.95)	_____
Quack! ($19.95)	_____
Silent Echoes ($24.95)	_____
What's Buggin' You? ($12.95)	_____

Shipping & Handling:	
1 book $3.00	Subtotal _____
Each additional book is	CA residents add 8.25% sales tax _____
$ .50	Shipping and Handling (see left) _____
	TOTAL _____

Name _____

Address _____

City_____ State _____ Zip _____

❏ Visa ❏ MasterCard   Card Number _____

Exp. Date _____ Signature _____

❏ **Enclosed is my check or money order payable to:**

Santa Monica Press LLC
P.O. Box 1076
Santa Monica, CA 90406

1-800-784-9553

www.santamonicapress.com

Get Offbeat!

Offbeat Museums

"A great book!"
— *Good Morning America*

"What a book! . . . Offers an abundance of alternatives to predictable places like the Getty."
— *Los Angeles Times*

"As delightful a coffee table/reference/bathroom/travel/popular culture tome as you'll ever discover."
— *The Edmonton Journal*

"The best and the weirdest and the quirkiest of homespun Americana is on display in Offbeat Museums."
— *Wisconsin Public Radio*

Offbeat Golf

"One of the funniest books to come across my desk during the past year is Bob Loeffelbein's *Offbeat Golf*, and, by gosh, it lives up to its billing . . . . If you're looking for a book to make you laugh, this one's for you . . . . This book's very interesting and funny. I highly herald this book as a 'must get' book if you want to see the hilarity involved in our passion."
—*Golf Today*

"Sam Snead meets Rube Goldberg!"
—*Golf World*

"Quality content . . . entertaining."
—*Los Angeles Times*

Offbeat Marijuana

"Zanily on the legalization side of the debate is *Offbeat Marijuana*. Like a stoner after a few hits, the main text of the book kicks back and lets go. There's a bowlful of pop culture here, including a discussion of druggie pulp fiction novels of the 1940s like *Marijuana Girl* ("She traded her body for drugs and kicks!" said the publisher's blurb). Rubin does tackle weightier issues such as medical marijuana and scientific findings on pot use."
—Jennifer Howard, *Washington Post*

"Let me offer praise for *Offbeat Marijuana*. Finally, a book on the decriminalizing side of the marijuana debate that doesn't take itself too seriously—sort of a giggling high."
— Robert Scheer, *Los Angeles Times*

"[An] entertaining and provocative cultural history of pot . . . with many illustrations, glib boxed features, and a snappy style."
—Booklist

Offbeat Food

"If you're wild about food, and we are, you'll love this culinary adventure. Alan Ridenour takes us through history and around the world learning delicious tidbits that surprise and tantalize."

— MarySue Milliken and Susan Feniger, Chefs, Restaurateurs, Cookbook Authors, TV and Radio Personalities

"The author serves up an intriguing assortment of foods that are little known or rarely consumed in America as well as familiar ones whose origins have long been forgotten. His facts are right, both historically and ethnographically. The book makes fascinating reading."

—Michael Owen Jones, Chairman, Folklore and Mythology Program, UCLA

Featured on National Public Radio with Scott Simon